I0866996

THE HELLER SOCIAL IMPACT CASE COLLECTION

THE HELLER SOCIAL IMPACT CASE COLLECTION

Reimagining Capitalism through Case-Based Learning

EDITED BY CAROLE CARLSON,
MATTHEW KRIEGSMAN,
& JOEL CUTCHER-GERSHENFELD

BRANDEIS UNIVERSITY PRESS | WALTHAM, MASSACHUSETTS

Brandeis University Press

Manufactured in the United States of America
Designed and typeset by Julie Allred, BW&A Books, Inc.
Typeset in Source Sans and Source Serif

Funding from the Doris Duke Foundation has supported the publication of *The Heller Social Impact Case Collection*.

Library of Congress Cataloging-in-publishing Data
Names: Carlson, Carole, editor. | Cutcher-Gershenfeld, Joel, editor. | Kriegsman, Matthew, editor.
Title: The Heller social impact case collection : reimagining capitalism through case-based learning / edited by Carole Carlson, Matthew Kriegsman, and Joel Cutcher-Gershenfeld.
Description: Waltham, Massachusetts : Brandeis University Press, 2024 |
Summary: "This is, to best of our knowledge, the first collection of social impact business cases. At a time of deep and pervasive global challenges, it is essential for future leaders to apply management principles to social impact cases. It is equally important to ensure that the protagonists and authors of the cases reflect diverse identities and locations from around the world." — Provided by publisher.
Identifiers: LCCN 2023038242 (print) | LCCN 2023038243 (ebook) |
ISBN 9781684581764 (paperback) | ISBN 9781684581757 (cloth) |
ISBN 9781684581771 (ebook)
Subjects: LCSH: Social entrepreneurship—Case studies. | Entrepreneurship—Technological innovations—Case studies. | Business planning—Case studies. | Leadership—Case studies.
Classification: LCC HD60.H44 2024 (print) | LCC HD60 (ebook) |
DDC 361.7/65—dc23/eng/20230907
LC record available at https://lccn.loc.gov/2023038242
LC ebook record available at https://lccn.loc.gov/2023038243

5 4 3 2 1

CONTENTS

SECTION 4. SOCIAL IMPACT STRATEGY CASES

SECTION 5. SOCIAL IMPACT OPERATIONS CASES

SECTION 6. SOCIAL IMPACT MARKETING CASE

SECTION 7. SOCIAL IMPACT HUMAN RESOURCES CASES

LIST OF EXHIBITS AND TABLES

EXHIBITS

TABLES

PREFACE

During our time teaching and learning at the Social Impact MBA program at Brandeis University's Heller School, there has been one consistent source of frustration: the lack of relevant teaching cases to help students examine organizations and leaders through a social impact lens. Our students are hungry to learn in ways that explicitly address social equity. Further, we know from experience that a wide array of social impact organizations face management challenges that can create strong learning experiences, and not just in the nonprofit sector. In this collection, we include cases that examine organizations and leaders in aviation, agriculture, garment manufacturing, and finance alongside cases that explore issues in healthcare, social services, and advocacy.

The lack of diversity in existing case offerings is well-known. While one of the reasons case teaching is so effective is that it enables students to place themselves at the center of the dilemmas faced by featured leaders, students won't learn as much if they can't see themselves in the examples they study. Most cases are focused on large, established for-profit organizations, and the majority of them feature white men as protagonists. We regularly hear from our students that the absence of cases featuring diverse leaders creates a gap in their learning because they miss the opportunity to envision themselves as high-impact leaders. If we take our obligation to educate diverse future leaders seriously, we can't rely exclusively on cases our students don't personally relate to.

This is a time of deep challenge in societies around the world. All of the United Nations's Sustainable Development Goals (SDGs) demand broad and far-reaching social impact advances. The social impact cases in this collection map onto many of the UN's SDGs, including "no poverty"; "good health and wellbeing"; "gender equality"; decent work and economic growth"; "reduced inequalities"; "peace, justice, and strong institutions"; and "partnerships for the Sustainable Development Goals."

In deciding to create this collection, we were motivated and inspired by current students, alumni, and faculty who wanted to share their experiences and tap into their expertise and networks. Incorporating these voices opened up a broad range of organizations, perspectives, and experiences while also making cases relevant to current students. The opportunity for collaboration also motivated us. In addition to cases authored by individual faculty, alumni, and students, this collection features collaborations among faculty, students, alumni, and practitioners.

Based at Brandeis University's Heller School, we knew that we were uniquely positioned to develop a collection that focuses on social impact. The Heller School for Social Policy and Management is a top-ranked policy school, one of the top 10 in the nation according to *U.S. News and World Report*, and our social impact MBA program is one of the leading programs of its type. Heller's motto "knowledge advancing social justice" is the north star for our teaching and research. In creating this collection, our world-class faculty wanted to write cases that would advance their teaching and scholarship, and our alumni and students were eager to explore high impact organizations that share their passions. Our students were motivated to produce the kinds of social impact cases that they would like to see in the curriculum. The editors bring decades of experience in case teaching and subject matter expertise in operations, strategy, leadership, negotiations, and entrepreneurship. To our knowledge, *The Heller Social Impact Case Collection* is the only collection of its type that has been published, and we look forward to having this edition be the first of many.

As case method educators know, it isn't enough to have excellent cases at their disposal. It is also important to have teaching resources that link the cases to existing and emerging theory, and it is valuable to have guidance on how to manage the case discussion in class. Most of the cases in this collection have been "road tested" multiple times in the classroom by some of our best case instructors. All of the cases have teaching notes, and several have supplements connecting them to underlying theories or models (available by request from University of Chicago Press).

We hope that this collection conveys our enthusiasm for using case teaching to connect the dots between theory and practice while elevating social impact leaders. It is our hope that by providing foundational learning, frameworks, inspiring protagonists, and diverse examples, we are providing a unique set of teaching tools that will inform and inspire students and faculty for years to come.

In closing, we would like to thank the many contributors to this project and gratefully acknowledge the important work of instructors who join us in using cases to educate the next generation of social impact leaders.

Carole Carlson
Matthew Kriegsman
Joel Cutcher-Gershenfeld

ACKNOWLEDGMENTS

We begin with deep appreciation to the many students, faculty, and alumni who have contributed cases to *The Heller Social Impact Case Collection*. We are grateful for their passion and creativity, as well as for their commitment to creating a case series with the highest standards.

Both the prior dean of the Heller School for Social Policy and Management, David Weil, and the current interim dean, Maria Madison, have encouraged and supported our work, which is deeply appreciated. The development of this collection was made possible with a grant from the Brandeis Center for Teaching and Learning, and we are thankful for their support. We would also like to thank our editor at Brandeis University Press, Sue Berger Ramin, her colleague Anthony Lipscomb, and production editor Hannah Krasikov for their guidance and expertise.

We appreciate the many Heller students who were engaged in testing these cases in their classes, driving continuous improvement in the case materials. We convey appreciation to our many colleagues and former instructors for sharing their wisdom and deep skills in case method teaching. Hilary Niles '23, a student in our Social Impact MBA program, deserves special recognition for her editorial review of the cases; she provided insights with fresh eyes by surfacing valuable questions and increasing consistency across the collection.

We also appreciate the support of the Doris Duke Foundation and its commitment to a more creative, equitable, and sustainable future.

Lastly, this collection could not exist without the cooperation and assistance of the organizations featured in this collection. Now more than ever, with broad need for social impact leadership, we are grateful that their participation will enable new teachings across the globe to shape the next generation of social impact leaders.

CONTRIBUTORS

Editorial Team

Carole Carlson, lead editor, is professor of the practice and MBA program director at the Heller School for Social Policy and Management at Brandeis University. She is an expert in case method teaching and entrepreneurship and currently teaches courses in social entrepreneurship, global social entrepreneurship, and health care entrepreneurship at Heller. She holds graduate degrees from MIT and Harvard Business School. She is the author or co-author of dozens of published cases and recently published a textbook on social entrepreneurship and innovation.

Matthew Kriegsman, editor, is a senior program manager at Amazon, where he leads strategic projects and network design for Amazon Air's network planning team. Prior to this role, he worked in the air ambulance sector, first as a senior strategy and operations analyst at Boston MedFlight, and thereafter as a senior analyst in strategy and analytics at Atrium Health's MedCenter Air. Matthew earned a BA summa cum laude/ Phi Beta Kappa from Brandeis University, a JD/LLM from Cardozo School of Law, and an MBA from Brandeis University with mentorship and classroom instruction from MIT's International Center for Air Transportation. Matthew is a licensed private pilot, drone pilot, and attorney.

Joel Cutcher-Gershenfeld, editor, is professor and Florence G. Heller Chair in the Heller School for Social Policy and Management. Joel is the award-winning author of a dozen books and over 100 articles and book chapters on large-scale systems change, stakeholder alignment, high-performance work systems, labor-management partnership, new technology, negotiations, and conflict resolution. He has facilitated change initiatives at enterprise, industry, or national levels in Australia, Bermuda, Canada, Denmark, England, Iceland, Jamaica, Panama, South Africa, and the United States. Joel holds a BS in industrial and labor relations from Cornell University and a PhD from MIT's Sloan School of Management.

Hilary Niles, editorial assistant, is a Social Impact MBA candidate at the Heller School for Social Policy and Management at Brandeis University. She holds a BA in Environmental Studies and Biology from Middlebury College. Prior to Heller, she spent 5 years working in fundraising at the Appalachian Mountain Club, the nation's oldest conservation and recreation organization.

Contributors

Archita Adlakha is an investment manager for the SAMRIDH Blended Finance Facility, an initiative by USAID with the technical support unit at IPE Global. In this role, she manages the investment portfolio of the facility, conducts the financial evaluation of social enterprises, manages partnerships with financial institutions and private investors, and structures innovative financing and blended financing instruments. She has over 5 years of experience working in the financial services and development finance sectors. She is the lead author for India's first policy white paper on blended finance, "Reimagining Healthcare in India through Blended Finance." She received a master's degree in International Business and Management from Delhi University and holds a graduate degree specializing in business and finance from Narsee Monjee Institute of Management Studies in Mumbai.

Achin B. N. Biyani leads the fund mobilization for SAMRIDH Blended Finance Facility, an initiative by USAID with the technical support unit at IPE Global. In SAMRIDH, Achin is also involved in deal sourcing to closing, managing partnerships, and structuring innovative financing and blended financing instruments. He brings extensive experience in the development and infrastructure sectors, including working in the areas of Public-Private Partnerships (PPPs), fund mobilization, policy research, infrastructure financing, procurement, and capacity building. Through partnerships and engagement with non-traditional stakeholders, he has played an active role ranging from the development stage to implementation of the programs. He is a co-author of the papers "Panorama of the Urban and Municipal Sector in India, Focales, French Development Agency" and "Bibliometric Review of Blended Finance and Partial Risk Guarantee: Establishing Needs and Advantages" published in the *International Journal of Financial Studies*, and he contributed to *PPP Practitioners Guide: Contract Management Toolkit and Renegotiations Framework* developed by Ministry of Finance, Government of India. He holds an MBA from the Faculty of Management Studies, University of Delhi.

Avery Brien is a public policy professional with experience providing strategic coaching and technical assistance to organizations and campaigns regarding advocacy strategies, coalition building, policy analysis, and messaging and communications. Avery has worked at the local, state, and national levels on issues such as health policy, housing, LGBTQ+ rights, and racial and economic justice. They hold a Bachelor of Arts from the University of New Hampshire and a Master of Public Policy from Brandeis University's Heller School for Social Policy and Management.

Naomi Bromberg Bar-Yam is founder and director emerita of Mothers' Milk Bank Northeast and past president of the Human Milk Banking Association of North America. Her professional training is in childbirth education, social work, and social policy, with a focus on family policy and advocacy. Naomi's training and personal experience as the mother of four children, two of whom were NICU babies, have informed her work in milk banking locally, nationally, and internationally.

Laura Burroughs is a Social Impact MBA candidate and committee member of the Impact Investing and ESG Group. Prior to Heller, Laura spent 6 years at an international NGO. Laura's expertise is in international development, sustainable resource management, monitoring and evaluation, and gender equity. She selected the Heller MBA program to translate her background into advancing impact for the private sector. She is currently interning at Corporate Citizenship, an ESG consulting firm where she contributes to sustainability research, ESG reporting and materiality assessments, and client proposals. She is a certified project management professional, with experience leading projects in the US and Somalia.

Jon A. Chilingerian (1951–2023) was a professor of health care management at Brandeis University and an adjunct professor of family and community medicine at Tufts School of Medicine. His subject matter expertise was in the management of health care organizations, strategic thinking, leadership and team development, performance measurement, and organizational change. His work brings an alternative perspective to the much-studied subjects of leadership, hospital management, crisis management, strategy, and the dynamics of individual and organizational change. He received a PhD from the Sloan School at the Massachusetts Institute of Technology and was the founding director of the executive MBA program for physicians and the MD-MBA program. He was a former assistant health commissioner for the City of Boston.

Monique DeSimone is a Social Impact MBA candidate and president/co-chair of the Impact Investing and ESG Group at the Heller School for Social Policy and Management at Brandeis University. She has 8 years of experience in the finance sector, with expertise in wealth management, financial planning and modeling, investment analysis, and ESG portfolio development. Monique was recognized as an Emerging Leader at GreenFin22 and is passionate about centering social equity within the investing landscape. She is a Chartered SRI Counselor and a Series 7 and 66 holder, and she received a BBA in Management with a concentration in Sustainability from the University of Massachusetts Amherst.

Keshia Engwenyi is a senior program officer at CARE USA, where she manages business operations for the education team. In this role, she provides program and grant management support to CARE education projects globally. She has over 5 years of experience working in the international development sector. She is passionate about social entrepreneurship and writes on sustainable approaches to creating impact on the African continent via her blog Connect the Dots. She received a dual Social Impact MBA/MA in Sustainable International Development from the Heller School for Social Policy and Management.

Marji Erickson Warfield is senior scientist and lecturer and chair of the Children, Youth, and Families concentration at the Heller School for Social Policy and Management at Brandeis University. Her research seeks to understand and evaluate programs and services designed to promote the well-being of children, youth, and young adults from marginalized communities, often centering individuals with disabilities and youth in foster care. She currently teaches courses in research methods, child and family policy, and disability policy at Heller. She holds a PhD from Heller and has authored several book chapters and published papers in a range of academic journals.

Mónica García is an education consultant specializing in early childhood education, conflict resolution, and qualitative research. Mónica has over 10 years of experience working in the public and private sectors designing curricula, projects, and qualitative surveys rooted in intersectional social justice. Mónica holds a Bachelor of Arts in Psychology and Sociology from Gonzaga University. Mónica is an alumna of Brandeis University's Heller School for Social Policy and Management where she earned a MA in Conflict Resolution and Coexistence.

Douglass Guernsey is a Social Impact MBA candidate and co-chair of the Impact, Investing, and ESG Group at Brandeis University. He brings a passion for entrepreneurship, governance, and sustainability to the impact investing space. Douglass has opened several restaurants, started a media company, and is the co-founder of the fundraising fintech Missionable.

William (Bill) B. Gunn Jr. is a health and organizational psychologist in private practice in Portsmouth, New Hampshire. He worked as a behavioral health specialist in family medicine education for 30 years and has expertise integrating public health and behavioral health into the primary care setting. Bill is co-author of *Models of Collaboration* and *The Collaborative Psychotherapist*, books designed for mental health professionals working in medical settings. He has also published articles about the integration of behavioral health into primary care. Bill leads organizational change projects that are uniquely designed to collaborate with the individual, team, or department in setting a vision and following through with strategic plans. He was the clinical director of Region 6 in New Hampshire for 5 years, and this work led to the development of the case in this collection.

Lauren Hajjar is assistant professor of public management at the Sawyer Business School at Suffolk University. Her research is focused on organizational change and human resource practices that support high performing teams, organizations and communities. She spent over a decade in the nonprofit sector providing behavioral health services to clients and now works directly with leaders, managers, and frontline staff in the implementation of various policies, practices and initiatives—facilitating both inter- and intraorganizational change and development efforts. Her publications are geared toward an international audience of scholars and practitioners. She holds degrees in psychology, public administration, and social policy and completed her doctoral work at the Heller School for Social Policy and Management at Brandeis University.

Jody Hoffer Gittell is professor at Brandeis University's Heller School; faculty director of the Relational Coordination Collaborative, a global community of researchers and change leaders; and co-founder of Relational Coordination Analytics. Gittell developed Relational Coordination Theory, proposing that highly interdependent work can be effectively coordinated through relationships of shared goals, shared knowledge, and mutual respect and supported by frequent, timely, accurate, problem-solving communication. The relational model of organizational change shows how stakeholders can design structural, relational, and work process interventions to support more effective coordination of their work. She received her PhD from the MIT Sloan School of Management.

Della M. Hughes, visiting research scientist, is former associate director of and senior fellow at the Center for Youth and Communities at Brandeis University's Heller School. Throughout her career, she has served in a mix of leadership positions, working in partnership with local and national nonprofits, foundations, educational organizations, governments, and businesses to level the playing field for youth and young adults facing social, educational, and economic disparities. She uses logic models to achieve results-oriented initiatives in program planning and implementation, evaluation and learning, continuous improvement, leadership development, systems change, and best practices in programming. She holds graduate degrees from Vanderbilt Divinity School and the University of Tennessee School of Social Work. She is a regular peer reviewer for *The Foundation Review* and has published a number of articles about her work.

Sonia Kikeri is the national director for policy and civic engagement at Emerald Cities Collaborative, working on equity-based policy analysis, development, and implementation and specializing in just transition, energy democracy, and community engagement. They have prior experiences ranging from working with refugees on the Turkish-Syrian border to serving as a legislative director for a Pennsylvanian senator. Sonia is committed to naming, confronting, and dismantling systems of oppression, colonization, and white supremacy and is honored to work with those who are actively building a reality of equity, reparations, and liberation. They hold a Bachelor of Science in Foreign Service from Georgetown University as well as an MBA and Masters in Conflict Resolution and Coexistence from Brandeis University.

Jess Lynch-Foust is a Social Impact MBA candidate at the Heller School for Social Policy and Management at Brandeis University, where she is a committee member of the Impact Investing and ESG Group. She has held roles in the financial industry at Atlas Impact Partners and Wellington Management and is currently interning with Ceres on their Corporate Sustainability Performance Analyst Team. She holds a BA in International Affairs and Human Services with a minor in Global Social Entrepreneurship from Northeastern University.

Ninna Meier is associate professor in organizational sociology at the Department of Sociology and Social Work at Alborg University. She uses case-based and problem-based teaching methods and currently teaches courses in organizational sociology, advanced qualitative methods, and academic writing. She holds a degree in philosophy and business administration (cand.merc.phil) and received her PhD from Aarhus University. She has studied the collaboration, leadership, and management of inter-organizational coordination in and across public sector organizations since 2009 and publishes for practitioners as well as scholars.

Sudheer Nadipally is the monitoring, evaluation and learning expert at the SAMRIDH Blended Finance Facility, an initiative by USAID with the technical support unit at IPE Global. He brings 19 years of experience across monitoring, evaluation, learning, and project management in the public health and social development sectors. In his previous assignments, Sudheer has been associated with several government, non-government, and non-profit funding organizations as well as research and academic institutions. He has presented his work at industry-wide conferences and has been published in multiple peer-reviewed journals. Currently, Sudheer is pursuing his PhD in Health Sciences. He holds an MPhil and an MA in Social Anthropology.

Ritika Pandey is an associate director at IPE Global and the lead post award at the SAMRIDH Blended Finance Facility supported by USAID. She has more than 14 years of experience with an eclectic mix of technical know-how, research acumen, project management, partnership, people management skills, social behavior change, and communication development. She has implemented large-scale projects funded by international multilateral donors for family planning, maternal-child health, and nutrition outcomes. She has managed multiple projects across Africa and Asia and is currently mentoring more than 35 start-ups and healthcare enterprises. She has authored case studies and contributed to articles in magazines including "Promoting Agriculture, Nutrition Convergence through Participatory Extension Videos" for the World Bank. She has a master's degree in Development Studies from Tata Institute of Social Sciences, Mumbai, India.

Neeta Rao is a senior health lead with USAID/India, where she focuses on innovative financing portfolios, including blended financing and pay-for-performance models. She provides strategic oversight to USAID's health investments in the western region of the country. She has worked on health systems strengthening, health financing, research and evaluation, policy, advocacy, community engagement, and program management with the World Health Organization, multinational agencies, governments, and non-government organizations. She has a Masters in Health Administration from Tata Institute of Social Sciences, India and has co-authored articles and chapters on health insurance, health accounts, and HIV/AIDS.

Julia Robinson-Rosendorff is an associate at TDC, where she works as a management consultant for nonprofit organizations. Prior to this role, Julia was an economics researcher with a focus on the intersection of education and inequities. Julia holds a Social Impact MBA with a concentration in Social Policy and Management from the Heller School for Social Policy and Management at Brandeis University as well as a BA in Economics from Brandeis University.

Mark I. Rosen is a teacher, consultant, researcher, and author. For more than three decades, he taught principles of management and organizational behavior to undergraduate and graduate students at Brandeis University and Bentley University. He earned his PhD in Organizational Behavior and Human Resource Management from the University of Wisconsin-Madison. Mark has also served as a consultant and researcher for businesses, nonprofits, and philanthropic foundations. He is the author of two books and the lead author/co-author of more than fifty research and consulting reports, case studies, and professional publications. Mark joined the board of Mothers' Milk Bank Northeast in 2017 and became the board chair in 2023.

Sean C. Rush is the former chairman and partner of PricewaterhouseCoopers' education and non-profit practice in the United States. He was named general manager of IBM's Global Education Industry Group in 1994, where he grew the business to $2.2 billion in sales by 2006. In 2008, Sean was appointed president and CEO of JA Worldwide. He now serves as president emeritus of JA, which was nominated for a Nobel Peace Prize in 2022. Sean currently serves as a director, trustee, or overseer for numerous educational, civic, and cultural institutions, including the Heller School for Social Policy and Management at Brandeis University, the National Leadership Institute, the Frank Lloyd

Wright Foundation, the Boston Symphony Orchestra, the Kibera Girls Soccer Academy, and the Harvard Kennedy School. He also has been an active constituent in the World Economic Forum and a guest lecturer for the Rhodes Scholars at the University of Oxford. Sean is the author, editor, or contributor to over 20 books and articles on the mission, governance, leadership, and operations of institutions in higher education. Sean holds a BA and an MBA from Boston College, an MS from Boston University, and an MPA from Harvard Kennedy School.

Elizabeth V. Sessions is a freelance writer and an instructor at the Heller School for Social Policy and Management at Brandeis University. She previously worked in social services with persons experiencing housing and behavioral health challenges and is now transitioning to a career in education. She holds an MA in Conflict Resolution and Coexistence and MA in Sustainable International Development from the Heller School for Social Policy and Management at Brandeis University.

Jennifer Stewart is the owner of Breaking Expectations, LLC. She has a passion for supporting transition-aged young adults with disabilities navigate both education and adult systems. Jennifer has worked with young adults with disabilities over 15 years in various capacities, from providing vocational counseling, supporting families, developing programming, building system capacity, and evaluating impact. Jennifer is a LEND Fellow; she has a master's degree in Public Policy from the Heller School for Social Policy and Management at Brandeis University and a Bachelor of Arts from the University of Colorado.

Maher Tabba is a professor of medicine and surgery at the Medical School and the University College at Tufts University in Boston, Massachusetts. He is the director of interventional pulmonology at Tufts Medical Center and chief of critical care medicine at the Melrose-Wakefield Health Care System in Melrose, Massachusetts. He completed an executive MBA degree at Brandeis University in Waltham, Massachusetts. He has served as associate curriculum dean at the University of Missouri in Columbia, Missouri and as the director pulmonary of the Critical Care Fellowship Training Program at Tufts Medical Center. His area of interest is health care economics and policies.

Miya Ward is a consultant with Nexight Group, specializing in stakeholder engagement, communications strategies, data collection and analysis, and technical writing and editing. She has been an active participant and organizer in social movement spaces for nearly two decades. Aside from the Ford Hall 2015 case study, she is a co-author of BYP100's Agenda to Build Black Futures. She holds a Bachelor of Arts in Comparative Literature from Haverford College and a MBA with a focus on non-profit management from Brandeis University's Heller School for Social Policy and Management.

Rachael Weiker is a project manager with the City of Saint Paul Department of Planning and Economic Development, where she focuses on building its entrepreneurial ecosystem. She has worked on community engagement, civic participation, economic development, and entrepreneurship at local, national, and international levels. She has an MBA and an MPP from the Heller School for Social Policy and Management at Brandeis University. She is also a fellow with the Eli J. and Phyllis N. Segal Citizen Leadership Program.

THE HELLER SOCIAL IMPACT CASE COLLECTION

SECTION 1

Social Impact Case Method Teaching

Advancing Social Impact Through Case Studies

CAROLE CARLSON

A Brief History of the Case Method

The case method is a well-honed approach for teaching and learning in MBA programs. After it was pioneered as a teaching approach in the late 1800s at Harvard Law School, its use rapidly expanded to business, medicine, and other disciplines. This evolution is unsurprising—law, business, and medicine are three fields where pattern recognition and the ability to understand situations from multiple perspectives are critical skills. But the roots of the method go back further—all the way to Greek philosopher Socrates (470–399 BC), who developed a method where the professor relentlessly questioned students in order to expose logical flaws in their arguments and uncover their underlying beliefs. Today's case method is less harsh and, as a result, is widely used because of its many benefits: the case method develops quick thinking and critical thinking skills, teaches the value of in-depth analysis, and fosters inclusivity by elevating differences of opinion.

Why Use the Case Method?

Today, in most graduate business programs, the case method is the foundation of participant-centered learning: active, discussion-based learning that puts students at the center of the equation. Cases provide the raw materials that enable students to apply their knowledge and skills to a situation and draw on their experience, analysis, and ability to connect ideas. Nitin Nohria, former dean of the Harvard Business School, described seven "meta-skills" that are developed through case discussions:

1. Preparation: To be effective, students are required to be prepared, prioritize information, and develop a point of view.
2. Discernment: Students must sort through information to determine what is relevant.
3. Bias recognition: Learning with their peers and through debate, students often learn that their initial conclusions are flawed.
4. Judgment: Students are called upon to develop strategies and recommend courses of action in ambiguous and uncertain situations
5. Collaboration: Discussion participants gain skills by practicing give-and-take debate.
6. Curiosity: Exposure to multiple situations and problems in a wide range of industries and sectors prompts students to be more inquisitive.
7. Self-confidence: Students gain confidence in their problem-solving skills and ability to clearly convey ideas and influence others.[1]

The case method taps into an important characteristic of adult learning: adults learn best when they can apply new material to things they already know. Case discussions build upon students' experiences and existing knowledge by exposing them to a new situation that they can diagnose using past experience and skills, as well as recently acquired knowledge and frameworks. Students bring their experience to the classroom, and new case situations enable them to stretch their understanding. The experiential component makes cases memorable, and by connecting learning to action (for example, preparing a case analysis or arguing for a point of view in class), students retain more knowledge. Simultaneously, students learn rapidly from a broad range of arguments and examples offered by their classmates. Finally, by putting themselves in the shoes of the case protagonist, students can visualize themselves making a decision and acting upon it.

As the late David Garvin—a well-known scholar and case method expert—observed, there is another benefit, which is practice. He believed that "a steady diet of cases leads to distinctive ways of thinking—and acting . . . Day after day, classes revolve around protagonists who face critical choices. Delay is seldom an option."[2] Garvin mentions the "bias for action" that results from using the case method, observing that it enables students to practice taking risks and decide and implement decisions courageously.[3]

How does the instructor fit in? By guiding the discussion to ensure that students fully engage, that the debate in class is robust, and that student ideas connect to key teaching points. "Students are on a journey of discovery and I'm the tour guide," said Ivey Business School professor Robert Austin. "Case method is an approach I like to call inductive. It starts with specifics of a particular situation and asks the students to extract some generalizable principals they can re-use in other situations. It's discussion based; it's the Socratic method; it's engaging for the students."[4] With this last bit, Austin reminds us that case discussions are also fun.

Cases are a unique platform for learning and practicing influence skills. Students gain extensive experience articulating and defending their logic to persuade others. And they have a real time platform to observe the reactions of others. Moreover, they do this in a low-risk environment where in a single day they might be on the executive team of three different organizations making decisions, persuading others, and analyzing the consequences. This rapid cycle allows students to build skills quickly while enabling them to reflect about what works and what doesn't.

Perhaps the greatest opportunity created by cased-based learning is bringing diverse experiences to the classroom. In our current Social Impact MBA class at Brandeis's Heller School, the average student has 6.5 years of work experience, students represent half a dozen countries, and about one third of students were the first in their family to graduate from college. Their professional experience spans sectors that include banking, philanthropy, law, health care, data science, education, and entrepreneurship. Students bring experience from large corporations, start-ups, government organizations, nonprofits, and NGOs. The case method enables the instructor to bridge the gaps among student backgrounds and, if they are skilled, to leverage those backgrounds to enable engaged exchange and learning among students with vastly different experiences. Students learn to collaborate with and learn from peers who stand in for a broad range of stakeholders, an essential skill for emerging leaders.

Why Use Social Impact Cases?

Cases with a social impact focus are particularly valuable because of the complexity of the management issues they address. For future leaders, the ability to consider not only the financial returns or operational efficiency of organizations but also their impact on society is a critical skill that is becoming increasingly vital.

Cases put the moral and ethical dilemmas faced by protagonists into high relief. For example, the first case in this collection centers around 99Degrees, a startup garment manufacturing company founded by Brenna Schneider. Although it is a for-profit venture, Schneider founded it to create jobs that teach advanced manufacturing skills, aiming to break cycles of intergenerational poverty. When we discussed this case in class, students raised questions that included whether providing jobs was sufficient for achieving the social mission goals of the founder, what the responsibility of a mission-oriented employer to provide benefits should be, and whether entrepreneurship is a good career path. We had an in-depth discussion about how entrepreneurs make early-stage formation decisions and identified the challenges and tradeoffs faced by the protagonist as she sought to scale the organization. Finally, we had a robust discussion about whether the organization should have selected a for-profit or nonprofit organizational form, and students had a lively debate as they shared their rationale for these choices. It was wonderful to see all of this learning in one short class and hear the nuanced perspectives brought by the students.

The case method teaches students about the value of preparation and developing a point of view. As a former colleague related (paraphrased): "One of the biggest things I took away from my MBA was the need to always show up well-prepared, to always have an agenda, and to always come armed with facts that supported it. In a wing-it world, this habit, more than anything else, has helped me be successful in my career." This orientation toward thoughtful and deliberate influence is even more important when leading or interacting with social impact organizations because of the complexity of their work and the wide range of stakeholder interests that should be considered.

To capture the "magic" of any case, the instructor needs to do many things at once: encourage students to participate and collaborate in the discussion, connect the case to underlying points of theory, manage the discussion to ensure broad participation, and manage the tone of the class. For social impact cases, it is even more important to drive conversations toward examining the implications of the choices at hand and, often, to moderate heated discussions that arise from differences among students. A social impact case also relies heavily on students sharing their experiences and how they inform their perspective. In our classrooms at Heller, we typically have students with significant global experience, and this can add a valuable dimension to the discussion.

Other reasons for using social impact cases include the growing importance of the social impact sector, the complexity and ambiguity that comes from decision-making that must balance profit with socially desirable outcomes, and the fact that even leaders who work exclusively in the commercial sector are likely to have volunteer leadership positions or board roles at nonprofits. Social impact cases have also been made more relevant by the blurring of lines between the commercial and social impact sectors, a fact that is illustrated by the case in this collection on ESG (environmental, social, and governance) standards at Trillium, a large investment advisory firm.

In many of the cases in this volume, the protagonists are diverse in many ways, matching the breadth of the social impact sector.

For students, social impact cases offer, among other things, the benefits of increased and generative participation with peers, opportunities to grapple with complex issues, and preparation to act as future leaders of a wide range of organizations.

Different Case Types

In addition to traditional cases, this collection includes analytic cases, role-play simulations, and a case written as a series of first person narratives by students participating in a social movement. Cases feature local, multi-nation, and global organizations. For-profit, nonprofit and government organizations are also featured. Cases span disciplines that include finance, human resources, operations, and entrepreneurship, among others. Teaching modes for the cases in this collection include mini-lectures, case discussions, role-play instructions, and breakout groups. What they all have in common is that they present engaging stories designed to lead to lively classroom debates and intense student learning.

For Instructors: Teaching with Cases Overview

In my experience, there are two things an instructor must bring to case discussions: preparation and flexibility. With respect to preparation, even though the instructor is not typically lecturing, deep knowledge of the case and its related frameworks and theories is important. Good instructors approach each case with intent; they have clarity about the themes they will cover (with approximate timing) and the learning points they plan to extract, and they have a plan for engaging students in the discussion.

At the same time, the best case method instructors balance their planning with flexibility, showing a willingness to follow the students' lead and adjust the discussion plan in real time. My case discussions often go into uncharted territory. For example, I recently taught a case where the protagonist had started a nonprofit school for orphans and disadvantaged youth in Vietnam that teaches skills that prepare them for hospitality careers in large hotels. While many of the students lauded his efforts, others argued that they found the hospitality business inherently exploitative. Luckily, the case protagonist was visiting our class and was able to explain that hospitality positions in Vietnam are indeed high-quality opportunities (particularly for those with limited education), with starting salaries comparable to those earned by college graduates starting teaching jobs. This gave the students valuable insights about the importance of context and the perils of a rush to judgment. In another recent case, we examined how a consumer technology startup had launched and marketed its product at multiple price points online before it was available to gather information about what the best pricing would be. One student pointed out the ethical concerns of raising consumer expectations for a product that does not yet exist, while another countered that this was a great example of lean thinking and was an excellent strategy for testing customer price sensitivity to derive a demand curve.

For Instructors: Three Steps to Effective Case Teaching

To teach cases well, instructors should think beyond the class and have a plan for before, during, and after each case discussion.

Prior to Teaching

Before the instructor and students enter the classroom, expectations should already be set by the clarity of the syllabus or teaching plan. Instructors who present their cases in an organized way show that they value students and want to respect their time.

Some instructors find it helpful at the beginning of the first class to establish a social contract. For example, one of the co-editors of this volume, Joel Cutcher-Gershenfeld, asks three questions: What should you expect of me? What can I expect of you? And what can we expect of each other? He records the answers in a digital document visible to the full class. This mutual sharing of expectations becomes the social contract for the class and motivates both the students and the instructor to be accountable for class outcomes. It is also the foundation of an agreed-upon set of norms for classroom discussions: for example, mutual respect, careful listening, and candor. Halfway through the semester, he reintroduces this social contract to discuss how they are all doing with respect to what they set forth at the beginning of the course.

Instructors should carefully plan each class to identify specific themes (also called pastures) with key learning points. Well-prepared instructors also have a plan for transitioning between themes. Instructors should think about which students they will call on initially and why.

During Teaching

The instructor is responsible for directing the discussion, asking questions, maintaining the flow between themes, punctuating themes to reinforce learning, and maintaining class energy. To keep the energy level high, great instructors know when to change pace by using breakout discussion groups or a physical activity. Like Socrates, great case instructors also ask good questions (though perhaps not as relentlessly as he did) and use them to guide debate and extract learning. Good questions are open-ended and inspire discussion, debate, and reflection.

The instructor also plays a critical role in maintaining a safe learning environment. The instructor should be on the alert for disruptive behavior and address it head-on or move the class away from it. A good instructor always has a set of tactics prepared to deal with disruptive, offensive, or long-winded participants—these tactics might range from diversion to changing the topic to opening up a situation for class discussion.

After Teaching

At the end of class, the instructor can take advantage of many options for extending learning. Perhaps the simplest and most effective way is to finish with a question, inviting students to continue to reflect on the issue at hand outside of class. Other ways to extend learning include assigning homework or video viewing and asking students to participate in post-class discussions or blogs. The instructor may want to follow up with specific students to offer encouragement, suggest ideas, or simply congratulate them on a job well done. I keenly remember, over 2 decades later, the first handwritten note I received from a professor. And, of course, it is helpful to take a few notes after each class about what went well or poorly and how to improve the structure, material, questions, or flow for the next time the course is offered.

For Students: Learning with Cases Overview

Prior to Class: Preparation Is Key

Students won't be well-prepared for a fast-paced case discussion if they quickly skim a case. But it is also unnecessary to read and re-read a case multiple times, memorizing details and taking pages of notes. Instead, to use their case preparation time effectively, students should use a process of *active reading* to absorb case information and be ready to participate actively in class.

Active reading is a purposeful and interrogative approach to reading a case. This technique involves quickly reading a case and then developing a point of view on the nature of the problem and the options confronting the protagonist. The student's point of view will vary by case, but questions they can ask to inform their opinion might include:

- What industry or sector does this organization operate in?
- What are key trends germane to this case?
- What are the options facing the protagonists?
- What have they done so far? Have their actions been effective or ineffective?
- What choices lie ahead? Which choices would you recommend?
- What evidence supports your recommendation?
- What choices or social impact issues are involved?

After developing their initial ideas, a student can use their time well by developing a set of theories (also sometimes referred to as hypotheses) about the case and then carefully re-reading it, collecting evidence that supports or disconfirms their ideas. This creates a framework that allows the reader to efficiently extract meaning from the written case. There is a lot of information in cases, some of which is extraneous, and using this hypothesis-based approach allows students to use their time efficiently, putting them in the best position to participate in class effectively.

Students should also push themselves beyond considering only high-level decisions facing the protagonist: cases have multiple dimensions, and students should go deeper to develop a nuanced perspective on a layered set of decisions and options, evaluating the consequences of each.

A few additional tips for preparation:

- Identify the full set of decisions faced by the protagonist or organization. In doing so, consider the options and assess each one to identify key tensions.
- Consider the case's connections to theory: if there are additional readings assigned, read them and consider their relevance.
- Consider connections to topics discussed in prior classes.
- Numbers don't lie: if the case supports it, perform some high-level analysis to check your ideas, and conduct more detailed analysis where appropriate using facts from the case text and exhibits.

- Develop recommendations: write down your ideas, stress test them, and develop supporting arguments.

Some students find it helpful to form study groups to discuss cases prior to meeting, especially in large classes. This three-step approach to participation (individual learning followed by small group learning followed by large class learning) is a highly effective learning technique, particularly for students that hesitate to speak up in larger groups.

During Class: Effective Participation

Perhaps the most important key to getting the most from a case discussion is to be fully present. This starts with listening carefully to the points made by others. Keep in mind that debate is encouraged in case discussions, so pay close attention and contribute by agreeing, adding additional insights, or disagreeing. Try to participate in a way that follows the discussion flow and stays within the theme being considered. You may have a brilliant point, but if it is poorly timed, it will not have an impact.

There are multiple ways to contribute. The lowest value comments are repetitions of points already made by others. Acknowledging case facts, while potentially valuable at the beginning of a discussion, loses its impact as the discussion deepens. Sharing experience and relating it to the case can also be beneficial, but only if you are concise. Valuable and influential contributions usually involve analysis, links to other cases or theory, original insights, and connections between ideas. One way to assess a contribution is to ask yourself: "Is the class better off because of the point I just made?"

Students should avoid the mistake of thinking "I learn best by listening." Nearly everyone learns best by expressing their ideas as part of a discussion. It helps students clarify and elaborate their ideas and share their perspective and experience with others. A related principle is "step up; step back." If you have already made more than one contribution, consider stepping back to hear from others. If you have not yet contributed, consider stepping up.

Case discussions are most effective when students stay in the time of the case. Cases are written about the past, and while it is always tempting to look up organizations to see what has happened, I encourage students to resist this. Nothing throws cold water on a case discussion like an update of how the organization has succeeded or failed since the time of the case. Instructors will often provide updates at the end of discussions.

For social impact cases, students are encouraged to bring their own lived experiences, identities, and values to the discussion—even more so than in a traditional business case.

Finally, trust the instructor. An experienced instructor will work to even out participation over time, enable students to bring their best ideas to the discussion, and moderate the discussion to keep it constructive and respectful.

After Class: Reflect and Review

For students, one way to deepen learning is to take a few minutes at the end of every class to record key lessons, reflect on important insights, and consider connections to other cases or class concepts. Some students also have "case buddies" who they trade post-class feedback with. Case buddies can offer external perspectives on the quality of your participation and encourage you to further develop your influence skills.

Closing Thoughts

The case method is a high-intensity, but highly effective, way to learn critical thinking, management, leadership, and influence skills. I hope that the cases in this volume will add the important dimension of social impact to your case discussions and make them even more impactful.

NOTES

1. Nitin Nohria, "What the Case Study Method Really Teaches," *Harvard Business Review* (online), December 21, 2021.
2. David A. Garvin, "Making the Case: Professional Education for the World of Practice," *Harvard Magazine* (September–October 2003): 56–65.
3. Garvin, "Making the Case."
4. Paul Mayne, "Austin: Making a Case for a Different Approach," *Western News*, April 15, 2019, https://news.westernu.ca/2019/04/austin-making-case-different-approach/.

SECTION 2

Social Impact Entrepreneurship Cases

CASE 2.1

Brenna Schneider at 99Degrees

CAROLE CARLSON AND RACHAEL WEIKER

It was July 2013, and Brenna Schneider considered with pride the social impact business she had created. She had just been selected to present her new social enterprise, 99Degrees, to senators Elizabeth Warren and Ed Markey as part of the MassChallenge business accelerator program. After many months of planning, reflection, concentrated mentorship, and guidance, Schneider had launched 99Degrees, a highly customizable clothing goods manufacturer with a social mission. Now 4 months into production with four full-time employees, Schneider had brought the company to market with genuine momentum and support. But she knew that she had many management and strategy challenges yet to consider.

The Garment Manufacturing Industry in Merrimack Valley

The economies in Northeastern Massachusetts grew and declined in tandem with the United States manufacturing industry. In the early 1800s the Merrimack River cities of Lowell and Haverhill took advantage of their highly accessible location, a skilled local workforce, and an innovative mass manufacturing process to create the first textile mills. In 1840 Lawrence was the first city to be built as a planned industrial city, and within 70 years it had grown to be a manufacturing leader with more than 95,000 residents. Thus, the Merrimack Valley had become the cradle and hub of the American Industrial Revolution, building economy and infrastructure around textile mills that attracted thousands of immigrants to their well-paying jobs.

However, by the middle of the 20th century, manufacturing jobs had started to move south and overseas, where labor and transportation costs were cheaper. This, along with the advent of the Great Depression, forced significant population and economic decline in Merrimack Valley. Though it remained a "gateway city," by 2012 Lawrence's population shrank to 77,000, and only 35% of its economy was manufacturing-based.

The absence of the industrial economy left its mark; in 2012 nearly 28% of Lawrence's population lived below the poverty level, and 14% were unemployed. The city remained a multicultural hub, with 36% of residents foreign-born and nearly 75% who spoke a language other than English at home. Yet, the limited economy narrowed job and career prospects for many residents.

However, manufacturing was on the cusp of a revival. To spur economic activity, the state governments of Massachusetts and New Hampshire collaborated to create economic incentives that would make Merrimack Valley a leading advanced manufacturing cluster in New England, projecting more than 100,000 advanced manufacturing jobs by 2020. These jobs brought significant opportunities for economic growth: the average advanced manufacturing salary of $77,000 more than doubled the median income in Lawrence of $31,500.

Yet, the majority of these positions required an associate degree or a background in science, technology, engineering, and math (STEM) coursework. While 65% of Lawrence residents had a high school diploma, only 12% had a bachelor's degree or higher. In addition, the new industry demanded skills like problem-solving, critical thinking, English language proficiency, and math proficiency. The region lacked a workforce development program to build the pipeline of skilled workers. The city would need a large-scale on-ramp of manufacturing training to meet the incoming labor demand.

Schneider's Background

Brenna Schneider's upbringing was tightly woven in with the manufacturing and apparel industry. She was closely involved in her parents' small manufacturing company in Pennsylvania, first as an embroidery machine production technician and eventually as manager of the firm's operations. Inspired by how the experience evolved her technical and managerial skills, she also witnessed firsthand how employees improved their social and economic stability by working in a manufacturing setting.

Then, as a William J. Clinton Fellow for Service in India, she worked with textile artisans to reposition traditional crafts into viable market-based businesses. When Schneider returned to the United States in 2008, she continued her career in service and manufacturing by working through the Iacocca Institute at Lehigh University in Pennsylvania to build up the manufacturing base in Lehigh Valley. Her experiences using manufacturing as a tool to build skills, increase employment, and alleviate poverty strengthened her conviction that the United States' manufacturing base could be used to "create pathways to social mobility and economic independence for American families while achieving business goals."

In December 2011, after completing her MBA in Social Impact Management at Brandeis University's Heller School, Schneider found a seemingly perfect opportunity to realize these goals as the Vice President of Operations for American MoJo, a socially responsible apparel manufacturer in Lowell, Massachusetts. The social enterprise aimed to provide living-wage jobs and onsite childcare for single mothers and therefore an opportunity for economic growth and stability. However, the manufacturing industry's high operating and capital costs combined with low margins made it difficult to maintain profitability. By the time a viable strategy emerged, the capital had run out and the company was faltering. After an expected acquisition fell through, the founders decided to close their doors.

Schneider was still deeply devoted to MoJo's social mission and was convinced that the company had potential. When MoJo ceased operations and its founders left to start new ventures, Schneider was left at a crossroads.

Between Ventures

Shortly before MoJo closed, Schneider was invited to participate in the Aspen Institute's "ThinkXchange" program on two-generation approaches to intergenerational poverty alleviation. Despite the firm's shuttering, she decided to attend, and although her experience with MoJo was not the success story that her peers shared, the exchange reinvigorated her belief in combining business with social justice.

While in Colorado, she learned more about social entrepreneurship models like the Tulsa Community Action Project and the Family Independence Initiative: nonprofits that use collaborative and innovative methods to stabilize families and communities. Learning about their broad range of models and perspectives, she felt challenged and inspired by the urgency of intergenerational poverty and the need for bold approaches to address the problem. Schneider felt that there could still be a chance for socially responsible manufacturing to succeed. She recognized that programs for job placement and skills were a piece of the puzzle, but someone needed to create the jobs necessary to break the cycle of intergenerational poverty.

Based on her experiences and historical trends, she knew that apparel manufacturing had been the economic gateway to more advanced manufacturing industries for regions in the United States and developing countries. Thus, applying an established workforce development pattern to a brand new market opportunity in domestic manufacturing could break the cycle of poverty for families in the United States. Schneider reflected:

> My interest was creating jobs that go somewhere. Advanced manufacturing has that—these jobs can pay \$50,000–\$80,000 per year, and they are right on the doorstep of old mill towns like Lawrence. But to get the jobs, applicants need a work history and some demonstrable skills in manufacturing. That's where we (apparel manufacturers) come in.[1]

Schneider knew that wages alone would not boost families out of poverty. Employees would need a variety of benefits to increase their social and economic capital. She identified childcare, professional mentoring, education, health care, and social networks as the five key factors she wanted to include in her social impact model, but she was unsure how she could afford to provide all of these to her employees while making a profit.

Just before MoJo terminated operations, the company had experienced a brief success with "me-commerce," a form of online retail in which customers could personalize and customize their orders. In this model, customers placed their order through an online retailer, who then contracted a cut-and-sew manufacturer to fulfill the order. Schneider felt that this niche would be the best opportunity to help Merrimack Valley's labor force meet a growing demand for onshore apparel manufacturing.

"Me-commerce" apparel manufacturing, projected to be worth \$3.4 billion by 2018, was an industry largely defined by turnaround time. In this market, the time between customers "checking out" from their online shopping cart and receiving product was limited to 2–5 days. Offshore manufacturers took an average of 4–6 weeks to deliver, and online retailers naturally faced high customer attrition (22% of customers were regularly lost to abandoned shopping carts and 5% of online orders were canceled). As demand for customized manufacturing grew, retailers were expected to look for high-quality onshore manufacturers to fulfill orders.

However, this rapid turnaround was dependent on highly skilled employees who could demonstrate critical thinking, problem-solving, and good communication skills on the manufacturing floor. Schneider would need substantial support to implement and finance a manufacturing company that could deliver on quality, time, and social impact.

While in Aspen, Schneider went on a solitary 17-mile hike through the mountains to sort through her thoughts. After returning to Massachusetts, she gave herself 2 months to reflect and plan on what a sustainable, socially just manufacturing company could look like. Though she still did not know how such a venture would evolve, she applied to the Merrimack Valley Sandbox Business Accelerator Program (Now Entrepreneurship for All) to help her consider the possibilities.

Finding an Entrepreneurial Ecosystem

Merrimack Valley Sandbox was an entrepreneurship empowerment program that sought to build businesses and entrepreneurs outside of the Boston metro area. Desh Deshpande, founder of the Deshpande Foundation and President Obama's appointee to the National Advisory Council on Innovation and Entrepreneurship, was the visionary and primary funder of the Sandbox. The accelerator's mission was to boost "the economic and social well-being of greater Lowell and Lawrence by advancing entrepreneurship and innovation." Participants in the program were placed in cohorts of 20–25 entrepreneurs and assisted by a team of three to four mentors to develop their business plan. Entrepreneurs in the program then gave a final "pitch" to Sandbox judges to win a startup grant.

One of the most important things that Schneider learned from the Sandbox program was lean startup methodology, also known as hypothesis-driven entrepreneurship. Pioneered by Harvard Business School professor Thomas Eisenmann and entrepreneur-in-residence Eric Ries, this methodology enables entrepreneurs to minimize the resources they spend during the startup phase of a new venture by building the business through a series of experiments. Rejecting alternate, less efficient approaches to startups that included what they call "build-it-and-they-will-come," "waterfall" (phased, siloed product development), and "just do it" (improvisation in the absence of vision and planning), Eisenmann and Ries instead propose a seven-step process for a lean startup:

1. Develop a vision;
2. Translate the vision into hypotheses;
3. Specify tests of a minimum viable product;
4. Prioritize tests to sequence them based on high-priority rise elimination;
5. Learn from minimal viable product tests;
6. Act on the data: preserve, pivot, or perish; and if hypotheses are validated,
7. Scale and optimize the venture.[2]

Together, these steps allow the prospective entrepreneur to validate key elements of the business model and, where necessary, make adjustments or terminate the venture before expending significant resources on a product that might not be accepted in the marketplace.

David Parker, co-executive director of Sandbox, reflected that it is important for entrepreneurs to learn lean startup methods and begin testing products with customers early. He stated, "Often, in their mind, the entrepreneur's idea or product is perfect and they won't go to market until it is 100% their vision." Yet, this takes time and money that startups don't have, and customers often quickly reject products or require changes. Parker said that it is "more efficient to minimize the investment in the first product, put something out to customers that is 80% of the core concept, and then adjust from there."[3]

Schneider spent the next 3 months developing her hypothesis by attending Sandbox classes and entrepreneur networking events while building a team of mentors. Her expert team of advisors—Scott McKenzie, CPA at Moody, Famiglietti, and Andronico, LLP;

Bob Zimering, director of Six Sigma at Raytheon; and Michelle Macaux of Next Street—helped her refine the concept and develop her business pitch.

Schneider also networked with her peers, former MoJo employees, consultants, and manufacturing and retail CEOs to develop an effective and profitable model for 99Degrees. It would be a custom-manufacturing company that provided living wages, benefits, and job training to its employees in addition to serving as a launching pad for workers to move on to advanced manufacturing jobs. As a for-profit corporation, the company would emphasize its innovative production methods, quality products, and fast turnaround to gain customers. A higher markup would allow for its socially responsible employment practices.

Parker noted that Sandbox had taken a big risk in including Schneider in their first class since her business idea was much less developed than her peers', yet by the end, they counted her as a model alumna and success in the making. She had won first place in the pitch competition and $7,500 in seed capital to start her venture. With an additional investment of $1,500 from family and friends, she took the plunge to launch her startup and launched in early April 2013.

Financing the Venture

Schneider had built a team of supporters and mentors who shared her vision, but she had to consider how to finance the venture. She reflected:

> One of the hardest things to realize is that so much of the business is about me. I guess this is true for most new ventures—partners are investing in both the venture and the entrepreneur.

American entrepreneurs typically fund their ventures through personal assets. In 2012, more than 60% of startups were financed by savings, and nearly 24% were guaranteed by personal credit or equity. Less than 0.5% obtained venture financing. For this reason, even entrepreneurs who are aided by accelerator programs are usually encouraged to employ "bootstrapping" techniques (such as special financing deals with vendors and customers), taking paid employment, or approaching friends and family for personal loans in order to stretch their resources as far as possible.

Social ventures have been even less likely than purely for-profit startups to attract external equity investment. Investors may be concerned that ventures with a mixed mission of profits and social impact may not maximize their returns, and social entrepreneurs like Schneider were understandably concerned about investor motivations and a potential loss of control. A lack of equity financing means that "bootstrapped" startups scale more slowly and in many cases are unable to invest in systems, equipment, or marketing that would help them be successful.

Jess McLear, a mentor through MassChallenge—a well-known incubator program—with experience in contract manufacturing, reflected that manufacturing inherently involves the use of capital expenditures, debt financing, and flexible credit lines.[4] Without outside financing, Schneider would have to rely on her customers' help to purchase, lease, or borrow equipment until she could build credit. For better or worse, bootstrapping would force Schneider to be strategic in how and when she could take on certain customers.

Since its inception, MoJo had self-financed, eliminating the risk and intervention of investors. But Schneider's initial capital was nowhere near the same level. Angel investors could provide a similar, significant amount of capital but would require that Schneider cede some control over her vision to an investment board. She decided that her priority was the potential for 99Degrees to achieve social impact, so she resolved not to seek equity investors.

That left Schneider with the three most time-intensive funding options: crowdsourcing, government loans, and bootstrapping. The City of Lawrence provided financing to support ventures just like 99Degrees, so Schneider applied for a $36,000 loan. However, the application process took 3 months and required Schneider to submit extensive documentation, including her financial projections, cash flow analysis, income statement, balance sheet, resume, personal credit history, executive summary of the business, sales pipeline, project summary, project budget and its impact on revenue and cash flow, 3 years of past tax returns, and a record of personal assets and liabilities. Once approved, Schneider had to co-sign and guarantee the loan and then submit entirely new documents to the underwriter. After the loan was in place, Schneider had to submit quarterly financials to the city, get their consent on any capital purchase over $5,000, hire at least two low- to moderate-income people within the duration of the loan, and request consent from the city if she intended to move the business out of Lawrence.

In search of more flexible funding, Schneider decided to leverage her networks and pursue partners that would help her grow operations but maintain control.

Commencing Operations

As she started operations, Schneider found an inexpensive space in a mill in Lawrence—a blessing of the city's poor economy and abundant underutilized mill properties—with the option to expand for little money. Working with six donated sewing machines and two workers (a cutter/shipper and a stitcher, both former MoJo employees), she had the capacity to take on orders.

She also reached out to Ross Lohr, a classmate from the Heller School and former coworker (they had waited tables together to support their MBA studies). Lohr was CEO of Project Repat, a social enterprise that provided customers with the opportunity to recycle old clothing into, among other things, new, personalized t-shirt blankets. Project Repat's specialty was connecting consumers to socially responsible manufacturing partners to support "jobs with dignity." Project Repat had experienced consistent growth in sales but needed additional partner manufacturers to achieve their mission and capacity. They chose to team up with 99Degrees and advanced $10,000 to pay for the first month's order.

After 3 months with monthly up-front financing from Project Repat, 99Degrees became cash flow positive with $13,500 in gross revenue in May, $14,000 in June, and $15,000 in July. They were targeted to gross $27,000 by October. However, Schneider remained concerned about stability: 99Degrees was highly dependent on this single customer contract and she still had not drawn a salary.

Operations and Management

Schneider emphasized that she had a clear strategy and understanding of the finances needed to achieve a sustainable scale, keeping a tight record and reign on the company's financials to gauge their progress. She reflected, "It is important to know your numbers and your strategy—really well. I don't think I had a full appreciation of this before actually running a business."

While filling the CEO role, Schneider also served as manager of marketing, operations, and production. This meant that she sometimes had to fill in for sewing, cutting, and shipping orders when necessary. At times her role even included equipment maintenance. One day the die-cut machine malfunctioned, so instead of attending a scheduled meeting with her Sandbox mentors, she spent the evening rewiring the equipment. But this was still a happy outcome of her bootstrapping and networking capabilities—through her network of fellow entrepreneurs and mentors, she had been able to learn the rewiring from an electrician rather than pay for repairs.

Nonetheless, the stress was considerable. Running the venture made for long days, and in the first 3 months she averaged 80 hours per week. She related, "The work is incredibly 'unsexy' and incredibly difficult but equally rewarding. Each day I see progress and steps taken toward my vision."

Her efforts began to pay off, and by late July she had hired six employees, freeing some of her time to deal with the management and development of the business. Her time spent away from the manufacturing floor was dedicated to building a community of people who would support her vision.

This networking leveraged immediate results; for example, she was able to get a significant equipment upgrade—the die-cut machine—for considerably less than market value due to a professional connection. This incremental scaling in machinery and capacity also helped her to develop a customer pipeline. In July she signed on two new customers (ReFried Tees and Wild Things) to begin contracts in the fall.

That same month she began speaking with a nationally known athletic clothier on production options. But she was worried: these agreements would require her to invest in higher-capacity equipment to successfully meet the production schedule as well as force her to seek new financing options. While it was difficult not to diversify 99Degrees's revenue base, she was not sure exactly how and where they fit into a target customer profile or portfolio. While every day she had to deal with immediate operational issues, she knew they distracted her from making these kinds of decisions.

As a social entrepreneur, Schneider also had to consider how to grow the venture in the next few years, sustain that growth, and then either continue to scale or exit. By the end of 2013 she expected to gross $450,000 and create 10 living-wage jobs. If she could get the model right, she projected that she could employ over 200 people by 2018. Beyond that, she was unsure how to continue to enable 99Degrees to achieve its social and economic mission.

Next Steps

Leveraging the Ecosystem

In May 2013, Schneider learned that she had been selected as a finalist in the world's largest accelerator program, MassChallenge. That year, 1,300 businesses worldwide applied to be a part of MassChallenge and only 128 finalists were selected to participate. As a finalist, she had access to free office space, mentorships, corporate discounts, and a support network of peer entrepreneurs for 4 intense months to develop her pitch. In October, she would have the chance to compete for $100,000 in grant funding in the final pitch contest.

Having learned from the Sandbox program that the mentorships were invaluable to the hypothesis process, Schneider quickly built a team of four advisors and set up a schedule and meeting plan for the group. She hoped to use their experience to her advantage and either make their mistakes faster or avoid them entirely. Two of her MassChallenge advisors, the former CFO of Clarks Shoes in the Boston region, Mark Bouckley, and venture investor Jess McLear, stressed that building a customer pipeline would be a big issue for 99Degrees. Although Schneider would have to chase a specific customer profile, working in a niche market would require her to be able to react quickly to opportunities as they arose.

Despite the challenges, Bouckley adamantly supported Schneider and her venture:

> You can't separate Brenna from 99Degrees. She's so authentic and it's so obvious that she has a passion and belief in what she's doing . . . that's why I was willing to be part of her mentor team. On the customer side and employee side it's all about Brenna, and until the company hits a proof point it will remain that way.[5]

Social Impact

Schneider developed a theory of change to guide her work, and with the help of a team of consultants from the Heller School, Schneider also hoped to narrow in on a sustainable growth strategy to achieve her social mission. The consultants helped her to create "tiers" of possible benefits to provide for each of 99Degrees's core social components (health care, childcare, social capital, education, and mentoring). For example, the childcare tier would progress from a basic benefit (offering assistance in finding childcare) to a premium benefit (like providing nanny care). The team mapped out the cost of each tier for each benefit along with a revenue map so that she could progress the benefit structure as revenues grew.

Scaling

Schneider also considered vertical integration—branching out into branded products and online sales as MoJo had done. But, after considering her strengths, she decided to hold back on this option. She believed that her strengths lay in operations management rather than brand-building and marketing. Lacking a strong employee or partner who would lead that part of the business, she decided it was premature to pursue this option. She was also chastened by MoJo's failure, which had occurred in part, she believed, because they had tried to do so many things at once.

The Road Ahead

Schneider left her meeting with Warren and Markey feeling empowered and inspired, but as she returned to her mill in Lawrence she wondered about several things. Primarily, she contemplated how best to grow 99Degrees. Based on her Heller consulting team's research, having a real impact would depend on growing, but what would be sustainable? Though demand for custom and build-to-order manufacturing was accelerating, her high cost of labor meant worrisomely low profit margins. While having a goal of $300 million would reach the most families, she may only be able to sustain a $10 million business. Once she decided on a revenue goal, would 99Degrees reach that scale in Lawrence, or would she need to move outside of the Merrimack Valley? Would she (or should she) have an exit strategy after 5 years like most startups?

She also reminded herself that she needed to address the diversity of her clients. She worried about how to scale her client base incrementally and sustainably, given that sales and marketing were not her favorite activities. While she recognized the risks of being dependent on one customer and the benefit of a well-established and predictable relationship, she anticipated struggling with how much time to invest in customer development and whether she should do this herself or engage others.

A related problem was financing. Schneider had effectively bootstrapped to date but felt the frustrations of this every day as limited equipment investments inhibited her productivity. But she was also wary of growing the venture too quickly and making poor scaling and investment decisions. While she was confident about her ability to attract some level of external financing (debt or equity) and was sure it would enable her to scale much more quickly, she worried about the costs. Her experience with the City of Lawrence loan had demonstrated that while growth capital was valuable, it could come with a hefty dose of external control.

As she thought about other potential outside investors, she worried: Would they share her vision in the long run? How involved would they want to be in decision-making? Bouckley had suggested that her limited financing options would quickly weed out financiers who were not aligned with her vision. Yet, how much precious time would it take to cultivate investor relationships and then work with their expectations?

As she prepared to revisit the same Heller classroom—this time to talk about 99Degrees—she also worried about herself. It had been months since she had taken the time to relax, read a good book, or go out with friends for dinner. She recognized that it was important to stay fresh so that she could maintain perspective, but she also knew that 99Degrees was at a fragile and important inflection point. How long could she sustain the 80-hour weeks? Did she need to slow down? As she said goodnight to her stitchers for the evening and swept the floor in the production room, she wondered how she would deal with the pressure.

Discussion Questions

1. How do you define social entrepreneurship? What are the essential elements?
2. What is your assessment of Schneider's effectiveness at the time of the case?
3. What do you see as the primary challenges ahead for 99Degrees? How should Schneider address them?
4. What lessons are there generally from this case for aspiring social entrepreneurs?

NOTES

1. Brenna Nan Schneider, interview with the authors, August 1, 2013.
2. Thomas Eisenmann, Eric Ries, and Sarah Dillard. "Hypothesis-Driven Entrepreneurship: The Lean Startup." HBS Case Collection Background Note 812-095. Boston: Harvard Business School, December 2011 (Revised July 2013).
3. David Parker, interview with the authors, August 10, 2013.
4. Jess McLear, interview with the authors, August 8, 2013.
5. Mark Bouckley, interview with the authors, August 20, 2013.

The Kindness of Human Milk

CASE 2.2

The Founding of Mothers' Milk Bank Northeast

NAOMI BROMBERG BAR-YAM AND MARK I. ROSEN

Naomi Bromberg Bar-Yam sat in a quiet booth at the back of the hotel restaurant preparing for her meeting with a new potential merger partner. As she took notes for the upcoming meeting, she reflected on all that had been accomplished since the founding of Mothers' Milk Bank Northeast in 2007, 5 years earlier.[1] Not only had she been able to find mothers willing to donate their excess milk, but she had also convinced hospitals to use human milk for fragile newborns rather than infant formula created from cow's milk. But she was concerned about the milk bank's future. This new proposed partnership, if finalized, would help her address some significant challenges. Demand was increasing. Would the milk bank be able to scale up production to meet this demand? Or would it make more sense to merge with other nonprofit milk banks in the country to centralize production? The stakes were high for the organization she had founded and cared deeply about—so she wanted to make the right decision.

The Birth of a New Organization

Naomi Bar-Yam was trained as a social worker, childbirth educator, and doula (someone who supports new mothers through labor and childbirth). Both of her two youngest children had a low birthweight and needed to spend time after birth in a hospital neonatal intensive care unit (NICU), where specially trained staff could provide 24-hour care and monitoring.

For both babies, Bar-Yam produced more milk than her babies needed. When the first was born in an overseas hospital, Bar-Yam was the only mother in the NICU with excess milk, so, at the physician's request, she gave some of it to another baby in the NICU who needed it.[2]

Later, Bar-Yam earned a PhD with a focus on Children and Family Policy from the Heller School for Social Policy and Management at Brandeis University. Her dissertation was a study of breastfeeding in the workplace.

Despite her personal and professional background, Bar-Yam was not aware that human milk banks existed until she began to seek a source of breast milk for a close family member. Investigating further, she was surprised to discover that the nearest milk bank to Boston was in Ohio and wondered why Boston did not have one. As she began to learn more about human milk banking, she was also surprised to find that hospitals rarely fed human milk to fragile preterm babies in NICUs if their mothers could not produce milk. The normative practice was for hospitals to feed babies infant formula made from cow's milk. This was not just the case in NICUs—the use of infant formula for newborn babies was pervasive in hospitals.

These considerations led Bar-Yam to think about starting a milk bank in Boston.

Infant Formula, Human Milk, and Human Milk Banks

Ever since commercial infant formulas were first developed in 1865, businesses have marketed infant formula based on cow's milk to doctors, hospitals, and parents. These marketing efforts have largely succeeded at making infant formula the norm to which other feeding methods, including breastfeeding and human milk, were compared. Manufacturers extolled the qualities of their particular formula, including how close their brand was to mothers' own milk, its convenience, standardization, scientific development and production, ease of measuring, nutrient balance, and more.

There is extensive research about the value of human milk, especially for preterm and fragile babies.[3] Despite this research, the largely volunteer and nonprofit breastfeeding community, as well physicians and academic researchers who advocate for the use of human milk, could not compete with the corporate research and marketing budgets of profit-oriented formula companies.

Human milk and breastfeeding are more than nutrition. Mothers' milk is medicine, containing immunological as well as neurological benefits that promote a variety of growth factors that cannot be reproduced in infant formula. The composition of each mother's milk supply adapts to a growing baby's needs, protecting the baby's immature immune system, supporting its brain growth, and priming its gut microbiome. None of these factors are found in commercial formulas. These components of human milk are crucial for the growth and development of all babies, but they are especially critical for preterm babies. Some of the short-term and long-term benefits of human milk include:

- Nutrients in human milk are better absorbed and used by babies than nutrients in infant formula.
- Human milk contains nutrients and other components to support a baby's brain growth and nervous system development. Studies showed that babies fed human milk performed better on intelligence tests when they grew older.
- Babies are born with immature immune systems. The disease-fighting qualities of human milk support infants' immune system development and help to prevent mild to severe infections and hospitalization.
- Babies fed formula have a far greater number of digestive, lung, and ear infections.
- Premature babies fed human milk are less likely to get a serious, often fatal infection of the intestines called necrotizing enterocolitis (NEC).

Informally, human milk is called "liquid gold" because of its value and golden hue, which is distinctly different from the familiar white hue of cow's milk. And while it is clear from research that babies benefit greatly from human milk, not all mothers are able to nurse their babies. Milk banks fill this gap. A milk bank is a nonprofit organization that accepts donations of mothers' milk from mothers who produce more than their babies need. Mothers are initially screened for health, lifestyle, and medications, and if the donating mother meets the screening criteria, her excess milk is shipped to a milk bank, where it is pooled with other mothers' milk, bottled, pasteurized, and tested. It is then dispensed primarily to fragile, premature, hospitalized babies. Mothers are not paid for the milk they donate so that their motivation is purely altruistic.

The need for human milk in hospitals is extensive. Modern medicine and technology enable preterm babies to survive and thrive when, only a decade or so ago, these babies—including babies born 3 or more months early and weighing less than a pound—would not have survived. Mothers of these premature babies may not yet be lactating, so babies require lifesaving milk from another source. In addition to preterm babies, full-term babies might also need milk at home if their mothers are unable to produce a sufficient quantity.

Mothers have shared milk among family, clan, and community for millennia. The first human milk bank in North America opened in 1910 at the Boston Floating Hospital for Children.[4] The movement continued to grow, and by the early 1980s there were over 50 milk banks throughout North America, most affiliated with a hospital.

However, the uncertainty of whether HIV/AIDS could transmit through human milk forced many milk banks to close in the early 1980s. In 1985, the remaining milk banks came together to form the Human Milk Banking Association of North America (HMBANA).[5] HMBANA's initial mission was to develop a set of evidence-based guidelines to assure that the donor milk fed to fragile preterm babies was safe. These were developed in compliance with Food and Drug Administration (FDA) and Health Canada regulations and in conversation with the Centers for Disease Control and Prevention (CDC). Safety standards were updated biannually based on continuing research and updated FDA and Health Canada regulations. Today, the FDA considers donor milk to be a food and regulates it as such.

Modern nonprofit milk banks in North America follow one of two models: hospital-affiliated and free-standing. In 2021, there were more than 30 nonprofit human milk banks in North America and more than 750 around the world.[6]

From Idea to Organization

Bar-Yam felt strongly that Boston, with its world-class medical centers, should have a human milk bank. In 2006, after years of thinking about the topic and conversations with friends and family, she gathered a group of people at her dining room table to discuss the possibility of starting one. The group consisted mostly of lactation consultants and nurses.

It turned out that there had previously been a human milk bank in Massachusetts for 25 years based at a hospital in the city of Worcester. It had been closed abruptly in 2001 after a change of ownership despite its importance. Based on that history, it was clear that a new milk bank in Boston should be free-standing rather than affiliated with a specific hospital.

To officially become a nonprofit milk bank, the organization needed to be approved by the IRS. Bar-Yam took one look at the lengthy application, shut off her computer, and avoided the process for months. Finally, in 2007, a friend who was also an attorney specializing in nonprofit law helped her to complete the 501(c)(3) application, create a fledgling board, and develop bylaws.[7]

Learning and Advocating

The science of human milk banking was complex, and Bar-Yam spent a great deal of time educating herself. She started to visit hospitals, often making cold calls to anyone involved with lactation or neonatology who would talk to her. It was a process of trial and error. She found that lactation nurses, who were trained in helping new mothers feed their babies after birth, were very interested in her quest, but physicians were more reluctant.

Bar-Yam began visiting other milk banks around the country, in one case piggybacking a visit on a wedding trip. It was becoming clear that this was not going to be easy. It would be complicated to screen donors before the milk bank could receive their milk. It would also be necessary to create a milk intake process, obtain equipment for storing and pasteurizing the milk, and establish a mechanism for shipping it safely to hospitals and parents receiving milk at home. She would need to develop relationships with each hospital. Someone would need to focus on the financials.

At this point, even though Bar-Yam and the Board had raised a modest amount of funding, she had little experience fundraising and was uncomfortable with the prospect of asking for the sums of money that would be needed to cover startup costs. Plus, there was still little demand by hospitals for what the new Mothers' Milk Bank Northeast (MMBNE) would be offering. She would need to advocate extensively, drawing upon the existing body of research on the medical benefits of human milk.

Finding and Equipping a Facility

MMBNE found its first space, rent-free, in 2008. As the organization slowly developed a process of screening donors and pasteurizing milk, it received processed milk from the recently established Ohio Mothers' Milk Bank to dispense, at a small markup, so that it could establish relationships with local hospitals in anticipation of starting its own operation. To safely store milk, MMBNE needed freezers. Tufts Medical Center donated an industrial freezer, and MMBNE also purchased several scratch and dent household freezers.

The physician and nurse involved in the defunct Worcester milk bank were both generous with their time, advice, and expertise. The physician became MMBNE's medical director and helped to create a medical advisory board. Bar-Yam was also mentored by the executive director of the Ohio milk bank.

MMBNE created a small but functional milk processing lab and began to screen donors and process milk. Demand from hospitals was slowly developing. In 2011, MMBNE received certification from the Human Milk Banking Association of North America.

Initially, MMBNE operated on a shoestring budget. Individuals volunteered their labor and gave in-kind donations. MMBNE also won a $10,000 grant from Ideablob, an organization that supported social entrepreneurial startups. To cover the costs of building the milk processing lab, several board members made low-interest loans, which were repaid by the milk bank within a couple of years. When MMBNE could finally afford to hire staff, it hired two individuals, one to process the milk and one to conduct donor screenings.

Got Breast Milk? The Challenges of Finding and Screening Milk Donors

In many ways, milk banking is similar to blood banking. Both require acquiring unique renewable body fluids that cannot be replicated in a lab. But while blood donors can donate multiple times a year throughout their lives, only individuals who are lactating can donate milk, and they can only donate while they are nursing. MMBNE needed human milk to operate, but human milk cannot be ordered from a vendor in the same way that a manufacturer can order raw materials. There was an ever-present need for MMBNE to find new donors.

MMBNE faced two challenges:

1. It needed to make the concept of milk donation widely known to bring in milk donations.
2. It needed to create a process for medically screening milk donors before accepting their donations. Then, it needed to create a process for milk donors to easily ship their milk to the new milk bank. Both processes would need to be cost-free and relatively simple for the donor, while being cost-effective and error-free for MMBNE.

When MMBNE started, the concept of blood donation was universally accepted by the public, but the concept of milk donation was almost completely unknown. MMBNE began by using multiple approaches to get the word out, including social media, stories on its website, coverage in newspapers and on television, and information provided to hospitals and pediatricians.

These approaches proved to be successful early on—once mothers knew about the option of donating their excess milk, they were very willing to do it and tell their friends, neighbors, colleagues, and family members about it. Momentum started to build.

HMBANA had already developed standards and guidelines for screening milk donors, in large part based on blood donor screening procedures. Donors answered a series of questions about their medical history, provided bloodwork, and had paperwork signed by the donors' and babies' physicians. MMBNE customized these standards and guidelines, found labs to do the blood testing and milk testing, and developed a precise and detailed set of recordkeeping procedures.[8]

The cost of screening for MMBNE was \$100–\$125 per mother and took, on average, 2–3 weeks.

Later, MMBNE began to establish milk depots, where screened donors could drop off their milk locally rather than ship it. Milk depots became an important community presence, increasing visibility and enhancing recognition of the importance of milk donation and breastfeeding.

The Yuck Problem: The Challenges of Getting Medical Buy-In

As it was becoming established, MMBNE not only needed to generate a supply of milk, but it also needed to educate hospitals about the benefits of human milk so that they would use it instead of infant formula made from cow's milk. Over the last century, the infant formula industry had effectively made its product the norm for infant feeding. The industry engaged in sophisticated efforts to educate medical providers so that they would choose infant formula as the default for babies rather than supporting mothers to breastfeed or use donor milk. Yet research clearly indicated that human milk had superior outcomes, particularly for fragile newborns.

While breastfeeding was very familiar to medical providers, the use of donor milk was not, in spite of the fact that mothers had shared milk in various ways for millennia. The concept was uncomfortable for highly trained, technologically advanced medical practitioners in the 21st century.

Medical practitioners generally raised two objections to the use of donor milk:

1. The first was labeled as the "yuck" problem. Physicians thought it was weird for babies to get milk from someone other than their own mother. Bar-Yam

countered with a compelling argument—it was also weird to give human babies highly processed milk from a cow that was originally intended for consumption by a calf.

2. Providers and hospitals had many legitimate questions about the safety of donor milk and the differences between donor milk and milk provided by the mother of a baby.

Educating the medical community would be crucial to the success of MMBNE. One of the earliest efforts to educate the medical community took place in 2010 when MMBNE hosted the international HMBANA conference in Boston. Hosting the conference locally made it easier for local providers and researchers to attend. The conference conferred legitimacy to concepts that were initially unfamiliar to the local medical community. It also inspired local medical professionals to attend other conferences sponsored by HMBANA and bring back cutting-edge research and best practices to their institutions and colleagues.

The first real breakthrough took place when three major hospitals in Boston—Massachusetts General Hospital, Brigham and Women's Hospital, and Boston Children's Hospital, all teaching hospitals for Harvard Medical School—started using MMBNE's donor milk in their NICUs. All had international reputations, and when other hospitals learned that these three hospitals were using donor milk, it gave MMBNE instant credibility locally. It also gave the concept of using donor milk credibility nationally.

Bar-Yam's personal and academic background proved to be critical. She could speak intelligently and credibly to medical professionals about the issues and address their concerns. Increasingly, she was invited to hospitals, where she would explain the steps involved in using donor milk, offer staff training, and speak to physicians about the science and medical research.

MMBNE established active medical and research advisory boards with top practitioners in neonatology, infectious disease, nursing, nutrition, lactation consulting, and pharmacology as well as researchers in human milk, breastfeeding, epidemiology, and public health. These boards also generated cross-communication and collaboration among institutions and colleagues.

In addition, MMBNE began to host a listserv for hospital-based nurses, physicians, dieticians, and lactation consultants. This forum allowed them to ask questions and share information with colleagues specifically related to hospital donor milk policies and best practices.

Once a booklet was written to help hospitals start using donor milk, more and more hospitals began to sign on. The tipping point came when hospitals started reaching out to MMBNE, including hospitals outside of New England.

The Urge to Merge

Unlike the vast majority of nonprofits, the milk bank was now operating almost entirely on a fee-for-service basis; revenues from hospital purchases were sufficient to keep the organization afloat.

Now that both the supply and demand for human milk were established and growing and the organization was financially sound, production became the central focus of the milk bank. Donor milk needed to be bottled, pasteurized, and shipped on a daily basis.[9]

However, Bar-Yam and her staff lacked operations expertise. There was only one board member who had this experience, but he could only do so much as a volunteer.

Because of the production challenge, Bar-Yam's thinking turned to the possibility of a merger with one or more of the other milk banks in the United States. While the ongoing process of finding donors and building relationships with hospitals needed to be done locally, a central milk processing and shipping facility for multiple milk banks would offer economies of scale and could be located anywhere that had overnight shipping access. Much like a commercial dairy, it would be run by individuals with production and food manufacturing expertise. The process would be more efficient and reduce waste, and, overall, more milk would be produced.

One barrier was public relations. When individuals visited the milk bank, seeing the big freezers and watching the milk being processed was the primary draw. If there was a central processing facility, from a visitor perspective, the milk bank would just be another office. This barrier could be potentially overcome through the use of videos that would explain and illustrate how the milk was processed.

There was also the challenge of determining how costs and revenues would be distributed among the various milk banks who would join in this proposed merger. Bar-Yam saw this as a difficult but solvable problem.

A group in a nearby state was thinking about starting its own milk bank. Bar-Yam saw them as natural partners for a merger. But conversations were not making any headway. They wanted to operate independently.

Should Bar-Yam press forward on finding other partners for a merger? Or should she take on the challenge of ramping up production locally?

Discussion Questions

1. Put yourself in Bar-Yam's shoes. If you were starting a new milk bank, how would you have educated yourself about human milk banking if you had no knowledge or experience in the field?
2. How would you have responded when you learned that interest and knowledge among physicians in prescribing donated human milk for babies was limited? Would you have persisted? How would you have convinced them of its value, creating demand for your organization's service?
3. Bar-Yam indicated that she was uncomfortable fundraising. What should she do?
4. The milk bank had a constant need for new donors, since mothers only lactated for a fixed period of time. What should Bar-Yam do to ensure an ongoing supply of human milk?
5. How important were the medical and research boards to the success of the milk bank?

NOTES

1. The organization was founded as Mothers' Milk Bank of New England, and the name was changed to Mothers' Milk Bank Northeast in 2013.
2. Although, at the time, Bar-Yam's milk was cultured to determine if it contained bacteria that would be harmful to another baby, milk sharing would not have taken place in U.S. hospitals largely due to concerns about milk safety, liability, and unfamiliarity with and qualms about the practice.

3. Fabio Mosca, and Maria Lorella Gianni, "Human Milk: Composition and Health Benefits," *La Pediatria Medica e Chirurgica* 39, no. 2 (2017): 155, https://doi.org/10.4081/pmc.2017.155; Joan Younger Meek and Lawrence Noble, "Technical Report: Breastfeeding and the Use of Human Milk," *Pediatrics* 150, no. 1 (2022), https://doi.org/10.1542/peds.2022-057989; Johns Hopkins Medicine, "Breast Milk Is Best," n.d., https://www.hopkinsmedicine.org/health/conditions-and-diseases/breastfeeding-your-baby/breast-milk-is-the-best-milk; Margaret G. Parker, Lisa M. Stellwagen, Lawrence Noble, Jae H. Kim, Brenda B. Poindexter, Karen M. Puopolo, "Promoting Human Milk and Breastfeeding for the Very Low Birth Weight Infant," *Pediatrics* 145, no. 5 (2021), https://doi.org/10.1542/peds.2021-054272; "Section on Breastfeeding: Breastfeeding and the Use of Human Milk," *Pediatrics* 129, no. 3 (2012): 827–41, https://doi.org/10.1542/peds.2011-3552.
4. Guido E. Moro, "History of Milk Banking: From Origin to Present Time," *Breastfeeding Medicine* 13, no S1 (2018), https://doi.org/10.1089/bfm.2018.29077.gem.
5. "Human Milk Banking Association of North America - HMBANA," n.d., https://www.hmbana.org/.
6. Mirriam Tyebally Fang, Efstratios Chatzixiros, Laurence Grummer-Strawn, Cyril Engmann, Kiersten Israel-Ballard, Kimberly Mansen, Deborah O'Connor, Sharon Unger, Marisa Herson, Gillian Weaver, and Nikola Biller-Andorno, "Developing Global Guidance on Human Milk Banking," *Bulletin of the World Health Organization* 99, no. 12 (2021): 892–900, https://doi.org/10.2471/blt.21.286943.
7. 501(c)(3) refers to the part of the U.S. tax code that designates an organization as nonprofit and tax-exempt.
8. "Donor Milk Safety and Screening," n.d., Mothers' Milk Bank Northeast. https://milkbankne.org/safety/.
9. Human milk was bottled first before it was pasteurized. Pasteurizing the milk in vats and then bottling it was not feasible for a small operation like a milk bank.

SECTION 3

Social Impact Finance Cases

CASE 3.1

Engage or Divest?

Trillium Asset Management, Facebook Governance, and Shareholder Advocacy

MONIQUE DESIMONE, JESS LYNCH-FOUST,
DOUGLASS GUERNSEY, AND LAURA BURROUGHS

The tension at Facebook's annual meeting in 2019 was unusually high. Following an onslaught of controversial events involving Facebook—including the Cambridge Analytica scandal, the proliferation of false information on the platform, and Russian meddling in the 2016 United States presidential election—many shareholders began to see Facebook's CEO, Mark Zuckerberg, as a serious governance risk.

For 3 years, the shareholder advocacy team at Trillium Asset Management had been trying to address this risk through the processes of shareholder proposals. Each annual meeting, the team at Trillium would submit a proposal to improve Facebook's Environmental, Social, and Governance (ESG) performance, but Zuckerberg and his super majority of voting shares quashed each proposal. The Shareholder Advocacy Team faced a pivotal decision:

- Would next year be the tipping point for Trillium to divest from Facebook and avoid potential losses? Or would the Shareholder Advocacy Team recommend continuing to engage with the company to improve governance from within?

Trillium Asset Management Background

Trillium Asset Management, established by Joan Bavaria in 1982, was one of the first socially responsible investing firms to integrate material ESG factors into its investment analysis (Exhibit 1). Within the industry, material ESG factors are considered to be those that impact the bottom line. Bavaria was considered a founding thought leader in the ecosystem of social impact investing. As of 2022, Trillium offered a multitude of actively managed mutual funds with exposure to a diversified array of asset classes.

ESG analysts and portfolio managers at Trillium utilized their own metrics, as well as data from various third-party providers such as Sustainalytics and MSCI, to source information for holistic investment evaluation. Exclusionary (negative) screens were used to eliminate companies with high, material ESG risk embedded in a company's value chain. On the other hand, a positive attribute screener was utilized to identify companies with best-in-class ESG performance that had the potential for superior market returns in the long-term.[1]

Shareholder Advocacy

Trillium's Shareholder Advocacy Team used several strategies including dialogue, public policy, proxy voting, and shareholder proposals, which effectively let it "lobby" its holding companies. Dialogue could foster change broadly by building rapport and increasing corporate engagement. Shareholder resolutions were submitted as documents with support from large institutional investors who may be internal or external to Trillium. While shareholder proposals with majority support were not binding decisions for a company, they did apply pressure on the organization. Trillium also promoted change on the policy level when public support and large sweeping action were more suitable strategies.

Trillium and Governance Factors

Governance factors include criteria that typically drive strong fundamental performance via internal structures, systems, and policies. Organizational infrastructure and management practices such as board diversity, separation of CEO and board chair, executive pay, and corporate transparency are core governance issues that can impact financial, social, and environmental risks.

Historically, Trillium had found that governance risks were a leading indicator of poor performance. Trillium CEO Matt Patsky recounted, "Enron early on had positioned itself as a player in the traditional energy space that was focused on energy efficiency. It became a darling of the Socially Responsible Investment movement back in the 1990s."[2] However, Trillium's fundamental ESG analysis identified Enron's governance issues as a risk to its investment viability. Despite Enron's popularity and seemingly strong mission fit, Trillium divested from its holdings by the mid-1990s due to lack of transparency in the organization's governance. As Patsky explained, "The corporate governance structure had deteriorated to where you really couldn't tell what was happening."[3]

Trillium's Investment in Facebook, Buy-Side Indicators

At the time of Trillium's initial investment in the second quarter of 2017, Facebook was a promising "buy." It surpassed a landmark of 2 billion active monthly users on its platform.[4] Facebook's acquisition of Instagram provided additional advertising revenue, which analysts estimated at nearly $4 billion in 2017.[5] By the middle of the fourth quarter of 2017, Facebook's share price had increased by over 50% since the beginning of the year.[6] Facebook's 2017 full-year financial highlights revealed strong fundamentals with a revenue increase of 47% year over year (Exhibit 2).[7]

Initially, Trillium identified several positive social factors with Facebook. As a social network with unprecedented reach, Facebook brought a new level of interconnectivity to nearly every corner of the globe. While Trillium recognized risks around issues of privacy and governance, the fundamental performance of the company and social benefits it provided qualified Facebook for Trillium's buy-list of investments.

Facebook's Background

Facebook was founded in February 2004 when Mark Zuckerberg and his roommates coded "The Facebook" in their Harvard dormitory. The Facebook differed from other contemporary social networking sites like Friendster by restricting access to students at universities, allowing for greater privacy protection.[8] After experiencing rapid growth, Zuckerberg dropped out of Harvard and moved to California, where he successfully raised $500,000 in seed funding from PayPal founder and investor Peter Thiel.[9] Zuckerberg significantly shaped the culture and environment of Facebook through his tight control of the company. Until 2008, he presided over both the engineering and business sides of the company as CEO, encouraging new hires to be "hackers," to "move fast and break things," and to "think like Zuck."[10]

Facebook Governance

Zuckerberg continued to consolidate his control of Facebook. In November 2009, Facebook enacted a dual-class stock structure in which both Zuckerberg's shares and current Facebook employees' shares were converted to "Class B" shares, which had the voting power of 10 votes per share.[11] When the company went public in 2012, it issued "Class A" shares, which had a 1:1 vote to share ratio.[12] The voting power differential between share classes effectively diluted the voting power of public investors relative to Facebook insiders.

Zuckerberg was the CEO and chair of the Board of Directors due to his majority of Class B shares, meaning no individual or group could have oversight of Zuckerberg. Under the corporate governance rules of NASDAQ, Facebook was a "controlled company" and as such was not required to have a majority of independent board members.[13] Zuckerberg used this power to make several fast-paced decisions. For instance, when Facebook purchased Instagram for $1 billion in 2012, Zuckerberg did not consult Facebook's Board of Directors, leading one Forbes contributor to compare the Facebook board to "the indulgent parent of Zuck."[14] Zuckerberg moved to consolidate power further by creating a new "Class C" stock with zero voting rights in 2016. However, non-insider investor action including litigation by Sjunde AP-Fonden and the Amalgamated Bank—a union-founded, socially responsible bank—as well as public pressure stemming from Facebook's mishandling of misinformation campaigns on the platform during the 2016 presidential election swayed the board to abandon their plan in 2017.[15]

In 2017, Facebook's Board of Directors consisted of two Facebook executives, Mark Zuckerberg and Sheryl Sandberg, and six independent board members (Exhibit 3). At the time, Dr. Susan Desmond-Hellman held the position of lead independent director, whose primary role was to act as a liaison between the chairman and the independent board members. The board also had specified committees designated for audit and compensation and governance.[16] As Facebook's CEO, board chair, and largest, controlling stockholder, Zuckerberg held near total control of the company with 60% of Facebook's voting shares.[17]

Additional Facebook ESG Risks

In 2009, the public began to unearth concerns about Facebook's privacy policies.[18] Unbeknownst to users, the platform was collecting their data and sharing the information with other third-party applications (apps). Additionally, Facebook's website updates transitioned users' private information to public without user consent. The resulting 2011 settlement with the Federal Trade Commission prohibited Facebook from making misrepresentations about privacy and required them to independently audit its privacy program every 2 years.[19]

As previously mentioned, following the 2016 presidential election, Facebook was caught providing data to Cambridge Analytica, which sold user data to the Trump campaign. The data of 87 million people were leaked through the use of a third-party quiz app that exposed the information of users and their friends.[20] Facebook also revealed that prior to the election, 470 fake accounts linked to Russia spent $100,000 on advertisements that fueled divisiveness.[21] The controversy surrounding Facebook's advertising practices also involved Facebook's exclusion of Black users from seeing relevant and local employment and housing ads.[22] Additionally, Facebook's self-service and ad-buying system allowed advertisers to target users interested in explicit, antisemitic topics.[23]

Engagement With Facebook

Recognizing Facebook's governance structure as a fundamental risk to the company's ability to assess their societal impact and respond to controversy, Trillium filed a shareholder proposal in 2017 requesting the establishment of a Risk Oversight Committee (Exhibit 4). Despite receiving 45% support from non-insider shares (11.55% of all shares), the board voted against establishing the committee at the 2018 annual meeting, citing that the board fundamentally managed risk and directly exercised this responsibility through its existing committee structure (Exhibit 5).[24]

Also in 2017, a shareholder proposal was filed to disband the dual-class share structure (who filed the proposal was not publicly disclosed). It received 83.2% support from non-insider shares at the annual meeting in 2018.[25] Despite the overwhelming support from outside investors, the board used their enhanced voting power to avoid the removal of the dual-class share structure.

Following the 2018 vote against the Risk Oversight Committee, Facebook engaged with Trillium on their integration of a risk oversight function within their Audit Committee. Given the significant duties of the Audit Committee, Trillium felt that Facebook's actions did not provide adequate risk oversight. With few governance mechanisms available to counterbalance Zuckerberg's power, Trillium believed that an independent board chair would allow the company to delineate oversight and strategic guidance from direct management.[26] With promising support from non-insider shareholders on governance related proposals, Trillium filed a proposal in 2018 that targeted the separation of Facebook's CEO and board chair position (Exhibit 5).

At the 2019 annual meeting, the proposal received support from 68% of non-insider shares (20% of all shares).[27] The board once again voted against changing the governance infrastructure, maintaining Zuckerberg's unchallenged control over the company. According to Facebook's opposing statement, separating the CEO and board chair position was unnecessary due to the presence of the lead independent director position.[28]

Despite the board's 2019 vote against the separation of CEO and board chair, Trillium was determined to improve Facebook's governance and oversight of management, believing that reducing Zuckerberg's power was necessary to rebuild public trust and brand reputation.[29] On October 30, 2019, Dr. Susan Desmond-Hellman resigned from Facebook's Board of Directors and vacated the position of lead independent director.[30] These factors, in concert with the promising support of and momentum behind its previous proposals, led Trillium to submit another proposal in 2019 to separate the position of board chair and CEO (Exhibit 6).

The results at the 2020 annual meeting delivered 63.8% support from broader investors (19.5% total shares). Although Trillium had proven consistent shareholder support of the issue, the board again rejected the shareholder proposal.[31]

Divest or Hold?

Upon returning from the 2020 annual meeting, Trillium reflected on its journey engaging with Facebook. For 4 years, they had tried to influence Facebook to provide oversight of the company's CEO through dialogue and shareholder proposals. While they had notable support from outside investors, with each proposal gaining traction, it was clear that Zuckerberg would still maintain control of the company.

On the other hand, Facebook was still a profitable investment for Trillium's shareholders and remained a strong platform for connectivity. Trillium had not developed a divestment coalition with other investment firms and its divestment alone was unlikely to influence Facebook. If Trillium maintained a stake in Facebook, it could continue to push for incremental changes to improve Facebook's ESG performance.

Trillium's Shareholder Advocacy Team pondered this complex decision. Should they maintain ownership of Facebook and continue attempts to improve their governance risks? Could they turn a blind eye to Facebook's controversies and focus on their financial performance? Alternatively, should they divest from the company? Was divesting now the right time? When would it be better to engage or divest to drive change?

Discussion Questions

1. At what point does governance oversight become a material question for ESG ratings?
2. Engagement versus divestment: What is the utility of each?
3. Are shareholder proposals effective?
4. In what ways can poor governance lead to compounded material risks for firms?
5. What were the tools at Trillium's disposal for influencing Facebook? Did you find one more effective than others?

APPENDIX A

Environmental, Social and Governance (ESG) Investing Overview

History

With the civil rights movement, the Vietnam war, and growing environmentalism in the 1960s and 1970s, the term socially responsible investing (SRI) was coined to denote the use of negative screens to avoid investment in industries like alcohol, tobacco, weapons, gambling, and fossil fuels. Driven by faith-based organizations' desire to place ethical parameters on their investments, values-based avoidance screens were initially utilized to forgo investment in "sin stocks."[32] The first sustainable mutual fund, Pax World Balanced Fund, was launched in 1971 to provide investors with an investment option that negated direct investment in Agent Orange and other controversial weapons of war.[33]

In the 1990s, Environmental, Social, and Governance (ESG) investing evolved from SRI by leveraging ESG analytics to identify attractive long-term investment opportunities and additional risk factors.[34] Fundamentally, ESG investing posited that companies who promoted long-term societal benefits also outperformed other companies financially.[35]

ESG Investment Strategies

ESG investing includes several investment strategies that vary in substance and scope: impact, thematic, engagement, negative screens, and integration strategies.[36] Also known as concessionary investing, impact investment strategies prioritize social and environmental outcomes over financial performance. Thematic ESG investments focus on a narrow ESG topic to provide direct investment in an ESG issue area, such as clean energy or diversity. Engagement strategies leverage company ownership to influence the ESG performance of companies, as was the case with shareholder advocacy. Negative screens focus on excluding companies with low ESG performance or undesirable characteristics. ESG integration combines ESG analysis with fundamental investment analysis to identify stocks with the potential for outperformance.

ESG investing can merge a number of these ESG investment strategies into a singular product. In short, ESG investing provides opportunities for investors to merge financial materiality with their desire to align investments with their values.[37]

Active Versus Passive Management

ESG investment products involving public equities come in three primary forms: exchange-traded funds (ETFs), mutual funds, and separate account strategies. The objective of actively managed funds is to outperform the benchmark, with portfolio managers *actively* selecting stocks they believe will provide alpha to their portfolio. On the other hand, passively managed funds simply follow a broad index, with no active trading involved. ESG ETFs that utilize a passive management strategy layer ESG screens on a specific index, such as the S&P 500.[38] While ESG ETFs can be more accessible to a broader array of investors due to their low minimum investments and fees, greenwashing is a serious concern. A recent analysis conducted in 2020 found that 83% of ESG ETFs had some form of fossil fuel exposure.[39]

Both active and passive investment allows for shareholder advocacy, yet active managers may have more leverage, as they can walk away from an investment, while passive fund managers cannot. Active managers might also have greater internal resources, such as fundamental analyst teams, to better understand the ESG risks executives face, and thus can better influence companies. However, many passive funds are accumulating capital at a more rapid pace and have large engagement teams. Historically, only a handful of social impact oriented firms have utilized the entire range of shareholder advocacy strategies—including company engagement, shareholder proposals, and proxy voting—though these practices have gained broader adoption in recent years.

ESG Investing Boom

According to the 2020 U.S. SIF Trends report, there was approximately $17 trillion in assets under management (one in three dollars) in the United States invested in sustainable investing strategies.[40] Since 2019, ESG funds had grown at twice the rate of the rest of the stock fund universe combined.[41] The momentum behind ESG investing had notably drawn skepticism regarding the merits of its environmental and social impact and ability to outperform the benchmark. Due to a lack of regulatory standards for what constituted ESG investing, how it was executed within an investment product varied significantly.

Trillium Investment Thesis Summary

Trillium's investment strategy focused explicitly on companies excelling in addressing material ESG issues, contending that capital investment should work to "advanc[e] humankind toward a global sustainable economy, a just society, and a better world."[42] Trillium used a robust, fully integrated, and proprietary ESG scoring system to determine which companies made it into its buy list and fit within its larger strategy. Trillium was also a leader in shareholder advocacy, maximizing engagement with companies.

EXHIBIT 1. Trillium Asset Management Investment Strategy

Evaluate Financial Integrity
Measure management and board quality by analyzing execution history and financial statement reporting

- **Growth** Focused, Strong Fundamentals
- **Reasonable** Valuations
- Cashflow and Balance Sheet **Strength**

Assess ESG Integrity
Analyze ESG risks and opportunities informed by our 30-year track record of proprietary data and insights

- Industry-Specific and Materiality-Based Benchmark **Review**
- External and Independent Information **Sources**
- In-Depth Peer and Competitive **Analysis**

Target Strategic Leaders
Identified through fundamental bottom-up selection

- Innovators with Competitive Advantages
- **Attractive**, Dynamic End Markets
- Long Term Strategy **Aligned** with Stakeholders

Advocacy
Conduct issue area and company specific analysis to engage with companies to promote positive ESG changes

- **Active** Ownership & Mission
- Strive to **Improve** Returns and ESG Performance
- Depth & **Breadth** of Team and Initiatives

Trillium Asset Management, "Socially Responsible Investing: Trillium Asset Management," Trillium Asset Management, 2023, https://www.trilliuminvest.com/esg/investment-approach.

EXHIBIT 2. Facebook 2017 Financial Highlights

	Year Ended December 31,				
	2017	2016	2015	2014	2013
	(in millions, except per share data)				
Consolidated Statements of Income Data:					
Revenue	$ 40,653	$ 27,638	$ 17,928	$ 12,466	$ 7,872
Total costs and expenses[(1)]	20,450	15,211	11,703	7,472	5,068
Income from operations	20,203	12,427	6,225	4,994	2,804
Income before provision for income taxes	20,594	12,518	6,194	4,910	2,754
Net income	15,934	10,217	3,688	2,940	1,500
Net income attributable to Class A and Class B common stockholders	15,920	10,188	3,669	2,925	1,491
Earnings per share attributable to Class A and Class B common stockholders:					
Basic	$ 5.49	$ 3.56	$ 1.31	$ 1.12	$ 0.62
Diluted	$ 5.39	$ 3.49	$ 1.29	$ 1.10	$ 0.60

(1) Total costs and expenses include $3.72 billion, $3.22 billion, $2.97 billion, $1.84 billion, and $906 million of share-based compensation for the years ended December 31, 2017, 2016, 2015, 2014, and 2013, respectively.

Quarterly Results of Operations Data, Facebook, Inc. 10-K (filed February 1, 2018): 48–50, https://www.sec.gov/Archives/edgar/data/1326801/000132680118000009/fb-12312017x10k.htm#s48AAAF4DE35658B6923840B08C98CE7B.

EXHIBIT 3. Facebook 2017 Board of Directors

EXECUTIVE OFFICERS, DIRECTORS, AND CORPORATE GOVERNANCE

The following table provides information regarding our executive officers and directors as of March 31, 2018:

Name	Age	Position(s)
Mark Zuckerberg	33	Chairman and Chief Executive Officer
Sheryl K. Sandberg	48	Chief Operating Officer and Director
David M. Wehner	49	Chief Financial Officer
Christopher K. Cox	35	Chief Product Officer
David B. Fischer	45	Vice President, Business and Marketing Partnerships
Mike Schroepfer	43	Chief Technology Officer
Colin S. Stretch	48	Vice President and General Counsel
Marc L. Andreessen(1)(2)	46	Director
Erskine B. Bowles(1)	72	Director
Kenneth I. Chenault	66	Director
Susan D. Desmond-Hellmann*(1)	60	Director
Reed Hastings(2)	57	Director
Jan Koum	42	Director
Peter A. Thiel(2)	50	Director

* Lead Independent Director
(1) Member of the audit committee
(2) Member of the compensation & governance committee

Facebook, Inc. Proxy Statement (filed April 13, 2018), https://www.sec.gov/Archives/edgar/data/1326801/000132680118000022/facebook2018definitiveprox.htm.

EXHIBIT 4. 2017 Trillium Shareholder Proposal: Risk Oversight Committee

Proposal Four: Stockholder Proposal Regarding a Risk Oversight Committee

Resolved: Shareholders request Facebook's Board issue a report discussing the merits of establishing a Risk Oversight Board Committee (at reasonable cost, within a reasonable time, and omit confidential and proprietary information).

Supporting Statement:
According to an article published by The Conference Board in the Harvard Law School Forum on Corporate Governance and Financial Regulation:

> A risk committee fosters an integrated, enterprise-wide approach to identifying and managing risk and provides an impetus toward improving the quality of risk reporting and monitoring, both for management and the board. This approach can assist the board in focusing on the "big picture." A risk committee can also provide greater support for company executives who are given broad risk management responsibilities, resulting in a stronger focus at the board level on the adequacy of resources allocated to risk management. Finally, it allows the audit committee and other board committees to focus on their respective core responsibilities.

Facebook's technological advances and scale appear to be significantly challenging the ability to understand its impact on society and may be creating numerous financial risks which could present material challenges to the company and its shareholders. Events illustrating this include, to name just a few:

- Research linking Facebook to depression and other mental health issues;
- Since 2011, Facebook has been operating under a 20 year Federal Trade Commission settlement agreement regarding user privacy practices;
- Investigations into Russian meddling in U.S. elections and its role in proliferating "fake news";
- Media coverage which demonstrated that its systems enabled advertisers to target users with offensive terms and other unintended consequences of its products;
- Concerns over censorship in Myanmar and India;
- Growing public and policy attention to the anti-competitive implications of platform monopolies;
- Smugglers reportedly using Facebook to broadcast the abuse and torture of migrants to extort ransom money from their families;
- Criticism from the Congressional Black Caucus over diversity and race relations; and
- The purported use of Facebook as a platform to incite terrorism.

Each of these individual cases may be addressable in a "whack-a-mole" fashion. However, they illustrate the growing concern that Facebook's Board lacks a strategic approach to risk. Unintended consequences seem to emerge daily, and indicate that the Board needs to have strong governance and risk oversight mechanisms to address these challenges and provide a "big picture" perspective.

Facebook's Board has chosen not to establish a separate Risk Oversight Committee. Instead, according to Facebook's Audit Committee Charter, the Audit Committee, "will discuss with the Company's management the Company's major financial risk and enterprise exposures and the steps management has taken to monitor and control such exposures, including the Company's procedures and any related policies with respect to risk assessment and risk management." This is standard boilerplate language, which does not capture the particular challenges faced by Facebook.

Given the importance of better Board risk oversight, we believe the Board should establish a separate Risk Oversight Committee, especially given the numerous other and important responsibilities of the Audit Committee.

Facebook Opposing Statement

We believe that a thorough and strategic approach to risk oversight is critical to our company and that our current approach to risk oversight ensures that we identify, evaluate, and address our unique risks while providing a "big picture" perspective through regular engagement with key members of management and appropriate delegation to our current board committees.

Our board of directors as a whole has responsibility for overseeing our risk management. The board of directors exercises this oversight responsibility directly and through its committees. The oversight responsibility of the board of directors and its committees is informed by regular reports from our management team, including senior personnel that lead a variety of functions across the business, and from our internal audit department, as well as input from external advisors, as appropriate. These reports are designed to provide timely visibility to the board of directors and its committees about the identification and assessment of key risks, our risk mitigation strategies, and ongoing developments.

The full board of directors has primary responsibility for evaluating strategic and operational risk management, and for CEO succession planning. Our audit committee has the responsibility for overseeing our major financial, legal, and regulatory risk exposures, which span a variety of areas including litigation, regulatory compliance, reputational and policy matters, platform integrity efforts, financial reporting, cybersecurity, and international operations. Our audit committee also oversees the steps our management has taken to monitor and control these exposures, including policies and procedures for assessing and managing risk and related compliance efforts. Finally, our audit committee oversees our internal audit function. Our compensation & governance committee evaluates risks arising from our corporate governance and compensation policies and practices.

Despite the proponent's suggestion to the contrary, our board of directors and committees currently spend a significant amount of time on matters relating to risk oversight as part of their existing duties. In particular, our audit committee focuses on many of the matters noted in the proponent's proposal. We believe that our board and committees have sufficient time and resources to address risk oversight matters along with their other responsibilities and that, given the size of our board of directors, it is inefficient to establish a separate risk oversight committee that would likely be comprised of some or all of the same directors that are already overseeing these matters.

The board of directors recommends a vote AGAINST the stockholder proposal.

Risk Oversight Committee Shareholder Proposal 2017, "Facebook - Risk Oversight Committee (2018)," Shareholder Proposal, Trillium Asset Management, October 26, 2017, https://archive.trilliuminvest.com/shareholder-proposal/facebook-risk-oversight-committee-2018/. Facebook Response to Independent Board Chairperson Shareholder Proposal 2017, Facebook, Inc. Proxy Statement (filed April 13, 2018), https://www.sec.gov/Archives/edgar/data/1326801/000132680118000022/facebook2018definitiveprox.htm.

EXHIBIT 5. 2018 Trillium Shareholder Proposal: Separation of Facebook CEO and Board Chair Position

Proposal Six: Stockholder Proposal Regarding an Independent Chair

Independent Board Chairperson

Resolved: Shareholders request the Board of Directors adopt as policy, and amend the bylaws as necessary, to require henceforth that the Chair of the Board of Directors, whenever possible, be an independent member of the Board. This independence policy shall apply prospectively so as not to violate any contractual obligations. If the Board determines that a Chair who was independent when selected is no longer independent, the Board shall select a new Chair who satisfies the requirements of the policy within a reasonable amount of time. Compliance with this policy is waived if no independent director is available and willing to serve as Chair.

Supporting Statement:

Facebook CEO Mark Zuckerberg has been Board Chair since 2012. His dual-class shareholdings give him approximately 60% of Facebook's voting shares, leaving the board, even with a lead independent director, with only a limited ability to check Mr. Zuckerberg's power. We believe this weakens Facebook's governance and oversight of management. Selecting an independent Chair would free the CEO to focus on managing the Company and enable the Chairperson to focus on oversight and strategic guidance.

The Council of Institutional Investors argues:

Having an independent chair helps the board carry out its primary duty—to monitor the management of the company on behalf of its shareowners. A CEO who also serves as chair can exert excessive influence on the board and its agenda, weakening the board's oversight of management. Separating the chair and CEO positions reduces this conflict, and an independent chair provides the clearest separation of power between the CEO and the rest of the board.

Facebook has resisted recent shareholder requests to separate these roles. In 2017, according to our calculations, a similar proposal received the support of 51% of the votes cast when excluding the shares of 13 executives and board members. However, the board has not acted on this important signal from its non-insider shareholders.

Google, Microsoft, Apple, Oracle, and Twitter have separate CEO and chairperson roles. More broadly, 59% of the S&P 1500 separated these roles as of April 2018.

We believe this lack of independent board Chair and oversight has contributed to Facebook missing, or mishandling, a number of severe controversies, increasing risk exposure and costs to shareholders. Examples from past years include:

- Russian meddling in U.S. elections
- Sharing personal data of 87 million users with Cambridge Analytica
- Data sharing with device manufacturers, including Huawei that is flagged by U.S. Intelligence as a national security threat
- Proliferating fake news
- Propagating violence in Myanmar, India, and South Sudan
- Depression and other mental health issues, including stress and addiction
- Allowing advertisers to exclude black, Hispanic, and other "ethnic affinities" from seeing ads.

In apologies, Mr. Zuckerberg has stated, "We didn't take a broad enough view of our responsibility." This broader view is what an independent Board Chair would provide, which we believe would benefit the company, its shareholders, and its global community of users.

Facebook Opposing Statement

We believe that our current board structure is effective in supporting strong board leadership. Implementing the proposal is unnecessary because the leadership structure of our board of directors already provides for independent leadership and oversight of management. Dr. Desmond-Hellmann currently serves as our Lead Independent Director. Our Lead Independent Director role includes the following authority and responsibilities, as described in greater detail in the section of this proxy statement entitled "Executive Officers, Directors, and Corporate Governance":

- presiding at all meetings of the board of directors at which the Chairman is not present, including executive sessions of the independent directors;
- calling separate meetings of the independent directors or special meetings of the full board of directors;
- facilitating discussion and open dialogue among the independent directors during meetings of the board of directors, executive sessions, and otherwise;
- serving as principal liaison between the independent directors and the Chairman;
- providing the Chairman with feedback and counsel concerning his interactions with the board of directors;
- providing leadership to the board of directors if circumstances arise in which the role of the Chairman may be, or may be perceived to be, in conflict;
- coordinating with the Chairman to set the agenda for meetings of the board of directors, taking into account input from other independent directors; and
- leading our board of directors in governance matters in coordination with our compensation & governance committee, including the evaluation of the performance of the CEO, the selection of committee chairs and memberships, and our annual board of directors and committee self-evaluations.

We believe that the role of the Lead Independent Director, including certain changes and enhancements that were recently adopted following a review by our compensation & governance committee, facilitates effective representation of the interests of all stockholders. Further, a majority of our directors are independent, and we have audit & risk oversight and compensation & governance committees comprised solely of independent directors.

Our board of directors currently has no established policy on whether or not to have a non-executive Chair and believes that it should make that judgment based on circumstances and experience. Our board of directors currently believes that the most effective leadership model is that Mr. Zuckerberg, our founder and controlling stockholder, serves as both Chairman and CEO. We believe our board of directors is functioning effectively under its current structure, and that the current structure provides appropriate oversight protections. We do not believe that requiring the Chair to be independent will provide appreciably better direction and performance, and instead could cause inefficiency in board and management function and relations.

In addition, our stockholders rejected a similar proposal at our annual meeting of stockholders in 2017.

We believe that our current board structure is in the best interests of our stockholders. Therefore, our board of directors recommends that our stockholders vote against this proposal.

The board of directors recommends a vote AGAINST the stockholder proposal.

Independent Board Chairperson Shareholder Proposal 2018, "Facebook, Inc. - Independent Board Chairperson (2019)," Shareholder Proposal, Trillium Asset Management, July 2, 2018, https://archive.trilliuminvest.com/shareholder-proposal/facebook-inc-independent-board-chairman-2019/. Facebook Response to Independent Board Chairperson Shareholder Proposal 2018, Facebook, Inc. Proxy Statement (filed April 12, 2019), https://www.sec.gov/Archives/edgar/data/1326801/000132680119000025/facebook2019definitiveprox.htm.

EXHIBIT 6. 2019 Trillium Shareholder Proposal: Removal of Zuckerberg as Board Chair

Proposal Five: Stockholder Proposal Regarding an Independent Chair

Independent Board Chairperson

Resolved: Shareholders request the Board of Directors adopt as policy, and amend the bylaws as necessary, to require henceforth that the Chair of the Board of Directors, whenever possible, be an independent member of the Board. This independence policy shall apply prospectively so as not to violate any contractual obligations. If the Board determines that a Chair who was independent when selected is no longer independent, the Board shall select a new Chair who satisfies the requirements of the policy within a reasonable amount of time. Compliance with this policy is waived if no independent director is available and willing to serve as Chair.

Supporting Statement:

Facebook CEO Mark Zuckerberg has been Board Chair since 2012. His dual-class shareholdings give him approximately 58% of Facebook's voting shares while holding only 13% of the economic interest, leaving the board, even with a lead independent director, with only a limited ability to check Mr. Zuckerberg's power. We believe this weakens Facebook's governance and oversight of management. Selecting an independent Chair would free the CEO to focus on managing the Company and enable the Chairperson to focus on oversight and strategic guidance.

Facebook has resisted recent shareholder requests to separate these roles. At the 2019 annual meeting, according to our calculations, this proposal received the support of 68% of the votes cast when excluding the shares of 13 executives and board members. However, the board has not acted on this important signal from its non-insider shareholders.

Alphabet, Microsoft, Apple, and Autodesk all have separate CEO and chairperson roles.

We believe this lack of independent board Chair and oversight has contributed to Facebook missing, or mishandling, a number of severe controversies, increasing risk exposure and costs to shareholders.

Concentrating power in the hands of one person—any person—is unwise. Looking forward to future growth opportunities, we believe Facebook needs strong risk oversight and to rebuild trust with investors, employees, users, and regulators. Transitioning to an independent board chair is necessary to rebuild the company's reputation and to create a governance environment with the benefits of genuine accountability and meaningful oversight.

Facebook Opposing Statement

We believe that our current board structure is effective in supporting strong board leadership. Implementing the proposal is unnecessary because the leadership structure of our board of directors already provides for independent leadership and oversight of management. Susan D. Desmond-Hellmann served as our Lead Independent Director from 2015 to 2019, and our independent directors recently designated Ambassador Kimmitt to serve as Lead Independent Director upon his appointment to our board of directors in March 2020. Our Lead Independent Director role includes the following authority and responsibilities, as described in greater detail in the section of this proxy statement entitled "Executive Officers, Directors, and Corporate Governance":

- presiding at all meetings of the board of directors at which the Chairman is not present, including executive sessions of the independent directors;
- calling separate meetings of the independent directors or special meetings of the full board of directors;
- facilitating discussion and open dialogue among the independent directors during meetings of the board of directors, executive sessions, and otherwise;
- serving as principal liaison between the independent directors and the Chairman;
- providing the Chairman with feedback and counsel concerning his interactions with the board of directors;
- providing leadership to the board of directors if circumstances arise in which the role of the Chairman may be, or may be perceived to be, in conflict;
- coordinating with the Chairman to set the agenda for meetings of the board of directors, taking into account input from other independent directors; and
- leading our board of directors in governance matters in coordination with our compensation, nominating & governance committee, including the evaluation of the performance of the CEO, the selection of committee chairs and memberships, and our annual board of directors and committee self-evaluations.

We believe that the role of the Lead Independent Director facilitates effective representation of the interests of all stockholders. Further, we have recently appointed several new independent directors, a substantial majority of our directors are independent, and each of the committees of our board of directors is comprised entirely of independent directors.

Our board of directors currently has no established policy on whether or not to have a non-executive Chair and believes that it should make that judgment based on circumstances and experience. Our board of directors currently believes that the most effective leadership model is that Mr. Zuckerberg, our founder and controlling stockholder, serves as both Chairman and CEO. We believe our board of directors is functioning effectively under its current structure, and that the current structure provides appropriate oversight protections. We do not believe that requiring the Chair to be independent will provide appreciably better direction and performance, and instead could cause inefficiency in board and management function and relations.

In addition, our stockholders rejected a similar proposal at our annual meetings of stockholders in 2017 and 2019.

We believe that our current board structure is in the best interests of our stockholders. Therefore, our board of directors recommends that our stockholders vote against this proposal.

The board of directors recommends a vote AGAINST the stockholder proposal.

Independent Board Chairperson Shareholder Proposal 2019, "Facebook, Inc.– Independent Board Chairperson (2020)," Shareholder Proposal, Trillium Asset Management, December 3, 2019, https://archive.trilliuminvest.com/shareholder-proposal/facebook-inc-independent-board-chairperson-2020/. Facebook Response to Independent Board Chairperson Shareholder Proposal 2019, Facebook, Inc. Proxy Statement (filed April 10, 2020), https://www.sec.gov/Archives/edgar/data/1326801/000132680120000037/facebook2020definitiveprox.htm.

NOTES

1. "ESG Criteria," Trillium Asset Management, December 2021, https://www.trilliuminvest.com/documents/trilliums-approach-to-esg-integration-2021.
2. Matt Patsky (CEO, Trillium Asset Management), in discussion with the authors, Boston, Massachusetts, April 6, 2022.
3. Ibid.
4. Chris Neiger, "Why 2017 Was a Year to Remember for Facebook Inc.," *The Motley Fool*, November 16, 2017, https://www.fool.com/investing/2017/11/16/why-2017-was-a-year-to-remember-for-facebook-inc.aspx.
5. Adam Levy, "Instagram Is Set to Make a Killing in Advertising in 2017," *The Motley Fool*, March 28, 2017, https://www.fool.com/investing/2017/03/26/instagram-is-set-to-make-a-killing-in-advertising.aspx.
6. Neiger. "Why 2017 Was a Year to Remember for Facebook Inc."
7. Meta, "Facebook Reports Fourth Quarter and Full Year 2017 Results," January 31, 2018, https://investor.fb.com/investor-news/press-release-details/2018/Facebook-Reports-Fourth-Quarter-and-Full-Year-2017-Results/default.aspx
8. Shane Greenstein, Marco Iansiti, and Christine Snively, "Facebook: The First Ten Years," Harvard Business School Case 616-012, October 2015.
9. Julianne Pepitone and Stacy Cowley, "Facebook's First Big Investor, Peter Thiel, Cashes Out," *CNNMoney*, August 20, 2012, https://money.cnn.com/2012/08/20/technology/facebook-peter-thiel/.
10. Miguel Helft, Jessi Hempel, and Caitlin Keating, "Inside Facebook," *Fortune* 165, no. 4 (March 19, 2012): 112–122.
11. Brad Stone. "Facebook Will Form 2 Classes of Stock," *The New York Times*, November 24, 2009, https://www.nytimes.com/2009/11/25/technology/internet/25facebook.html.
12. Ingrid Lunden, "Facebook to Offer 388M Shares at IPO, at a Market Cap of between $93.2B and $104.2B," *Tech Crunch*, May 15, 2012, https://techcrunch.com/2012/05/15/facebook-files-new-s-1-pricing-34-38-per-share-adds-50-6m-shares-of-class-a-stock-raising-14-7b/.
13. Facebook, Inc., *Proxy Statement* (Washington, DC: United States Securities and Exchange Commission, April 14, 2017), 13, https://www.sec.gov/Archives/edgar/data/1326801/000132680117000016/facebook2017definitiveprox.htm#sBFAE3CD960369A7782138BEB75ED97BC.
14. Shayndi Raice, Spencer Ante, and Emily Glazer, "In Facebook Deal for Instagram, Board Was All but Out of Picture," *Wall Street Journal*, April 18, 2012, https://www.wsj.com/articles/SB10001424052702304818404577350191931921290. Eric Jackson, "Can the Millennial Zuckerberg Be a Great Leader?" *Forbes*, April 18, 2012, https://www.forbes.com/sites/ericjackson/2012/04/18/the-power-of-millennial-zuck/?sh=6f3beb3376b0.
15. Tom Hals, "Zuckerberg Nixes New Facebook Share Class After Shareholder Lawsuit," *Reuters*, September 22, 2017, https://www.reuters.com/article/us-facebook-stock-trial/zuckerberg-nixes-new-facebook-share-class-after-shareholder-lawsuit-idUSKCN1BX2PA.
16. Hals, "Zuckerberg Nixes New Facebook Share Class After Shareholder Lawsuit."
17. Facebook, Inc., *Proxy Statement*, 10.
18. Federal Trade Commission, "Facebook Settles FTC Charges That It Deceived Consumers by Failing to Keep Privacy Promises," November 29, 2011, https://www.ftc.gov/news-events/news/press-releases/2011/11/facebook-settles-ftc-charges-it-deceived-consumers-failing-keep-privacy-promises.
19. Federal Trade Commission, "Facebook Settles FTC Charges."
20. Sheera Frenkel, Matthew Rosenberg, and Nicholas Confessore, "Facebook Data Collected by Quiz App Included Private Messages," *The New York Times*, April 10, 2018, https://www.nytimes.com/2018/04/10/technology/facebook-cambridge-analytica-private-messages.html.
21. Sapna Maheshwari and Alexandra Stevenson, "Google and Facebook Face Criticism for Ads Targeting Racist Sentiments," *The New York Times*, September 15, 2017, https://www.nytimes.com/2017/09/15/business/facebook-advertising-anti-semitism.html.
22. Maheshwari and Stevenson, "Google and Facebook Face Criticism."
23. Sam Levin, "Facebook Allowed Advertisers to Target 'Jew Haters,'" *The Guardian*, September 14, 2017, https://www.theguardian.com/technology/2017/sep/14/facebook-advertising-jew-hater-antisemitism.

24. "Facebook, Inc.—Risk Oversight Committee (2018)," Trillium Asset Management, October 26, 2017, https://archive.trilliuminvest.com/shareholder-proposal/facebook-risk-oversight-committee-2018/. Facebook, Inc., *Proxy Statement*, 52.
25. Jake Kanter, "Facebook Investors Voted in Support of Proposals to Fire Mark Zuckerberg as Chairman, but Zuckerberg Still Holds Power," *Business Insider*, June 4, 2019, https://www.inc.com/business-insider/facebook-investors-vote-in-support-fire-mark-zuckerberg-chairman.html.
26. Jonas Kron (chief advocacy officer, Trillium Asset Management), in discussion with the authors, Boston, Massachusetts, April 13, 2022.
27. "Facebook, Inc.—Independent Board Chairman (2019)," Trillium Asset Management, July 2, 2018, https://archive.trilliuminvest.com/shareholder-proposal/facebook-inc-independent-board-chairman-2019/.
28. Facebook, Inc., *Proxy Statement* (Washington, DC: United States Securities and Exchange Commission, April 12, 2019), 58, https://www.sec.gov/Archives/edgar/data/1326801/000132680119000025/facebook2019definitiveprox.htm#s01F926C417505621961CDE3214E4713A.
29. Jonas Kron, in discussion with the authors, April 13, 2022.
30. Meta, "Dr. Susan Desmond-Hellmann Departs Facebook Board of Directors," October 30, 2019, https://about.fb.com/news/2019/10/desmond-hellmann-departs-board/#:~:text=Susan%20Desmond%2DHellmann%20Departs%20Facebook%20Board%20of%20Directors,-October%2030%2C%202019&text=Facebook%20today%20announced%20that%20Dr,%2C%20effective%20October%2030%2C%202019.
31. "Facebook, Inc.—Independent Board Chairperson (2020)," Trillium Asset Management, December 3, 2019, https://archive.trilliuminvest.com/shareholder-proposal/facebook-inc-independent-board-chairperson-2020/.
32. Blaine Townsend, "From SRI to ESG: The Origins of Socially Responsible and Sustainable Investing," *The Journal of Impact and ESG Investing* 1, no. 1 (2020): 5, https://www.bailard.com/wp-content/uploads/2020/09/History-Socially-Responsible-Investing-and-ESG-Investing.pdf.
33. Townsend, "From SRI to ESG," 3.
34. Andrew A. King and Kenneth P. Pucker, "ESG and Alpha: Sales or Substance?" *Institutional Investor*, February 25, 2022, https://www.institutionalinvestor.com/article/b1wxqznltqnyzj/ESG-and-Alpha-Sales-or-Substance.
35. E. Napoletano and Benjamin Curry, "Environmental, Social and Governance: What is ESG Investing?" *Forbes*, February 24, 2022, https://www.forbes.com/advisor/investing/esg-investing/.
36. King and Pucker, "ESG and Alpha."
37. "The Evolution of ESG Investing," MSCI, accessed August 29, 2022, https://www.msci.com/esg-101-what-is-esg/evolution-of-esg-investing#:~:text=The%20practice%20of%20ESG%20investing,the%20South%20African%20apartheid%20regime.
38. "What are ESG ETFs?" Royal Bank of Canada, accessed May 5, 2022, https://www.rbcgam.com/en/ca/learn-plan/types-of-investments/what-are-esg-etfs/detail#:~:text=ESG%20ETFs%20can%20support%20broad,of%20diversification%20into%20your%20portfolio.
39. F. Norresad, "Sustainable ETFs with the Highest Investments in Fossil Fuel Companies U.S. 2020," October 12, 2021, *Statista*, https://www.statista.com/statistics/1268563/esg-etf-fossil-fuel-exposure-usa/#main-content.
40. US SIF Foundation, *Report on US Sustainable and Impact Investing Trends* (US SIF Foundation, 2020), 1, https://www.ussif.org/files/US%20SIF%20Trends%20Report%202020%20Executive%20Summary.pdf.
41. Robin Wigglesworth, "ESG Rush Opens Opportunities for Betting Against the Angels," *Financial Times*, April 26, 2021, https://www.ft.com/content/262f2dfa-82bc-4454-96aa-bc5c38f82cdd.
42. "Our History," Trillium Asset Management, accessed August 29, 2022, https://www.trilliuminvest.com/about.

CASE 3.2A

SAMRIDH Blended Finance Facility

Accelerating Pandemic Response and Building Equitable Health Systems in India (A)

ARCHITA ADLAKHA, NEETA RAO, ACHIN B. N. BIYANI, RITIKA PANDEY, AND SUDHEER NADIPALLY

From the onset of the pandemic to mid-August 2022, India reported over 44 million cases and more than 500,000 deaths due to the coronavirus. At times, the number of daily new cases reached as high as 400,000, pushing health systems to the brink. While hospitals, clinics, and diagnostic laboratories faced the challenge of catering to an increased number of patients, supply chains and manufacturers had to quickly ramp up production and supplies. The country resorted to prolonged lockdowns to augment capacity and bridge the demand-supply gap.

As the number of COVID-19 cases increased, the Government of India (GoI) took measures to strengthen the nation's health systems for equitable service delivery to address current and future needs. Pandemics, by their very nature, require dynamic health systems that are capable of responding rapidly to absorb surges in cases that cause strain. India worked to augment its health infrastructure, strengthen the capacities of health care providers and community volunteers, and increase access to resources for innovators and manufacturers to better respond to the COVID-19 challenge and future public health emergencies.

The Ministry of Health and Family Welfare (MOHFW), GoI led the overall response to COVID-19. Their focuses included improving health system preparedness through facility and infrastructure strengthening, risk communication, and government health provider training. Supported by USAID, IPE Global implemented Sustainable Access of Markets and Resources for Innovative Delivery of Healthcare (SAMRIDH), one of India's first and largest blended financing facilities, for pandemic response. Their key question is whether this cross-sectoral partnership can unlock new pools of capital in ways that will achieve national health care priorities while simultaneously preparing the country for future health emergencies.

Background

From the World Health Organization's (WHO's) Millennium Development Goals to the UN's Sustainable Development Goals, building robust health systems has been a top priority for countries across the globe. The need to build comprehensive health care systems stems from the severe implications that the poor population's health has on the development and growth of a nation. Comprehensive health care can help end poverty and address socioeconomic inequalities in education, employment, and gender. However, despite the growing need to improve health outcomes, providing equitable access to affordable and quality health care services has been challenging, particularly in developing countries. In India, the problem of weak health systems has been further compounded by the imbalance between demand and supply-side factors, which adds to the nation's vulnerability in the face of sudden health emergencies.

As the world's most populous country, India has the advantage of a rich demographic dividend. However, it is threatened by the "triple burden of disease": non-communicable diseases, communicable diseases, and infectious diseases. While the mission to eradicate major infectious diseases remains unaccomplished, India's population also bears the high burden of non-communicable diseases and injuries. These challenges were further exacerbated by the rampant spread of COVID-19. This has led to an overall rise in the demand for effective health care services in the country. However, despite this demand, there continue to be acute shortages on the supply side.

The Indian health care landscape is characterized by an inadequate workforce, poor infrastructure, and low spending. With a doctor-patient ratio of one to 1,700, the country is well below WHO's prescribed ratio of one doctor per 1,000 people. Similarly, with 1.7 nurses per 1,000 people, India falls short of the WHO recommended rate of three nurses per 1,000 people. Furthermore, 70% of India's health care infrastructure is nestled in the top 20 cities, whereas 66% of the Indian population lives in rural regions.

To fill many of these gaps in the health care value chain, the Indian government has committed to increasing budgetary allocations toward health care infrastructure. The National Health Policy 2017 of India recommended increasing the government's health expenditure from 1.15% of GDP to 2.5% by 2025. However, progress has been slow, and government expenditure remains around 1.3% of the GDP. As a result, close to 63% of total health spending in India is out-of-pocket expenditures (OOPE), which not only deplete patients' savings but can also lead to catastrophic health care expenses that push people into a vicious cycle of debt and poverty.

Given the current inequalities in health care distribution, a glaring lack of trained health care personnel and infrastructure, and low government spending on health care, India has immense potential to implement innovative, sustainable, and scalable health care technology to improve the lives of its citizens. Yet in a country with 1.38 billion people, many of whom are now equipped with internet connections and smartphones, it is still a challenge to find more than a handful of examples of digital technology being used to improve health care outcomes. While the country has a robust entrepreneurial ecosystem with over 7,400 registered start-ups and innovations in the health-tech domain,[1] challenges like access to affordable capital, market access, regulatory roadblocks, and market inefficiencies limit their scale-up.

India's Central Bank has also offered to promote lending practices within the health care sector, especially in areas affected by COVID-19. Thus far, lending from public and private sector banks to health care organizations has been limited. The health care sector is often perceived to be risky due to the capital-intensive nature of its business, long gestation periods for researching and developing products, and regulatory clearances, among other factors, which delay the inflow of financial returns. The health care sector has been publicly scrutinized for undergoing dynamic shifts in tandem with the regulatory landscape, which further demotivates banks and commercial capital providers from lending to health care enterprises.

More than 100 private equity and venture capital investors have invested in the health care delivery space in India since 2010, with a total transaction value of USD $1.275 billion.[2] However, these investments have largely gone into metropolitan markets rather than toward improving accessibility and affordability for vulnerable people residing in semi-urban and rural communities. It is estimated that India will need an additional investment of USD $256 billion by 2034 to build equitable health systems, which is significantly higher than current spending levels. Even if health care systems just adopt new technologies and implement a focus on prevention and wellness, they will still need an estimated USD $166 billion.[3]

India's unique accessibility, affordability, and quality challenges could be addressed through innovative health care technologies or organizations and startups using innovative business models, solving for affordable and equitable health care distribution. Given the size of the sector, a quick rate of adopting these social enterprises would have an immense impact on improving access to health. But for this to happen, conventional modes of health care funding must be augmented by innovative funding methods. A tri-sector collaboration between public, private, and philanthropic capital is a promising option that could help resolve funding challenges.

The SAMRIDH Blended Finance Facility

At the time of its founding, SAMRIDH was a first-of-its-kind facility. The immediate goal of the SAMRIDH facility was to bridge the supply-side gaps in emergency health services and accelerate India's response to COVID-19. It offered both grants and debt financing provisions to health care enterprises and innovators to enable them to augment their capacities for producing and supplying high-impact health solutions for COVID-19. SAMRIDH's long term goal, however, was to strengthen comprehensive health services in India by improving access to affordable and quality health care for the most socioeconomically vulnerable portion of the population (40%, or approximately 540 million people). In turn, this would build resilient health systems that could effectively respond to future health emergencies.

SAMRIDH, through blended finance models, leveraged philanthropic funding as catalytic capital to mitigate barriers for private investment in high-impact, market-based solutions that sought to improve the health and well-being of vulnerable communities in India. This initiative was supported by the United States Agency for International Development (USAID) and implemented by IPE Global. In addition, it worked in technical collaboration with the Government of India (GoI), international philanthropies, financial institutions, academic organizations, social entrepreneurs, and accelerators.

The initiative was designed to achieve the following key objectives:

1. Identify and support sustainable, innovative business models by providing access to affordable capital
2. Mobilize grant pool and debt commitments to set up a blended finance facility that supports health care entrepreneurs and innovations
3. Reduce the out-of-pocket expenditure (OOPE) for poor and underserved communities
4. Encourage the participation of women in entrepreneurship to solve health challenges

5. Drive Environment, Sustainability, and Governance (ESG) principles through investment decisions

SAMRIDH followed a LEGO approach (implying "play well" in Danish) to its solutions, creatively using different building blocks to achieve a result-oriented outcome toward health systems strengthening. This required a central entity to design and drive the initiative's overall strategy to achieve the end goal. Responding to this requirement, USAID/India established a Technical Support Unit (TSU) for SAMRIDH that was managed by IPE Global.

The TSU followed a systematic evaluation approach to identify high-impact health solutions. It also played a direct role in mobilizing grants and facilitating debt funding support to health care businesses. In addition, following a "Capital Plus" approach—using public or philanthropic sources to increase private sector investment in UN Sustainable Development Goal 3, "good health and well-being"—SAMRIDH built networks to provide market access, business advisory, and technical assistance to advance the expansion and sustainability of proven health care innovations. To implement this multipronged approach, the TSU catalyzed diverse partnerships with over 100 ecosystem players from the government, financial institutions, philanthropies, incubators, academia, and industry associations.

SAMRIDH also had a robust governance structure in the form of an Advisory Committee that provided oversight, guided the efficient disbursement of funding, and ensured that funded solutions would be sustainable in the medium and long terms. The Advisory Committee was comprised of senior bureaucrats and experts from Atal Innovation Mission, NITI Aayog, the Principal Scientific Advisor Office of the Government of India, IIT-Delhi, the Rockefeller Foundation, and IndusInd Bank.

The Power of Collective Action: Forging Tri-Sector Partnerships

As India worked through the health, financial, and socioeconomic implications of COVID-19, it was evident that the country must dramatically increase and improve the quantity and quality of its spending on health care. Increasing investment would be critical to maintaining the nation's development trajectory and delivering inclusive, poverty-alleviating growth. In the immediate term, emergency government spending on social welfare and traditional development aid was crucial to minimizing the impact of COVID-19. But what about the longer term? How can the structural weaknesses in the health care and education systems—made stark by the pandemic—be improved in the long run?

Blended finance offers one possible pathway toward improvement in the Indian health care system. With tri-sector collaboration and partnerships between public, private, and philanthropic organizations, blended finance creates investment opportunities that can be channeled toward scaling impact for development, especially toward access to health care. Blended finance addresses the two main barriers that private investors face when considering to invest in health care in developing countries: (a) high perceived and real risks and (b) poor returns for the risks taken compared to other investments. The presence of public and/or philanthropic capital within a transaction improves its risk-return ratio, making these investments more attractive for commercial investors.

Cross-sectoral collaborations involving financial institutions, philanthropic funders, private investors, government stakeholders, and public funders on one side and social enterprises and innovations on the other are difficult to establish. To implement this collaborative approach, SAMRIDH needed to catalyze diverse partnerships with over 100 ecosystem players from government agencies, financial institutions, philanthropies, incubators, academia, industry associations, and health care organizations. Each stakeholder acts as a critical cog in the machine, bringing distinct objectives and motivations to their transactions.

Key Partners of SAMRIDH Health Care Blended Finance Facility

Philanthropic Donors | Contributors to the facility's grant pool

- United States Agency for International Development | The Rockefeller Foundation | Morpho Foundation | Ford Foundation | IndusInd Foundation | 360 ONE Foundation

Fund Hosting Entity | Host and operator of the grant funds received by SAMRIDH

- Indian Institute of Technology, Delhi

Debt Financing Partners | Contributors to the debt pool; the committed funds remain with the institutions, and they lend to health enterprises as per their respective rules and procedures

- Axis Bank | IndusInd Bank | HDFC Bank | Caspian Debt

Technical Support Unit | Manager of SAMRIDH's end-to-end operations, including identifying high-impact health solutions; mobilizing investments; and monitoring, evaluating, and disseminating project impact

- IPE Global Limited

Technical Partners | An expanding mix of partners, including the government, incubators, and industry associations, guiding the project with diverse expertise and networks

- Atal Innovation Mission, NITI Aayog | National Health Authority | Principal Scientific Advisor to the Government of India | Convergence Blended Finance | NATHEALTH

By bringing stakeholders under one umbrella, SAMRIDH's shared vision was to create a "Social Impact" by acting as a collective force to provide rapid and timely solutions to some of the country's most pressing development challenges.

The foundation for SAMRIDH was laid in the midst of the COVID-19 pandemic, when the world was going through lockdowns and altered ways of working. The SAMRIDH TSU formation is unique not only because the team comprises technical (medical and public health professionals) as well as financial (investment managers and corporate bankers) experts who bring in diverse experiences and backgrounds but also because the team was onboarded virtually. Team members did not meet each other for the first time in person until nearly 2 years after the project was founded. During SAMRIDH's 18-to-24-month-long foundational period, the TSU team worked remotely to identify, scale and support high-impact solutions. By bringing complementary and diverse skillsets together with the single motivation of "supporting social enterprises to make health affordable and accessible to the vulnerable," the team was able to positively affect the lives of those who suffered the most due to challenged health care systems.

Additionally, the governance structure of the SAMRIDH facility included an Advisory Committee comprised of senior bureaucrats, national-level government officials, academic experts, multilateral donors, and representatives from banks and financial institutions. These experts brought extensive experience from their respective fields, provided oversight, and guided the efficient disbursement of funding. In effect, the committee ensured that the funded solutions were sustainable in the medium-to-long term.

Making the Cut for the SAMRIDH Portfolio

The Indian health system is complex and fragmented. Profitable organizations, like corporate hospitals, and nonprofits, like mission and charitable hospitals, occupy the same milieu. Ensuring SAMRIDH's mission to serve vulnerable communities was a key challenge since these communities lacked purchasing power, and it was difficult to target them using market-ready health care facilities/services. To screen and shortlist such organizations, SAMRIDH had to rely on proxy indicators by targeting health care organizations that worked in semi-urban and rural markets, individuals covered under government-funded insurance schemes and who purchased generic medicines, and individuals with lower gross margins.

The COVID-19 pandemic was dynamic and fast-moving. Hence, SAMRIDH had to constantly realign its priority areas depending on the current situation. For example, early in the pandemic, it focused on oxygen supply, capacity building, and vaccination, but later it focused on health delivery and medical devices. The fast transition between waves made it impossible for the TSU to use geographic targeting to deploy solutions. Instead, it used the previously mentioned proxy indicators to guide actions.

In addition, some donors designated their contributions to particular areas, like diagnostics and surveillance. Others restricted SAMRIDH from using their funding to duplicate programs and interventions funded through other agencies or mechanisms. Some donors also had geographic restrictions (e.g., North Korea, China) on the sourcing of components. This further limited the possible methods for reaching the target population. Since SAMRIDH's focus was on scaling up market-ready solutions, it decided to only consider solutions with a Technology Readiness Level (TRL) of five or higher: health care technologies/organizations that had a ready product, were ready to hit the market, and had potential for immediate scale up. Health care solutions needed to be legally registered in India and have at least one year of operational history, and SAMRIDH followed a gender lens approach to enhance diversity in its investment portfolio. Additionally, while there were selection criteria for shortlisting the right mix of health care technologies/organizations to eventually receive support under the program, the application and selection process could not be confined to binary classifications. For example, there were applications that demonstrated intent to deliver social impact but lacked the financial capabilities to tackle the issue at scale.

As a tool, blended finance plays a crucial role, filling an investment gap for raising commercial capital for early-stage health care technologies/organizations that are experiencing early market traction. These organizations may be considered too early for private equity or venture capital investment, too risky for debt investment owing to no/low credit history, and too advanced for raising grants. The blending of capital under this program carves out a unique offering for early-stage health care organizations to access commercial capital at an affordable rate, helping to build long-term growth trajectory and financial sustainability for the organization.

Discussion Questions

1. How is SAMRIDH unique?
2. What are the points of common interest between SAMRIDH's partners?
3. What are the competing interests between SAMRIDH's partners?
4. Does SAMRIDH's product solve the challenge to access affordable and equitable health care?
5. How can SAMRIDH deliver health care effectively at a lower cost?
6. What are the incentives for SAMRIDH to pivot toward semi-urban and rural markets?
7. Is it possible to achieve social impact without compromising on financial returns? How can social enterprise strike a balance between the two?
8. Do you think the SAMRIDH facility can build an ecosystem where social enterprises have natural avenues to affordable capital and technical support in order to scale up high-impact solutions? Why or why not?

NOTES

1. *Tracxn HealthTech India Report 2020* (HealthTech, 2020).
2. NATHEALTH, *Financing and Funding Indian Healthcare: Navigating the Turbulent Tide* (New Delhi: PwC, 2018), https://www.pwc.in/assets/pdfs/publications/2018/financing-and-funding-indian-healthcare-navigating-the-turbulent-tide.pdf.
3. NATHEALTH, *Financing and Funding Indian Healthcare: Navigating the Turbulent Tide* (PwC, 2018), https://www.pwc.in/assets/pdfs/publications/2018/financing-and-funding-indian-healthcare-navigating-the-turbulent-tide.pdf.

SAMRIDH Blended Finance Facility

CASE 3.2B

Accelerating Pandemic Response and Building Equitable Health Systems in India (B)

ARCHITA ADLAKHA, NEETA RAO, ACHIN B. N. BIYANI,
RITIKA PANDEY, AND SUDHEER NADIPALLY

Sustainable Access to Markets and Resources for Innovative Delivery of Healthcare (SAMRIDH), supported by USAID and implemented by IPE Global, combines commercial capital with public and philanthropic capital to mitigate barriers to private investment in market-based health technologies/organizations that can improve access to affordable and quality health services for the vulnerable population in India.

SAMRIDH had been able to mobilize USD $300 million in grant and debt capital from philanthropies, leading banks, and non-banking financial companies, allowing for the rapid introduction and scaling of social and market-based health enterprises. This means that for every $1 of philanthropic capital it raised, SAMRIDH mobilized an additional $8–$10 through contributions from the private sector via project implementers, consumers, governments, and other development partners. SAMRIDH's blended finance approach had proved to be a major contributor toward maximizing finance for development. This approach is promising for the ways it could help countries pursue sustainable private investments to achieve the United Nation's Sustainable Development Goals (SDGs) while reserving scarce public resources for the areas where they are needed the most.

In a short span of time, SAMRIDH had made significant advancements in strengthening the access, quality, and responsiveness of health care delivery in India. The initiative received global recognition as one of "India's top 50 COVID-19 last mile responders" by the World Economic Forum. It was also the first Indian initiative to win the 2022 P3 Impact Award, led by the Office of Global Partnerships at the U.S. Department of State, Concordia and the University of Virginia Darden School of Business Institute for Business in Society to recognize innovative and impactful public-private partnerships (P3) that address societal challenges.

SAMRIDH was paving the way toward a conducive ecosystem for scaling-up market-based health care solutions targeted to improve services for vulnerable communities. Through its diverse and distinct initiatives, the initiative had made significant advancements toward strengthening the access, quality, and responsiveness of health care delivery in the country. Its partnerships leveraged significant results. For example, by providing support in the form of performance-linked payment, SAMRIDH helped one social enterprise meet its operating expenditure in the initial phase of its project, ensuring its financial sustainability. This social enterprise was also experiencing a cash flow crunch triggered by a long working capital cycle. Combining returnable grants with a commercial loan from a financial institution helped support the social enterprise to achieve its break-even point early. Cross-sectoral collaborations allowed SAMRIDH to provide a diverse range of support, including business advisory, mentoring, and market access opportunities.

Providing holistic support to social enterprises, generating 8 to 10 times leverage for each philanthropic dollar spent, and making medical breakthroughs accessible to vulnerable communities were some of the high points of the partnerships that those at SAMRIDH were proud of. SAMRIDH had also demonstrated the power of partnerships. Stakeholders' vision for SAMRIDH's sectoral and geographical expansion proved this conviction. Improving the lives of vulnerable communities and addressing sustainable development goals remained central to the initiative's vision. Looking forward, the SAMRIDH facility was excited to build an ecosystem where social enterprises have natural avenues to access affordable capital and technical support to scale up high-impact solutions.

Technical Screening Criteria

The SAMRIDH team believed that while there are new-age health technologies that aim for the moon, more often than not, most of these technologies need consistent time and effort to deliver the best results. It takes a careful eye to shortlist unique, market-ready, and scalable business models that can be well-positioned to alter health care access inequality within an economy.

To address this, the SAMRIDH Technical Support Unit (TSU) quickly developed a detailed technical and commercial assessment criterion. The technical assessment was an amalgamation of the requirements of a venture capital firm and the needs of the development agency. It had parameters like innovation score, technical risk, disrupter ability, market/development likeness to other organizations, and unique advantages, among others. The assessment also measured criteria such as alignment with SAMRIDH's vision; impact monitoring ability; project team and implementation capability; gender lens investing approach; environmental, social, and governance (ESG) score; and estimated scale of impact.

Blended Finance Evaluation Parameters

The broad eligibility criteria for applying for funding from SAMRIDH were developed to examine the applying organization's purpose and scope of work, registration, year of operation, financing standing, and other similar factors. Beyond the basic eligibility checklist, evaluation and selection criteria needed to be customized to each case due to the wide range of innovations and interventions proposed to be supported under the blended finance facility. In many cases, assessment is both contextual and subjective. Once a proposal is received, the SAMRIDH team prepares an investment case on the applying social enterprise and presents it to the Advisory Committee. Their broad evaluation criteria include:

Business Model and Sustainability: Revenue trajectory, operating margins, accreditation, unit economics, profit after tax, sales channels

Managing Capability: Management experience, qualifications, organizational structure

Capital Structure (Present and Future): Net worth, debt to equity, sources of debt, ability to raise commercial capital, debt service coverage ratio projections

Competitive Positioning and Innovative Quotient: Competitive edge in value chain, patents/copyrights, research and development budgets

Customer Segmentation: Segmentation and positioning, consumer purchasing power, concentration risk, geographical coverage

Market Opportunity and Growth Plan: Operating market size, market growth, projected revenue and profitability growth, strategic partnerships

Once the social enterprises have been screened from both technical and commercial perspectives, the shortlisted investment proposals move to the investment structuring stage. The SAMRIDH TSU then works alongside the social enterprise to help identify its prominent financial pain points and accordingly customizes a mix of blended financing products that can help solve some of its challenges.

Structuring the Blended Finance Product Mix

The choice of financing instrument to address each enterprise's challenges depends on multiple factors, including the enterprise's need for concessional capital to mitigate specific investment risks, help rebalance risk-reward profiles, and meet the working capital needs for solutions that have the potential to achieve the desired social impact. Therefore, depending on the case in consideration, the blended financing mechanisms are finalized using instruments like results-based financing, first loss default guarantees, loan buy down, pay for performance instruments, and interest subvention.

Other possible financing instruments are designed and finalized in consultation with banks and financial institutions to mitigate the high investment risks associated with early-stage and new-age social entrepreneurs. These instruments are considered when disbursing funds to eligible social enterprises and innovations that align with the overall project vision. Some of the considerations for designing each instrument are social impact (impact created per dollar), the financial standing of the business (business viability and sustainability), population groups served (focusing on vulnerable, hard-to-reach populations), and provision of equitable and affordable health care services.

Case Examples: Innovative Financing Structures

While financing instruments defining the use of grant and debt funds are finalized in consultation with banks and financial institutions, these cases include some examples of possible instruments.

Case 1. Collateral/Interest Subvention Support

A medical equipment manufacturer required collateral support to scale-up its manufacturing capacity for medical equipment and devices.

Problem Statement: A medical equipment manufacturer had a strong order book but lacked the manufacturing capacity to fulfill the orders. It was possible to scale-up manufacturing capacity in the short-term, but the manufacturer was unable to get financing facility (term loans) from banking institutions for two reasons:

a. Since the order book consisted of mainly government orders, the margin profile did not allow servicing high-interest pay-outs on term loans. Furthermore, given government payment cycles, higher moratorium periods were required.
b. The manufacturer's balance sheet did not have enough collateral to match the bank's requirement for the term loan.

Solution: SAMRIDH worked with its banking partners to structure the following arrangement:

a. SAMRIDH secured grant funds that the manufacturer could use for interest subvention and/or for an increase in the moratorium period. This allowed the manufacturer to invest in increasing its manufacturing capacity in a sustainable manner.
b. SAMRIDH created a bank guarantee that could be used by the lender (bank) as part collateral for the loan.

Social Return: In return for this arrangement, the equipment manufacturer provided assurance that 40% of the total kits sold during the project duration would be sold at subsidized rates to government hospitals, allowing for deeper penetration of the advanced testing kits into health care settings in semi-urban and rural markets, making affordable equipment available to the general public.

Case 2. Results-Based Financing/Working Capital Support

The means of providing financing to social enterprises are contingent on the verification of predetermined results, leading to coverage for working capital. The main aspects of results-based financing are: (1) payment is based on achieved results, and (2) the relationship between the payment and results is predefined. As and when the results are achieved, there is a cash inflow, which is used across business operations and utilized as working capital.

Problem Statement: An AI-enabled chest x-ray solution can identify up to 30 distinct lung abnormalities in under a minute. India faced a severe shortage of testing supplies and medical devices during the COVID-19 pandemic, which adversely impacted the ability of hospitals and health workers in low-resource settings to monitor and extend timely, appropriate treatment to patients. A social enterprise with a presence in urban locations in the country, however, did not have the demographics and logistics necessary to bring the solution to semi-urban and rural locations. Additionally, incentives were needed by social enterprises that would serve semi-urban and rural markets that operated with lower margins to cover the incremental working capital expenses and improve the overall cashflow viability for undertaking such projects.

Solution: SAMRIDH worked with the social enterprise and other stakeholders to structure the following arrangement:

a. SAMRIDH used grant funds to structure cash payments to cover the operational expenses for expanding into newer sites upon the achievement of pre-defined results. This allowed the social enterprise to increase its scale and operations and to expand into semi-urban and rural locations.
b. In addition, SAMRIDH offered incentives for over-achievement to encourage the social enterprise to go beyond and create higher on-the-ground impact. This would demonstrate the proof of concept in scaling AI-enabled solutions to screen for lung abnormalities in low-resource settings. Once the model was running and established, it would invite greater implementation of such projects by both the private sector and the government.

Social Return: As a consequence of the above arrangement, the social enterprise expanded its business and entered newer geographies, adding to the overall top line (revenues) of the enterprise. This, in turn, led to the increased use of screening and diagnostic technologies in semi-urban and rural areas. The AI-enabled technology was made available to the general public in the middle of the pandemic at relatively low testing prices.

Business Advisory and Advocacy

There is no one-size-fits-all solution to initiating or scaling blended finance. Each enterprise's journey is unique. Supporting innovative businesses and projects by utilizing concessional capital at an early stage, thereby attracting private capital in the medium-to-long term, can be truly transformational and can enable success stories of sustainable business models.

Beyond offering financial support to enterprises, the SAMRIDH TSU supported enterprises on their journeys of transforming ideas into action. The team took a lot of effort and pride in supporting enterprises by providing business advisory services including incubation and mentorship support, clinical and commercial validations, regulatory clearances, and government advocacy initiatives. SAMRIDH TSU also facilitated introductions between enterprises and venture capital and private equity investors. SAMRIDH TSU supported its enterprises at every step along the way.

Once an enterprise joined SAMRIDH's investment portfolio, the team carried out a 360 degree assessment to determine the exact requirements for providing that organization with customized support. This included but was not limited to:

- Performing needs assessments of the enterprise and its solution to understand its technical and business gaps
- Providing enterprises with services corresponding to their needs, which may include providing support and coaching by leveraging internal or external expertise in different areas (access to funding, business support, networking, etc.)
- Assessing the enterprise's work to implement the customized plan and suggesting remedial/mitigation measures where needed through advice and handholding
- Proposing facilitation activities for the enterprises to share experiences, engage in peer-to-peer sessions, have meetups with the ecosystem, etc.
- Developing and maintaining a knowledge bank for all the support offered to the enterprise and ensuring ready access to all relevant information regarding an enterprise's progress
- Creating cross-linkages through the network of partners, stakeholders, and industry professionals by scaling solutions into newer geographies and/or sectors
- Creating an ecosystem of start-ups that can contribute to the overall impact for the vulnerable population as well as lead to sustainability

One of SAMRIDH's main ideas for offering customized business advisory to each of its portfolio enterprises was to help them strike a balance between chasing business and financial goals and achieving some form of social impact. Since each enterprise's vision and journey are different, it is critical to give them the tools to turn what they wanted to achieve into a reality rather than just an illusion. Having the right partners on board to steer the enterprise and its promoters in the right direction is a rare superpower. The SAMRIDH initiative continued to build enterprises that achieve great performance heights through their participation in the portfolio.[1]

Measuring Impact: A Friend or a Foe

Given the complex nature of the SAMRIDH initiative and its intertwined, multi-part activities, it was challenging to develop the facility's monitoring, evaluation, and learning framework. Unlike a stand-alone project with clear objectives and defined outcomes to achieve, incorporating several project components and areas of work in SAMRIDH's theory of change and logical framework approach was difficult.

Another challenge was retaining the scientific and theoretical rigor in developing monitoring and evaluation (M&E) systems while maintaining flexibility to accommodate complex and multi-part project activities. These issues were compounded by the dearth of literature in these areas. Furthermore, the funds pooled from various philanthropic organizations and commercial capital providers demanded that health care enterprises honor donors' contributions to the project and ensure they are reflected in the M&E systems developed. With all these challenges, the TSU expended significant amounts of time and effort on developing customized reports that met the reporting requirements of their respective donors, financial institutions, and partners. In addition, the team developed M&E systems that were both robust and agile in nature to capture current project activities while accommodating for future needs of the proposed activities. These M&E systems included a theory of change (TOC) and logical framework approach (LFA), created by mapping results against project goals using indicators and performance metrics to capture the project accomplishments.

SAMRIDH typically required multiple rounds of iterative discussions with the enterprises it supported. It was challenging to make the enterprises understand the importance of M&E systems for their projects, owing to their often limited prior exposure to them. For the TSU, getting enterprises' buy-in and attaining their confidence in implementing M&E systems was another learning and rewarding experience. To achieve a common understanding of M&E among enterprises and make them aware of the system's importance, the TSU conducted capacity-building sessions for social entrepreneurs and partners. This activity helped improve the traction of data reporting and inculcated the feeling of shared responsibility. The TSU also conducted field visits to the intervention sites to interact with end users; this provided insight about how the entity was helping them access health care and acted as an opportunity to verify reported data.

After establishing the M&E systems, the data populated by each portfolio enterprise were recorded and captured through an online reporting system, which further aggregated facility-level impact numbers and developed a comprehensive facility-level dashboard. Even when enterprises achieved their expected outputs, tasks related to standardizing the end user/beneficiary level outputs remained. There was also a continuous need to increase the reach of these solutions in their respective intervention areas, using best practices and laid out parameters in the health care industry.

Although the TSU solved many of the outlined challenges in developing and implementing monitoring activities, there is a critical need to shift the evaluation approach to innovative and lateral thinking against conventional models practiced within the industry. To improve this outcome, the TSU team has been considering the business nature of the enterprise (for-profit/nonprofit), its purpose and amount of funding, geographical presence, target users/beneficiaries, and thematic areas of operations. It is also developing an impact evaluation framework to best capture the delta change that the enterprise could bring at the end user/beneficiary level, health care ecosystem level, entity level, and overall project level against the project outcomes. Using the enterprise-level impact evaluation results, the TSU team plans to aggregate the results at the thematic and overall SAMRIDH levels. This will help to share the project accomplishments in wider health care forums.

The Road Ahead

A variety of learnings, reflections, and opportunities have emerged so far in the journey of the SAMRIDH Blended Finance Facility. The TSU continues to remain excited about what's next in store on the path to increasing access to affordable capital for social enterprises to achieve scale and financial and commercial sustainability. Blended finance can be a positive tool for creating investment opportunities and promoting tri-sector collaboration between public, private, and philanthropic organizations toward scaling impact for development. Globally, blended finance is entering the mainstream; traditional policymakers and grant-making agencies are adjusting their perspectives and exploring opportunities that can be leveraged to revolutionize the development finance sector. Additional participation and involvement by the private sector is also magnifying the blended finance market, leading to improved scale in investing approaches and solutions. Although an enormous funding gap continues to exist in UN SDG financing, there is growing momentum for blended finance, and positive signals in capital markets suggest its greater adoption in the near future.

Discussion Questions

1. What will be the keys to sustain the SAMRIDH model?
2. To what degree could this model be applied in other parts of the world?

NOTES

1. For more information, visit: "SAMRIDH Healthcare Blended Finance Facility," n.d., accessed February 28, 2023, https://samridhhealth.org/.

SECTION 4

Social Impact Strategy Cases

CASE 4.1

HopeWell, Inc.

DELLA M. HUGHES AND MARJI ERICKSON WARFIELD

In January 2019, Shaheer Mustafa, CEO of HopeWell, Inc., reflected on the transitions he had led at HopeWell over the previous 3 years and what he planned to accomplish going forward. He and the HopeWell team had dramatically repositioned HopeWell during this time by co-creating a theory of change (TOC) and logic models to provide a best practice approach to change management and bring cohesion to their efforts. But he knew that new challenges would need to be addressed in the coming year. How could they bring cohesion to this large, multi-site organization and increase their effectiveness while infusing their efforts with HopeWell's social justice orientation, best practices, and learning culture?

HopeWell Background

Having turned 50 in 2016, HopeWell was at a pivotal juncture. Formerly Dare Family Services, the nonprofit organization had large state contracts and a history of providing well-regarded foster care for children and youth and residential programming for adults with disabilities. However, after a dynamic and highly entrepreneurial beginning, the organization's focus over time shifted to traditional approaches. Although Dare Family Services became financially well-resourced, its organizational systems and supports were siloed and underdeveloped—innovation was simply not a priority.

In 2016, the Dare Family Services Board of Directors and new CEO, Shaheer Mustafa, began to re-envision the organization for the 21st century. As part of that transformation, they adopted the name "HopeWell" as a symbol of their renewed commitment to positive, innovative models of care and their central mission: "to enrich the lives and expand the opportunities of individuals and families in need of love, support, and safe places to grow and thrive."

After recruiting and hiring a senior leadership team and beginning strategic planning, Mustafa knew that it was time to carefully craft a theory of change to articulate a new vision for HopeWell; how they planned to achieve that vision; and, just as importantly, the values that would drive their efforts. To build the foundation for a social justice and learning organization, HopeWell's evolution would need to include shifts in the roles and focuses of its Board of Directors, CEO, and senior leadership as well as in its organizational structure, practices, and culture. At the core, Mustafa knew that this evolution must center on addressing critical issues facing the individuals and families with whom HopeWell worked.

Theory of Change and Logic Models as Management and Learning Tools

Mustafa knew that while talk of organizational transformation was common when leadership changed, the systematic planning required for implementing the best practice elements needed to create deep and lasting change were often partially launched but not intentionally carried out. From the beginning, HopeWell's leadership embarked on plans to build on the organization's strengths. In addition, they built a collective vision, values, and framework for how the work should be carried out in every aspect of the organization, what their results should be, how their work could alter the human services landscape, and how the organization could be held accountable.

In 2019, HopeWell partnered with the Brandeis University Heller School's Center for Youth and Communities for organizational learning and capacity development. Part of this work involved guiding HopeWell's co-creation of a TOC and organizational and department-level logic models. Developing these tools required intensive effort from HopeWell's leadership team as well as extensive staff input. This concerted effort was carefully and thoughtfully grounded in values; best practice, management, and policy standards; systematic, strategic, and inclusive approaches; and HopeWell's community-based origins and history of excellence in programming. The one-page TOC graphic (Exhibit 1) depicts the overarching vision and contains a summary of their approach; accompanying organizational and departmental logic models laid out the approach in more detail to demonstrate the link between HopeWell's actions and impact.

The TOC summarized HopeWell's path to "The Promise": HopeWell's commitment to continuously reflect, learn, and evolve to promote wellbeing, self-efficacy, justice, and opportunity. HopeWell embraced a systemic, holistic, integrated, science-based approach to outcomes that would transform the lives of those with whom they worked, energize staff to continue to excel and innovate, and embolden the leadership team to push toward sustainable systemic change.

In addition to the TOC and logic model work, Mustafa asked the Brandeis team to prepare a case study to document the point-in-time status of the organization. The team reviewed a trove of documents from all aspects of the organization and interviewed 14 key stakeholders ranging from direct service staff, to senior managers, to board members, to funders. The information from these interviews—as well as from 10 meetings with staff, youth, family members, caregivers, and senior leadership—provided the information for this case study. Quotes that appear in this study are anonymous, as agreed upon up-front with case study interviewees.

HopeWell's process involved two phases: laying the foundation for change and gearing up for transformation.

Phase 1, Laying the Foundation for Change: Leadership Matters

Having worked at the Department of Children and Families (DCF) and leading other nonprofit organizations, Mustafa brought decades of experience in child welfare and human services. He also carried with him academic and mentorship connections that guided his work in transforming HopeWell. As both a former student and teacher at the Institute for Nonprofit Practice, he embodied a collaborative teaching and learning orientation that included a commitment to data and evaluation as mechanisms for identifying evidence-based practices and driving organizational development decision-making. Further, to ensure that his thinking and vision were not too caught up in day-to-day details, he relied on mentors to keep his eye on larger issues facing HopeWell and the field in general.

Mustafa knew well the complexities and challenges facing children and youth in foster care and adults with disabilities, as well as the common methods to address them, which are detailed in hundreds of volumes of research and commentary. He also understood that although engaging with these individuals so they may lead fulfilling and productive lives sounded like common sense, it challenged many of the underpinnings of traditional child welfare and disability policies and practices. "Protection" had been a dominant paradigm in both fields.

Services developed to "protect," by their nature, are reactive to the problems that individuals in care experience, and these services were typically designed to "fix" individuals. Mustafa's big challenge was: How could Hopewell, a traditional human service organization, make transformative changes to all aspects of its operations and have impact on the field while still balancing its day-to-day moving parts to be on track toward attaining The Promise?

Certainly, the CEO's leadership and credibility were critical. Participants consistently identified the same mix of traits to describe Mustafa: strategic, confident, ambitious, entrepreneurial, and courageous ("go big or go home"), typically combined with humble, curious, compassionate, collaborative, and a listener to diverse points of view. Further, they noted that he had a "rare quality" of being both visionary and focused on the details at the same time. They also shared that he was unafraid to think and act outside the box. He sought candid feedback from others, "was hungry for connection and new conversations," always thinking about who else should be at the table; he also believed that when you can "swallow your own ego and think big—good things can happen." Finally, they collectively perceived him as bringing his full self to work, living his values transparently, and encouraging others at HopeWell to do the same. They linked these traits to his penchant for hiring talent that could co-lead the HopeWell transformations. Further, he had the same level of care and concern for the individuals and families with whom HopeWell worked as he did for the staff—people were always at the center of his thinking and acting.

> An [adult] individual in one of the programs had a negative episode—HopeWell spared no expense to keep him safe and make him feel that he was still a part of the program even though he needed to reside in an alternate location. He was not kicked out of the program—as most other agencies would have done. HopeWell caters to people first—puts people and families at the center . . . HopeWell ensures happiness and stability for all of the people that we serve and their families, and maintains a devoted staff while doing so.

Phase 2, Gearing Up for Transformation

Executive Leadership Team for Management and Learning

Mustafa made significant changes early on to the leadership team to address a top-heavy staffing structure. This was not the usual "housecleaning" but rather a careful and respectful assessment of how to best create an Executive Leadership Team (ELT) aligned with HopeWell's emerging mission and values. Over time, departures and retirements opened opportunities for hires from outside of HopeWell, including the vice president of program impact and strategy; chief human resources officer; vice president of research, policy, and learning; and chief development officer.

Importantly, Mustafa promoted internally, affirming and engaging long-time staff who would thrive in the new work culture and were able to demonstrate dormant skills and abilities. Through these different processes, the larger leadership team was reshaped and the change process was ignited, without which nothing else would happen.

With his leadership team in place, Mustafa knew HopeWell could be nimbler in addressing pressing problems facing the individuals and families with whom they worked. One of these problems was finding better ways to support youth aging out of foster care (Exhibit 2).

Creating a Human Resources Department to Cultivate a Strong Workforce and Culture

Knowing that the people throughout the organization determined whether the outcomes would ultimately be attained, Mustafa acted quickly to establish the Human Resources (HR) department that previously had not existed. Hiring a chief officer for HR who was committed to and well-versed in best practice kick-started a series of sweeping changes not only to the basic procedures for hiring employees, providing supervision, and managing payroll but also, more importantly, to changing the workplace culture.

> With the recent increased focus in our country on social justice and racism, Shaheer and Leah [Chief Human Resources Officer] held town halls with staff to open spaces for them to share their experiences. It made a difference for this to be led by black and brown leaders. This shows they take this seriously—put a stake in the ground.

For starters, Mustafa and the ELT made it clear that employees at all levels were respected, cared about, and supported in all they did. Tangible examples of this included the establishment of multiple benefit programs for employees, such as professional development opportunities, student loan support, equitable and transparent salary adjustments, shifts to utilizing technology for easier reporting procedures, and employee assistance and wellness programs. Support for employees extended to their well-being and the well-being of their families.

In addition, the focused HR attention resulted in what one staff member described as an "increase in the overall values that we represent." One example was described in terms of "goal sharing." Before goals were set, feedback was gathered from staff through HR pulse surveys and site visits from members of the ELT, demonstrating organization-wide that employees did have input into important decisions. This infused energy into all levels and shifted "what people wanted for themselves and how hard they were willing to work." Speaking of Mustafa, one member of the staff observed:

> He trusted me to do what I thought best and gave me the freedom to make and implement change—this was a breath of fresh air. To go and do was amazing! Looking at the end result versus micro managing—that really drew me in. My ability to hire and create a team to build my vision.

HopeWell's diversity, equity, inclusion, and belonging (DEIB) strategy was rooted in the fact that systemic racism had an outsized impact on the communities they served, requiring the organization to take an anti-racist stance in its policies, practices, and procedures. The emerging organizational culture intentionally and directly addressed issues related to social justice and increasing the diversity of HopeWell's workforce. Mustafa and the Board of Directors committed to increasing the diversity of Black, Indigenous, and People of Color (BIPOC) and those with lived experience in foster care throughout the organization. As of September 2022, 33% of the Board were BIPOC, and 33% had lived experience in foster care; 57% of the Executive Leadership Team were BIPOC, with one member having lived experience in foster care; and a bit over half of staff identified as BIPOC, many of whom had lived experience. Says Mustafa: "This is intentional and, we believe, represents the manifestation of our equity stance. It's relevant in so many ways, but to have leadership and staff reflect the community we serve is essential to authentic partnership and collaboration with the community."

Further, HopeWell's deep roots in social justice were manifested by directly addressing racial disproportionality in the child welfare system. Mustafa articulated this organizational charge in this way:

> For HopeWell, institutional racism is directly responsible for why kids and families become engaged in child welfare. Full stop. You can't talk about foster care without talking about the lasting effects of slavery, genocide, and forced relocation of indigenous people and systemic efforts to oppress BIPOC communities through over-policing. Programs like RISE (Readiness, Inquiry, Scholarship, Education Initiative) that specifically tackle educational opportunity gaps, compounded by the very systems that are supposed to support youth, disproportionately affect Black and Hispanic kids. So, our DEIB work is more than just creating representation and belonging but using targeted interventions to disrupt systemic racism. This is deeply conscious and intentional on our part.

In addition to focusing on macro-level issues, HopeWell made DEIB come alive in the organization through small but significant actions that embraced and appreciated the differences among staff. One example was how HopeWell created a sense of belonging by implementing thoughtful communication and employee experience strategies to recognize ethnic, cultural, and religious holidays; employees were provided with information so they could learn about traditions different from their own and culturally sensitive ways to work with employees who celebrated those traditions. Further, Mustafa sent regular messages to staff regarding HopeWell's position on key events in the world (e.g., race relations, social injustices, etc.) that could be affecting those with whom they worked as well as the employees. One HopeWell staff member remarked,

> As social justice issues have risen, HopeWell really embraces DEIB at every level of the organization; they are intentional about DEIB and racial equity work. This is not true in all agencies.

Using a Theory of Change and Logic Models as Management and Learning Tools

Mustafa and the ELT expanded their attention to ensuring that their investment in reimagining HopeWell would gain traction, create organizational cohesion, and increase effectiveness. With Brandeis as an organizational development and learning partner, HopeWell's leadership chose an iterative, developmental process to create the TOC as well as the organizational- and departmental-level logic models (Exhibits 3 and 4). This process began in 2019 and, while major foundational elements (e.g., the TOC and strong drafts of the logic models) were in place by the end of 2021, the short-term outcomes and measures of the logic models still required vetting.

Key Steps in Developing the Theory of Change and Logic Models

1. Articulate the Goals and Design the Process

The TOC and logic models were clearly important tools for external purposes like communications and funding proposals, but Mustafa knew that the process was also critical to internal organizational development and capacity building. Engaging staff, caregivers, families and individuals in the programs, and other stakeholders to co-create HopeWell's vision and values—while generating a strong connection to how they could contribute to accomplishing the mission—would bring cohesion to their efforts and increase their effectiveness. He and his executive team also knew they were expected to provide a path for moving the organization forward. A foundation of best practice and their articulation of the TOC would be the guide, and the logic models would be the more detailed plans.

To ground their work in best practice, the Brandeis team was charged with conducting an extensive review of the research literature and preparing a synthesis. From there, HopeWell leaders carefully considered how to introduce the plan and its purpose, the timing and flow of the process, who should participate to represent the voices of their many constituencies, and how and when to engage them to make the process accessible (given workloads and life challenges) and participation meaningful.

2. Engage Stakeholders and Develop Working Drafts

Based on the experience and existing foundational values held by HopeWell leaders and found in the Brandeis literature synthesis, an initial TOC was drafted. Meetings with departmental leaders were organized to review the draft and to have structured conversations about values, beliefs, successes, and outcomes as well as the major strategies used to reach them.

Taking care to include the language of the people involved and synthesized by the leadership team, this input moved the TOC further along and informed the content of the organizational logic model. The "starter" logic model draft began to crystallize with more of a focus on operational values, approaches, and intended outcomes.

Next, to expand participation, smaller work groups in each department reviewed these organizational drafts, deliberated wording and priorities, and made their imprint on the content. These work groups included staff, caregivers, families, adults with disabilities, and youth in foster care.

In a second meeting of each small group, members were given updated drafts, now including a programmatic logic model format, and were charged with identifying measures of progress toward outcomes. The goal was to make sure the logic models had objective and realistic measures of progress that would ultimately require data collection but would not create unnecessary demands on the hard-working field staff. At this stage, input into the organizational and program logic models from all of the departments was assessed for alignment and synthesized into solid working drafts.

3. Finalize the Theory of Change

The TOC was again refined and shared with Mustafa for his consideration. A solid product was emerging, but it took numerous iterations to make the language and tone precise and to create a graphic that fully represented HopeWell's dynamic nature and its developmental and systemic approach. By October 2021, the graphic was finalized, and a communications firm was employed to create the final product (Exhibit 1).

HopeWell's iterative process and intentional structure were designed to develop key tools, laying the foundation for HopeWell to become a learning organization. In this structure, learning, courageously trying new approaches, and assessing whether those approaches succeeded or failed and why would be critical and valued tasks. One of these tasks included identifying what improvements could be made as an integral part of the work culture. An additional task prioritized centering all efforts for creating the essential supports and opportunities for those with whom HopeWell worked. The iterative process helped maintain the integrity of an organization in action—one that was growing while the foundation and tools were being developed. Yet, not everything went smoothly.

Defining Learning Organizations

Learning organizations and the people in them learn constantly from everything they do. They use their own experiences and those of others to improve their performance. They learn from their successes and also from their failures. Continuous learning is systematically built into the organization's DNA and infrastructure. The value of continuous learning is espoused, driven, and modeled by the CEO and senior management. There is no doubt in every organization member's mind that continuous learning is expected and will be rewarded.

Managing Process Challenges

Moving from concept to implementation always presents challenges. Key among the challenges for HopeWell's TOC and logic model development included juggling the schedules of busy people as well as merging their differences in learning styles, mindsets, skills, and values.

- Refining the TOC, especially when it came to the graphic, tested staff's perceptions of the written words and their understandings of the flow of the approach. The back and forth may have seemed endless, but it resulted in a dynamic TOC that was understandable and reflective of the organization at that point in time. HopeWell's leaders realized that as HopeWell transformed, the TOC and logic models would ultimately require modifications based on what the leaders had learned. In other words, they did not have to be, and could never be, "perfect" (or "finished").
- HopeWell leaders recognized that the individuals they planned to engage in developing the TOC and logic models would have differing learning styles; this was factored into the planning. They discussed in advance with each unit leader the purpose and benefits of the process. Their preparation also included selecting individuals for the small groups and assessing how to customize the approach for specific group conversations. This tactic largely worked well, but there were points where the process had to be paused and reworked to get to the desired outcome due to lack of familiarity with the tools and language.

- Clarifying values and beliefs helped staff understand their fit with the organization. For those ready to be challenged by using best practice, having a more explicit focus on outcomes, and engaging in ongoing learning, their excitement about the work deepened and they felt more connected. Others were not as prepared to work differently and made decisions to find other employment.
- Having a written aspirational document (the TOC) and guide for practice and management (the logic models) did not mean the change happened overnight. Each department, program, and unit had to digest what this meant in terms of staff development and develop support to move this multifaceted plan into action. Additionally, making the TOC and logic models a cornerstone of managing a social justice learning organization begged the question of how to construct a sustainable management information system with protocols for data collection, analysis, learning, and improvement. HopeWell leaders grappled with effective ways to move these tools to the next level.

Looking Ahead: Sustaining Leadership, Culture, and Quality to Attain Outcomes and Social Impact

HopeWell had accomplished a great deal since Mustafa became CEO in 2016. By 2022, HopeWell was able to define itself as a social justice and learning organization that had grown to engage 1,500 youth and individuals annually. It had become one of the largest providers of intensive foster care in New England, supporting families throughout Massachusetts. In addition to offering intensive foster care, HopeWell provided in-home support and stabilization services to families involved with the Department of Children and Families (DCF). The organization also supported youth aging out of foster care by providing stable housing, education, and employment support. In addition, HopeWell delivered residential care for adults living with disabilities. HopeWell's work was funded primarily via state contracts, but it also received significant funding from corporate and individual donors.

The organization continued to evolve and grow, guided at all levels by its ever-present mission, vision, and values. Significant new hires strengthened and diversified the leadership team, and new partnerships were engaged in launching grand initiatives.

Leading and managing an organization to maintain high standards, learn, adapt, innovate, and seek ambitious social change had its own set of challenges. These were multiplied by the redesign and growth process and, even more so, by the COVID-19 pandemic that started in 2020. The change process presented opportunities to learn and stretch boundaries, and it was a magnetic force for entrepreneurial leaders. How that force was managed would be critical to the long-term health of the organization, because attention to the core business and organizational culture was essential. HopeWell was now facing that challenge.

Readiness, Inquiry, Scholarship, Education (RISE) Initiative

As he looked ahead, Mustafa identified a serious issue that demanded attention: the academic opportunity gap for youth experiencing foster care was one of the largest gaps for any group of students in Massachusetts. This gap had far-reaching, long-term effects, including low rates of meeting academic milestones from elementary grades through adulthood, third grade English Language Arts state standards, high school graduation, and college degree attainment. He knew that to move toward The Promise, this issue needed to be dealt with head-on, which had implications for creating new programming for youth in foster care as well as for systemic change. Further, he knew that if they did their job well, the initiative could have expansion possibilities and be a model for addressing systemic change.

HopeWell prepared a concept paper and received funding first for extensive research on best practice and then for launching a pilot for the Readiness, Inquiry, Scholarship, Education (RISE) initiative (Exhibit 5). The Brandeis team came on board early in the initiative planning stages to partner in developing a programmatic logic model aligned with the TOC and organizational logic model and to conduct an implementation evaluation.

An all-new RISE core team of four was hired, with members having differing and complementary training and experience. Their job was to build out this initiative in the context of a social justice learning organization that would have positive outcomes for youth in foster care, improve public school systems' attention to these youth and their assets and needs, and provide a roadmap for others interested in a similar approach.

Discussion Questions

1. Well-thought-out TOC and logic models can provide clear management guidance and support a learning culture for the entire organization and its stakeholders. With multiple new inputs (policies, regulations, practices, etc.) and core programming occurring simultaneously, balancing the internal and external moving parts was essential to ensure that all HopeWell efforts were headed toward attaining The Promise.
    - What elements were necessary for this approach to be effective?
    - Who should be involved in designing and managing the process? Who should be involved in providing input for the models?
    - What supports were needed to make the development of these management and learning tools necessary?
    - What challenges should the leadership anticipate in this process?
    - What opportunities did this approach create?
2. HopeWell used the TOC and logic models as management and learning tools.
    - How could these tools and associated processes support HopeWell's entrepreneurial spirit and the systemic change it sought while managing the organization on a day-to-day basis at a high level of quality with a strong commitment to its values and focus on the people?
    - How could these tools and processes help create a learning culture?

EXHIBIT 1. HopeWell Theory of Change

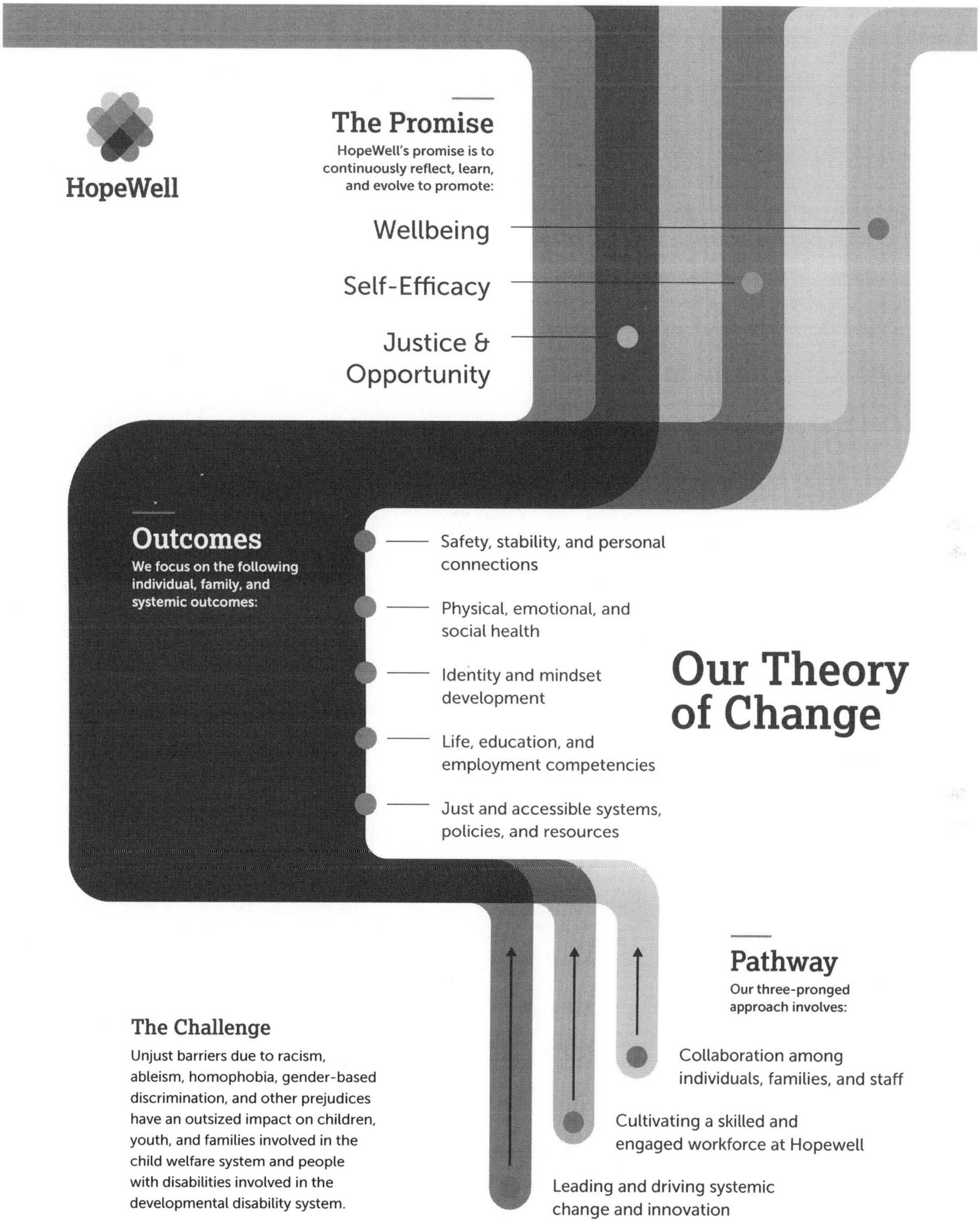

Used with permission of HopeWell, Inc.

EXHIBIT 2. HopeWell's My First Place for Youth Aging Out of Foster Care

My First Place™

For the more than 25,000 young people across the United States who transition out of foster care into adulthood each year, the future can be perilous and uncertain. Having gone without the consistent support of family to guide them in developing life skills and building a foundation for success, foster kids too often fall prey to homelessness, unemployment, and poverty.

- 40% of former foster kids will experience homelessness
- 25% will be arrested or incarcerated
- 54% will drop out of high school
- Fewer than 5% will earn a bachelor's degree

However, with the right support, more is possible for foster kids. At HopeWell, we help foster kids beat the odds. Our programs provide vulnerable young people with the tools they need to reach their full potential in school, work, and life.

My First Place™ is a nationally-recognized education and employment program that employs housing and intensive case management to support youth in developing the skills they need for a successful transition to self-sufficiency. Developed nearly two decades ago by First Place for Youth, a California-based nonprofit, My First Place has a strong track record of supporting at-risk foster youth at a critical time in their lives when they need to learn to support themselves. We believe that having a safe place to call home is a stabilizing factor that enables youth to focus on their education and employment goals, build community, and establish a foundation for long-term success in independent living.

Our program is delivered by a team of program staff—consisting of a Youth Advocate, an Education and Employment Specialist, and a Housing Specialist—who support each young person to identify, plan for, and work towards achieving their personal long-term goals in education, employment, housing, and healthy living. Currently working with youth who have aged out of foster care in Greater Boston and Greater Springfield, we support youth as they pursue their education and employment goals while offering rent-free housing in shared apartments for the duration of their time in program.

Used with permission of HopeWell, Inc.

EXHIBIT 3. Center for Youth and Communities Logic Model Development Process

A logic model is a picture of how a program or initiative will work—the theory and assumptions underlying it. A good logic model links outcomes with program or initiative strategies and activities as well as the assumptions. At its best, the logic model is based on lessons from research and experience.

Essentially, a logic model is a "theory-based" approach to organizational planning for change and evaluation—a process that creates a snapshot of how an initiative or program effects change and develop key interim outcomes that lead to longer-term outcomes or impacts. The logic model is intended to provide a framework that articulates the theories or "assumptions" about why the initiative/program will work (stemming from research as well as practical knowledge from the field), the strategies that will be used for implementation, and the outcomes (both intermediate- and long-term) expected.

The model used by the Heller School's Center for Youth and Communities seeks answers to the following seven questions:

1. Who will be served/who will benefit from our work?
2. Why are you doing this? Why does change need to happen? What are the political, economic, social, technological, and environmental conditions or factors that compel you to make change? What identified needs or assets led you to address the issue? What assumptions guide our work? What do you know, think, and believe about why you do what you do?
3. What outcomes do we want to achieve (individual, organizational, system/ community)?
4. What mix of programs, services, and activities will be needed to achieve the desired outcomes?
5. Who needs to be involved? What community resources can we draw upon? What other resources will it take (financial, human, material, etc.)?
6. How will we know if we're making a difference?
7. How will we measure it? How will we know we are making progress?

It is critical to track each assumption, strategy, and outcome across the model to see if each is supported by the other two; in other words, each assumption should have a strategy and outcome that tie to it and vice versa. There may be more than one strategy and outcome supporting an assumption, as there might be more than one assumption and strategy supporting an outcome. Finally, you may also develop an action plan with specific, realistic activities as well as a timeline and person(s) responsible for the strategies.

Used with permission of Susan P. Curnan and Della M. Hughes, Center for Youth and Communities, The Heller School for Social Policy and Management, Brandeis University.

EXHIBIT 4. Logic Model Template and Guiding Questions

What is the problem to be solved? It's important to be clear about this so that you don't end up solving the wrong problem.

DEFINING THE PROBLEM TO BE ADDRESSED		
Logic model category	**Explanation**	**Questions to think about**
For whom?	• Identify the population(s) and/or group(s) with and/or for whom you are working.	***For whom are you doing this work?*** • Who will benefit from your work and the changes you create?
Assumptions	• "Assumptions" are what you know, think, and/or believe. • Describe the assumptions underlying the initiative and the approaches you are taking. • These assumptions are likely to be the same or very similar across all years of the initiative.	***What assumptions guide your work?*** • Why are you doing this? Why does change need to happen? • What are the political, economic, social, technological, and environmental (PESTE) conditions or factors that compel you to make change? • What data and/or identified needs or assets led you to address the issue? • What is it about the initiative's approach that makes changes or differences happen?
Strategies	• Outline the strategies that will be needed to achieve the desired outcomes for the given year.	***What mix of powerful strategies will be needed to achieve the desired outcomes?*** • What systems need to be in place? • Who needs to be involved? • What resources can be drawn upon? • What other resources will it take (financial, human, material, etc.)?
Short-term and long-term outcomes	• Answer the question, "What is success?" Outcomes for the first year of implementation should be more specific, while outcomes for subsequent years may be more general. • Describe tangible changes sought for each population/group identified in the "For Whom?" row. Outcomes should be reasonably measurable. • Many outcomes will require much more than one year of work. Many will stay fairly constant across the years; some may be unique to each year.	***What outcomes do you want to achieve?*** • What changes do you want to see happen over the next few years? • What will be different if your strategy works?

DEFINING THE PROBLEM TO BE ADDRESSED		
Logic model category	**Explanation**	**Questions to think about**
Measures of success	• Answer the question, "How will you know the initiative has been successful?" year-by-year. • This row supports and informs the evaluation. It describes the information that initiatives will need to gather to know the extent to which each outcome is being achieved. • Some data will be available through existing systems but may need to be compiled and analyzed in new ways. Other data will require new approaches.	***How will you know if you're making a difference?*** • How will it be measured? • What data is already gathered and accessible? • What new data must be gathered, and how?
Long-term impact	• Describe what will happen after 10 to 15 years if the initiative is successful.	***What condition(s) do you ultimately want to create?***

Used with permission of Susan P. Curnan and Della M. Hughes, Center for Youth and Communities, The Heller School for Social Policy and Management, Brandeis University.

EXHIBIT 5. HopeWell's RISE Program

HopeWell's RISE Program

Readiness • Inquiry • Scholarship • Education

RISE is HopeWell's innovative approach to **advance educational equity for children experiencing foster care**. The program targets a critical intervention point — early literacy. RISE meets the distinct needs of children experiencing foster care through a combination of home-based tutoring, social-emotional skill development, caregiver support, and cross-system coordination.

Addressing a **3-Prong Challenge**

1. Academic outcomes are significantly lower for students experiencing foster care.

When compared to almost every other group of students, students in foster care are more likely to face educational inequities in academic achievement, school discipline, high school completion, and access to postsecondary opportunities.

> These disparities start early. For example, **here in Massachusetts, just 26% of third-graders experiencing foster care are on-track in reading**, compared to 50% of third-graders overall.

2. The very nature of being in foster care affects children's educational experiences.

Children experiencing foster care often move from home-to-home and school-to-school. These transitions mean they are repeatedly faced with rebuilding social networks and adjusting to new curriculum. Further, these challenges can often be exacerbated by a lack of effective coordination among school systems, caregivers, and child welfare systems.

> Children experiencing foster care change placements an average of 4-8 times, and **each placement change can disrupt learning by 6 months**.

3. These early systemic inequities accumulate and compound throughout their lives.

Early literacy is a critical intervention point. When students struggle to learn how to read, it can affect their behavior, self-esteem, and cumulative learning across subjects.

> Students who are behind in reading in elementary school **drop out of high school at a rate 4x greater than their peers**.

And the longer-term trajectories for youth who "age out" of foster care are alarming.

> Within 18 months of "aging out," **40% of youth will experience homelessness and over 50% will be unemployed.**

Sources are available upon request.

Used with permission of HopeWell, Inc.

Tufts Medicine Health Care System

CASE 4.2A

Merging Hospitals in a New Model (A)

MAHER TABBA AND JON CHILINGERIAN

The American health care landscape changed dramatically after the Affordable Care Act (ACA) was signed into law on March 23, 2010, leading to consolidation in the health industry. This new framework—combined with the mounting financial pressure on all hospitals that resulted from limited Medicare and Medicaid reimbursement rates, economic uncertainty, and new mandates by the ACA—demanded a new vision for care delivery and forced hospital integration.

Normand Deschene, CEO of Lowell General Hospital (LGH), and Ellen Zane, CEO emeritus and vice chair of the Tufts Medical Center (TMC) Board of Trustees, discussed a possible two-hospital affiliation in September 2013.[1] This conversation took place at a time when Tufts had a questionable ability to compete locally with multiple giant health care systems operating in eastern Massachusetts including Partners, Beth Israel Deaconess, and Steward. In addition, Tufts's failure to negotiate with Boston Medical Center in early 2013 had led to more uncertainty about the future of TMC.[2]

The goal of the proposed affiliation between TMC and LGH that became Tufts Medicine Health Care System (TMHCS) was to change the traditional health care model by focusing on community health, preventive medicine, and investment in technology instead of solely focusing on hospital equipment and buildings. Both hospitals were high-quality facilities on every parameter used to measure health care quality and were ranked as more cost-effective than other hospitals of the same caliber.[3] The primary difference in care after the affiliation would be that TMC would be able to provide higher-level services in Lowell so that, in Zane's words, "people can get the care they need closer to home."[4] Zane added that the affiliation would also improve both hospitals' abilities to provide patients with seamless, high-level care at a lower cost. Furthermore, the new entity would create an attractive model for other hospitals and medical provider groups to join in the future.

The Massachusetts Health Policy Commission (HPC)—which monitored changes in the health care marketplace and used a 30-day review period to analyze the potential effects of changes in hospital ownership—determined that this affiliation would not be likely to raise costs. David Seltz, the executive director of HPC, indicated that this affiliation would actually save patients money as a result of more patients being referred to TMC rather than more expensive hospitals in downtown Boston: "Both [TMC and LGH] have relatively low prices compared to their peers."[5]

Hospital Mergers, Acquisitions, and Affiliations

Health care mergers and acquisitions (M&A) have historically intended to combine multiple medical facilities and provider groups to expand patient volume; develop multiple health services; and provide complementary, multidisciplinary, specialized, and advanced medical care among the affiliated facilities. This model of practice increases the size of the health care market being managed by the new entity, providing more market power and a stronger negotiation position, minimizing administrative expenses, reducing acquisition costs, and improving financial revenue. Generally, hospital M&A has been driven by economics and supported by state and federal policies and regulations.

Hospital M&A has occurred since the 1960s, but on a more modest scale. A substantial increase in hospital mergers took place during two eras. The first was during the introduction of Health Maintenance Organizations and Preferred Provider Organizations (PPOs) in the late 1980s and early 1990s, which led to the implementation of new constraints on health care spending; the goals of these programs were to form networks of medical providers, monitor utilizations, and reduce unnecessary services. The second era was after the Affordable Care Act (ACA) was passed in 2010; the ACA focused on promoting system integration in health care by offering incentive programs and bonus packages when medical care was coordinated, efficient, and maintained high-quality standards.

Outcomes of Hospital Mergers

Between 2008–2014 there were nearly 400 U.S. M&A transactions that resulted in more than 750 acquired or merged hospitals. Several reports have concluded that hospital M&A were unsuccessful in producing the desired results. In many cases. they failed to provide better outcomes or decrease costs. They also led to higher negotiation prices and insurance policies. As a result, consumers became responsible for more premiums in exchange for fewer benefits.[6] A combination of different operational styles in the merging facilities, cultural resistance to change among providers and institutional leaders, and poor planning contributed to these failures.

According to a comprehensive survey by the Deloitte Center for Health Solutions and Healthcare Financial Management Association of mergers in the 7 years prior to the TMHCS merger, the primary reason among acquiring organizations was a desire to increase market share. Twenty-nine percent of acquired organizations (and 24% of acquiring organizations) cited delivering care more efficiently as a primary motivation. The financial outcomes were often not favorable. After two years, acquired hospitals had a post-transaction decline in operating margin, revenue, and expenses. Anticipated cost structure efficiencies often failed to materialize, with less than a third of mergers achieving even half of the transaction's projected cost structure efficiencies.[7]

That said, quality improved after many mergers, with 27% reporting increased HCAHPS (a standardized nationwide survey that reports patient satisfaction) scores, 23% reporting reduced readmissions, and 17% reporting reduced mortality. Of the hospital executives that completed the survey, over half (54%) said the acquired hospital experienced improved care quality.[8]

Academic vs. Community Medical Practice

Both academic and community-based medicine have played essential roles in delivering health care across United States academic medical centers (AMCs) by providing state-of-the-art care for a wide range of medical conditions, including complex and rare diseases. They typically recruit providers with advanced expertise and specialized training in challenging health conditions. They also provide adequate infrastructure, necessary resources, and ancillary services to enable physicians to deliver complex services. In addition, AMCs have contributed to training the next generation of medical professionals and have been responsible for initiating and coordinating various types of medical research. AMCs accounted for 20% of hospital admissions in the country and treated a significant portion of Medicare, Medicaid, and uninsured patients. Based on the adjusted case mix index[9], AMC care costs were 10–20% higher than the care provided in non-academic medical facilities.[10]

On the other hand, community medicine is structured to evaluate and treat the common medical conditions in a given region. It is also responsible for implementing all types of preventive medicine, including medical screening tests and vaccinations. Through outpatient clinics and inpatient services at community hospitals, community medical providers are typically the first line of patients' medical assessment. These providers are responsible for treating the majority of patients and manage more than 80% of hospital admissions. Their medical care has typically been underserved, and few specialists are available to support the primary care physicians. They manage the most common medical conditions, and their practice style relies on direct communication with patients and their referring physicians. The outcomes of health care provided in these communities were comparable to the outcomes of care provided in academic hospitals.[11]

The Potential of Academic/Community Mergers

Mergers between academic and community hospitals have great potential to improve the health and well-being of the communities they serve. These mergers enable patients to receive high-quality, academic-level medical care locally. Community practitioners benefit from the availability of academic medical specialists, who support their practices and retain more patients. Mergers of this nature can also generate financial benefits, better access to capital, greater leverage with insurers, and more expansion of the patient pool available for medical research. Furthermore, medical trainees may gain significant experience in community medicine.

However, this type of merger faces multiple challenges stemming from the different health care cultures of private and academic practices. While private practitioners often prefer to establish direct physician-patient relationships, physicians in academic programs provide patients with care in conjunction with medical residents, fellows, and professional extenders. One key to success lies in developing strategies that use tools for cultural assessment to create a new, blended working environment during academic-community hospital mergers. Institutional integration can be hindered by communication styles, decision-making structures, and nonprofit versus for-profit status. Cultural changes will not occur immediately; they take place gradually, requiring time for staff to adjust. A variety of approaches can be used to accomplish cultural modification. In some hospitals, changes may be mandated and implemented immediately, while in others, changes may be introduced subtly.

Potential Partners?

TMC was one of the country's oldest medical facilities. Its history dated back to 1796, when Boston Medical Dispensary was founded by Paul Revere and Samuel Adams, patriots in the American Revolution, to treat underprivileged patients in the New England area. TMC also served as the first children's hospital in Boston. During the last quarter of the 20th century, the hospital was recognized as one of the most prestigious nonprofit teaching hospitals in the region, with 400 beds that offered up-to-date academic health care, medical training, and research. It was also the primary training site for the Tufts University School of Medicine. The facility had a long-standing affiliation with a sizable number of community physicians, including 1,800 primary care physicians and specialists in the Greater Boston area. TMC had received multiple awards for patient experience quality and equity, including:

- Press Ganey, a highly reputable national survey company that aggregates validated patient survey data, gave TMC a five-star rating. The surveys conducted by this organization were more scientific than other review platforms and provided a more accurate representation of what patients had to say about their doctors and their care.
- TMC earned the distinction of being among the country's top 10 academic medical centers with respect to quality and safety, according to the University HealthSystem Consortium's (UHC) Quality and Accountability Study of 2010. The study, which examined clinical quality and patient satisfaction data across a broad range of measures, compared scores from 98 academic medical centers in the United States. TMC, ranked sixth, was the only UHC member hospital in New England to be ranked in the top 10 institutions nationally.
- TMC also achieved a number one ranking in United Health Care's "equity" category in 2010, indicating that all patients, regardless of race, gender, or socioeconomic status, received equal treatment.

Lowell General Hospital's parent company Circle Health (included in the merger) was a nonprofit community-based health care system that provided medical care to several communities in an area located 30 miles northwest of Boston. Its network of physicians and hospitals included Lowell General Hospital and Saints Hospital, and its inpatient service was considered one of the largest community practices in the state of Massachusetts. However, it was based in the city of Lowell, the nation's first manufacturing center for textiles in the 19th century. To receive a higher level of medical attention than Circle Health could provide, patients needed to travel to Boston, where most of the specialized and advanced medical care could be provided. Among the common challenges associated with these referrals to tertiary centers[12] were transportation, difficulty in accessing the clinics, and prolonged waiting time. Because these communities were home to a large number of immigrant communities, including a large number of individuals who had limited incomes, many patients suffered a significant financial burden as a result of these referrals. Additionally, each immigrant community had specific cultural and linguistic requirements that might not be accommodated outside their communities.

Supporters of the Tufts and LGH/Circle merger knew that the merger would not be easy. The potential benefits to patients in terms of increased access were compelling, but it would be challenging to bridge the differences between academic and community models. Were these the right partners to bring to the table? And what could they do to avoid the many pitfalls observed in other hospital mergers?

Discussion Questions

1. What is the logic behind hospital mergers? If this logic is sound, why have so many hospital mergers been unsuccessful?
2. How was the Tufts/Circle merger different from traditional hospital mergers?
3. What challenges would you anticipate?
4. What steps would you have taken, in the leaders' shoes, to ensure the merger met its goals?

NOTES

1. Audrey Michael, "Tufts Medical Center and Lowell General Collaborate on New Health Care System," *The Tufts Daily*, November, 5, 2014, https://tuftsdaily.com/news/2014/11/05/tufts-medical-center-lowell-general-collaborate-new-health-care-system/.
2. R. Weisman, "Tufts, Lowell hospital uniting," *Boston Globe*, April, 15, 2014.
3. Michael, "Tufts Medical Center and Lowell General Collaborate."
4. Michael, "Tufts Medical Center and Lowell General Collaborate."
5. Michael, "Tufts Medical Center and Lowell General Collaborate."
6. Raechel N. Warren, "What About the Patient? The Effects of Mergers and Acquisitions in the Hospital Industry on Patient Care," *SUURJ: Seattle University Undergraduate Research Journal* 3, no. 1 (2019): 10, https://scholarworks.seattleu.edu/suurj/vol3/iss1/10/. Martin Gaynor and Robert Town, *The Impact of Hospital Consolidation—Update* (Princeton, NJ: The Synthesis Project, Robert Wood Johnson Foundation, 2012), http://www.rwjf.org/content/dam/farm/reports/issue_briefs/2012/rwjf73261.
7. Clark Knapp, Jimmy Peterson, Rick Gundling, Chad Mulvany, and Wendy Gerhardt, *Hospital M&A: When Done Well, M&A Can Achieve Valuable Outcomes* (Report) (Deloitte Development LLC and Healthcare Financial Management Association, 2017) https://www.hfma.org/wp-content/uploads/2022/10/56348.pdf.
8. Knapp, et al., *Hospital M&A*.
9. Case mix index is a measure used by the Centers for Medicare and Medicaid Services to determine hospital reimbursement rates for Medicare and Medicaid beneficiaries. This measure reflects the diversity, complexity, and severity of patient illnesses treated at a given hospital or other health care facility. A higher index number means the hospital receives high reimbursement rate, and it also means the hospital is treating higher level of complex diseases.
10. Howard B. Fleishon, Jason N. Itri, Giles W. Boland, and Richard Duszak Jr., "Academic Medical Centers and Community Hospitals Integration: Trends and Strategies," *Journal of the American College of Radiology* 14, no. 1 (2017): 45–51, https://pubmed.ncbi.nlm.nih.gov/27815052/. Andrew J. Sussman, Jeffrey R. Otten, Robert C. Goldszer, Margaret Hanson, David J. Trull, Kenneth Paulus, Monte Brown, Victor Dzau, and Troyen A. Brennan, "Integration of an Academic Medical Center and a Community Hospital: The Brigham and Women's/Faulkner Hospital Experience," *Academic Medicine* 80, no. 3 (2005): 253–260, https://pubmed.ncbi.nlm.nih.gov/15734807/.
11. David M. Shahian, Paul Nordberg, Gregg S. Meyer, Bonnie B. Blanchfield, Elizabeth A. Mort, David F. Torchiana, and Sharon-Lise T. Normand, "Contemporary Performance of US Teaching and Nonteaching Hospitals," *Academic Medicine* 87, no. 6 (2012): 701–708, https://pubmed.ncbi.nlm.nih.gov/22534588/.
12. Primary medical care focused on general health and medical education and was provided by general practitioners. Secondary medical care focused on delivering more specialized care and was provided by specialists. Tertiary medical care focused on delivering highly sophisticated medical care and required more advanced health monitoring and a complex approach by multiple highly specialized providers.

CASE 4.2B

Tufts Medicine Health Care System

Merging Hospitals in a New Model (B)

MAHER TABBA AND JON CHILINGERIAN

Creating Tufts Medicine

On October 22, 2014, Tufts Medical Center (TMC) and Lowell General Hospital announced that they had finalized their agreement to create a new health care system, Wellforce Health Care System, to provide more integrated and coordinated care to patients at both hospitals. In 2022 Wellforce changed its name to Tufts Medicine Health Care System (TMHCS)

According to *Tufts Daily News*, "CEO of Lowell General Normand Deschene said that Wellforce 'turns the traditional health care model on its head' by focusing on prevention, community health, and investment in technology, instead of solely on hospital equipment and buildings."[1] The article cited CEO emeritus and vice chair of the TMC Board of Trustees Ellen Zane, who will also serve as chair of the Wellforce board, saying that the "proposal was a response to a changing health care landscape in light of the Affordable Care Act."[2] "Wellforce is aligned with the revolution occurring in health care," Deschene said in the statement. "The ACA and trends in health care costs in the United States demand a new vision for care delivery."[3] Wellforce was designed to be an innovative, community-based system for delivering medical care to patients in metropolitan areas who needed easier access to local, multidisciplinary medical care. Patients would be supported by academic medical expertise in a manner that would improve their quality of life.

To establish solid fundamental principles for the new affiliation, hospital leaders had many concerns to consider during the merger negotiation. However, the potential benefits were clear:

- While academic and community medicine had significant differences, they both achieved the same goals with similar outcomes.
- The community health care network provided sufficient patient volume to meet tertiary levels of care, which helped the academic center justify recruiting more specialized providers.
- The academic hospital had leverage in recruiting medical providers with advanced and talented expertise.
- The new health system would enable community hospitals to deliver complex care to the people in their neighborhoods. Patients and their families would be able to receive advanced medical treatment locally and avoid traveling long distances just to encounter long waiting times for medical appointments,

procedures, and tests at the academic center. Post-hospitalization care could also be arranged locally to provide continuity of care close to home.
- The merger would make it possible for the affiliated hospitals to provide health care with a broader scope and scale.

The intent of this merger was to share the financial benefits among the participating facilities rather than consolidating all the profits into the main facility.[4] But the leaders of both institutions were also well-aware that academic and community medicine had different delivery structures and cultures and that they would encounter challenges. How, they wondered, could they maximize the benefits of bringing these institutions together while avoiding the pitfalls?

Acknowledging Barriers

To ensure smooth merging between TMC and LGH, it was necessary to first recognize the most significant constraints and obstacles.

- It would be difficult to persuade some current academic practitioners to change to a community-style practice.
- Attracting academic physicians with a commitment to scholarly activities to work in community hospitals distant from their research laboratories and teams would be challenging.
- Academic physicians feared losing the support of their medical trainees while working at the community hospitals.
- The absence of some ancillary medical services—such as speech pathology, pulmonary rehabilitation, and addiction medicine—in the community hospital led providers to rely on creative solutions to achieve their desired objectives.
- To ensure equitable financial obligations and rewards among all contributing facilities, it would be necessary to construct reasonable arrangements in advance.

Implementation Process

At TMHCS, the directors of all clinical services provided direct supervision during the merger. Each departmental chief was personally involved in every aspect of the implementation process. This enabled a seamless transition of clinical services and set an example for other departments. A weekly report on the operation's status was distributed to the system leaders, who identified difficulties and developed solutions. High-ranking executives in both organizations monitored the details and stayed in communication with working staff. Additionally, community providers were delighted to receive consultations and specialized clinical expertise that would assist them in providing better care to their patients. Relationship coordination among providers was excellent. It promoted common goals, shared knowledge, and mutual respect, which brought about a very productive working environment.

Benefits Achieved

As a result of the merger, each site benefited in many ways. There was an increase in patient volume in emergency rooms, inpatient admissions, and outpatient clinics in all facilities. The case mix index, number of surgical procedures, and financial revenue also demonstrated significant growth. Using the academic-community affiliation model, more patients received treatment locally, and patients remained in the system for all levels of care. For those reasons, hospitals generated significant revenue through downstream care for these patients. In addition, all community hospitals were able to perform the majority of their diagnostic and therapeutic clinical procedures locally, which led to greater financial benefits. A variety of new medical services were developed for the first time in these communities through TMHCS, including critical care medicine, oncology service, advanced cardiovascular service, weight reduction surgery, women's health, and behavioral health. Finally, the system's hospitals served as valuable medical training facilities for medical students, residents, and fellows as well as sites for medical research activities.

Moreover, TMHCS understood the diversity of its patients in the communities it served. Several programs were developed to increase the staff's cultural humility and ensure understanding of patient needs and concerns. For example, the institutional Diversity, Equity, and Inclusion (DEI) Counseling Committee was formed to create effective strategies for meeting the organization's cultural enrichment needs and to ensure DEI values were understood and fulfilled. The committee also participated in the recruitment effort to develop a diverse workforce that reflected the system's surrounding communities.

TMHCS also modernized the delivery of health care by integrating technology into its operations. It replaced the appointment lines for each clinic with a centralized call center that offered assistance in multiple languages. A telemedicine service was also introduced to facilitate communications between physicians and patients. As a result, the clinic's volume of primary care physicians and specialists increased, as did patients' compliance with their appointments. Additionally, this service saved patients from long commute and waiting times for their appointments, leading to more efficient outpatient operation.

The COVID-19 outbreak prompted TMHCS to organize several medical mobile units to provide medical care to patients who were terrified to go to the hospital during the pandemic. This initiative helped prevent the progression of many medical conditions and limit the rise of irreversible diseases and complications.

Impacts of the Academic Center on the Merger

TMC, the leading academic center within TMHCS, was led by exceptional medical providers who delivered cutting-edge academic medical care in all merging facilities. It also contributed tremendously to the new system with its experience in monitoring patient outcomes and medical research. TMC had significant positive impacts on the merger in the areas of clinical care, postgraduate medical training, and research.

Quality of Clinical Care

Following the merger, TMHCS continued to receive awards for outstanding medical care and for its commitment to excellence in quality. Some highlights were:

- TMC was named the recipient of Vizient's five-star rating for quality and distinguished patient care in 2018. The award recognized the medical center as one of the top 10 academic medical centers in the nation, demonstrating superior quality and safety performance in more than 100 quality measures.
- Leapfrog, a national watchdog group committed to quality health care, awarded TMC the highest possible rating for hospital safety in the fall of 2020, making it the first hospital to receive A grades in four consecutive rankings. It recognized the medical center's achievements in patient safety, including meeting or exceeding the highest standards in the United States.

Postgraduate Medical Trainings

TMC also offered 45 nationally competitive postgraduate medical training programs with over 450 positions. Trainees rotated between all TMHCS facilities, bringing academic medicine to the hospitals within the organization. Integrating medical trainings with clinical operations emphasized the importance of high-quality, patient-centered, culturally sensitive, comprehensive care as well as excellence in clinical skills.

Research

TMC was consistently ranked among the top 10% of independent hospitals that received federal research funding. In addition, TMC was one of 25 medical institutions nationwide that received National Institute of Health (NIH) funding to develop the Clinical and Translational Science Institute. The objectives of this institute were to develop innovative solutions that improve the efficiency, quality, and impact of the process of converting observations made in the laboratory, clinic, and community into interventions that would enhance individual and public health. The NIH and pharmaceutical companies provided TMC with nearly 75 million dollars in research funding annually to support a wide range of basic research and clinical trials. Research development and advancements allowed patients in both academic and community hospitals to receive the latest therapeutic options. The proximity of this research to TMC also made it possible for medical investigators to involve more subjects in their research projects, giving their work more power.

Ongoing Challenges

Despite a smooth transition during the merger, the leadership of TMHCS continued to face several challenges in multiple managerial areas:

- Department chairs continued to struggle to recruit faculty who were willing to engage in community practice. This meant that they would no longer be able to undertake comprehensive research projects or participate in more scholarly activities. The geographic distance made this problem more apparent.
- A disparity existed between reimbursement rates for academic and community providers who delivered the same medical services at the same location.

- Triaging patients among facilities and reversing transfers had not yet been fully integrated on the system level.
- Sustaining and enhancing the system from the leadership level had been challenging, mostly due to the tremendous effort needed to complete the integration.
- Taking on new missions and implementing new service lines in an organization with multiple facilities that had different financial interests, goals, and targets occasionally created conflicts of interest.
- Multiple operational goals still needed to be integrated across the system.
- Aligning leadership and ensuring they shared common visions needed to be refined further.
- Investing in infrastructure tools and equipment in community facilities needed to be prioritized to provide more services and standardized care.

Areas for Improvement

To enhance the operational success of this merger, several areas were considered active priorities. These included:

- Coordinating the strategic importance of participating facilities to rationalize the implementation of new operational services.
- Enhancing diversity among leadership.
- Streamlining all internal operations, including negotiations and purchasing.
- Operating non-competitively with unified system-wide financial objectives.
- Promoting the new TMHCS brand in the health care markets within Massachusetts and neighboring states.
- Implementing aggressive diversity, equity, and inclusion initiatives at all levels of the system to reflect the needs of the diverse population in the system's surrounding communities.
- Supporting matrix-style operations in the new system to improve services provided by various facilities while delivering high-quality operation.
- Promoting workforce integration, including among providers, nurses, and others.
- Centralizing outpatient appointments among all clinics.
- Achieving a higher ranking in nationally recognized health care grading organizations such as U.S. News.

Status as of 2022

In addition to Tufts Medical Center, Floating Children's Hospital,[5] and Circle Health, Melrose-Wakefield, Home Health Foundation, and Hospice Service joined TMHCS. A clinically integrated network of private and employed medical providers formed among these facilities. Over 15,000 physicians, nurses, scientists, employees, and educators worked within the system as of 2022. Several new specialty services were established and made available to the affiliated hospitals. Medical care became more efficient in all participating facilities, and focused clinical experts became available to all patients.

Within each hospital, multiple medical record systems had been adopted to accommodate the needs of each specialty. As a result, patients' referrals were often delayed, pharmacological prescriptions were often fragmented, and medical information was spread among multiple records, affecting the quality of care patients received. In addition, this led to reimbursement losses, administrative inefficiency, and losses of vital laboratory information. For these reasons, a unified medical record was introduced, allowing hospitals and clinics to access patients' medical information easily. On top of that, system consolidation took place at multiple levels of the corporate operational structure including in administrative functions, human resources, and purchasing committees.

TMHCS implemented vertical and horizontal integrations by acquiring hospitals, physician practices, post-hospital care facilities, pharmacies, and other medical service providers, making the company the dominant health care provider and the largest employer in the local community. Since its founding, TMHCS had grown to become among the top three most prominent health care systems in the state of Massachusetts.

Despite there being strong competition in the health care market from other major academic centers in Massachusetts, adopting the strategy of moving academic medical care to the metropolitan areas enabled TMHCS to penetrate untapped markets, connect strongly with local providers and patients, and create a permanent clinical presence. As a result, local business owners were able to contract with regional health care providers to obtain medical insurance for their employees.

Because this affiliation formed a large network of hospitals and physicians, the system also possessed more marketing control and better negotiating power with insurance companies to secure higher reimbursement rates for medical services while guaranteeing lower prices for medical supply providers.

To ensure consistency in the implementation of medical guidelines and quality metrics, clinical committees became broader and included representatives from all participating hospitals. During the COVID-19 pandemic, this collaboration was put to the test. All facilities worked together to coordinate medical management and provide optimal care at time when the number of patients was unprecedented. Moreover, medical trainees benefited from the merger by gaining a greater understanding of medical illnesses that were common in the community rather than focusing on tertiary medical education at the academic hospital, which focused more on uncommon and complicated medical conditions. Finally, the merger provided patients with access to therapies under investigation and increased the number of subjects available for ongoing medical and scientific studies.

Prospects for the Future

To maintain a competitive position state-wide, TMHCS intended to continuously work on improving the three dimensions of its function: efficiency, effectiveness, and quality. It would also need to evaluate the regional health care market periodically, especially with a highly crowded territory involving strong challengers. Understanding changes in the local demographic's needs and market shifts would be the fundamental elements for maintaining the system's current level of function and advancing forward. Furthermore, there was a need to anticipate ways to expand and enhance TMHCS's medical services while maintaining a strategic approach to avoid future pitfalls that might damage its operation.

It is common for the leading medical facility in a merger to not expand fast enough to handle rising demands for referrals and needed medical services, resulting in longer patient wait times for specialty care, lower satisfaction rates, and loss of customers to out-of-system providers. It will be necessary for TMHCS to carefully plan the growth of its medical services and staff recruitment in order to meet increasing patient demands and adapt to new clinical capacities.

Reflection

TMHCS was established through a nontraditional merger model that was largely successful. Together, academic and community practitioners provided local patients with comprehensive medical services supported by academic experts, contrary to the traditional merger arrangement where academic medical centers viewed community hospitals as sources of referrals. Traditional referral practices had often led to significant losses of revenue in community hospitals, which ultimately had a negative impact on their survival. By creating a novel strategy, TMHCS was able to bring medical specialists into community facilities to enhance their growth and profits.

As the team at TMHCS had learned, three essential elements were the most important predictors of hospital merger success: comprehensive planning, proper implementation, and most importantly, an effective and accountable governance structure capable of making decisions with sufficient knowledge and an ability to minimize individual bias.

Discussion Questions

1. What is your assessment of Tufts Medicine's effectiveness at implementing a multi-hospital merger?
2. How well do you think Tufts Medicine was poised to handle ongoing challenges to achieve the merger's strategic goals?
3. How do you assess the value of each participating hospital's contributions to a successful merger?
4. What lessons can health care managers take away from this case?

NOTES

1. Audrey Michael, "Tufts Medical Center and Lowell General Collaborate on New Health Care System," *Tufts Daily News*, November 5, 2014, https://tuftsdaily.com/news/2014/11/05/tufts-medical-center-lowell-general-collaborate-new-health-care-system/
2. Michael, "Tufts Medical Center and Lowell General Collaborate."
3. Michael, "Tufts Medical Center and Lowell General Collaborate."
4. Laura Bozovich, Kathleen Knocke, George Pink, Ann Howard, and Kristin Reiter, *The Association Between System Affiliation and Financial Performance in Critical Access Hospitals* (Flex Monitoring Team, October, 2021).
5. The Floating Children's Hospital began as a ship in the Boston Harbor in 1894. Children were treated by volunteer physicians and nurses. In 1920, the floating hospital was brought to land alongside Tufts Medical Center. It closed on June, 30, 2022.

Aligning Transition Supports and Services for Students With Disabilities

CASE 4.3

JENNIFER STEWART

Providing individualized and comprehensive supports and services for students with disabilities, both while they are in secondary school and as they prepare to exit the school system, is a challenge of resources, knowledge, and perseverance. School systems, state agencies, nonprofits, community service providers, and family support networks are all working to meet the needs of students with disabilities, but they often run into capacity barriers to effectively support an individual to achieve their postsecondary goals. The lack of coordination, communication, and ultimately resources to support students with disabilities often results in an underserved individual wondering what possibly could be available to help them. Colorado is just one of many states that is working to figure out how to improve their systems of collaboration for students with disabilities.

Andrea and Robert Mills lived in Colorado and had a son with disabilities who had aged out of special education transition services associated with secondary school. They remembered hearing about the importance of preparing for when the yellow school bus no longer came to support their son Jack, but unfortunately, they lacked a plan, and they needed to figure out what to do next. Special education transition services in schools are an entitlement through the Individuals with Disabilities Education Act (IDEA),[1] and Jack was fortunate to benefit from these services for 21 years. However, when Jack exited from the school system and moved into the community and world of adult services, access was very different, and services and supports were provided based on eligibility. This transition from school to adult services was something for which the Mills family was not prepared.

Jack is now 22 years old and has a diagnoses of autism and a significant learning disability. He has many abilities, interests, and strengths as well as some significant support needs. During Jack's high school years, he loved learning, had many friends, and enjoyed being included as much as possible. Jack's days at school were often spent in a classroom segregated away from his peers without disabilities. The expectations of him were often low, especially regarding what he could do after high school. The school services he received were not focused on preparing him for being independent or for a life of employment. In conversations with the school, Andrea and Robert often felt there was not much discussion about what Jack could do after graduating, and they thought they might have missed the boat on helping him plan for a future that explores his aspirations. *What did we miss? Should we have paid more attention? Was this transition planning process supposed to happen earlier?*

Andrea and Robert want a full and engaging life for Jack, but they are overwhelmed by the process of navigating the adult services system that supports individuals with disabilities. *How can we get him supports? What is he eligible for? If he works, will he lose his Social Security benefits? Will he be safe?* Outside of the school supporting his education, the family did not know who else to turn to. Andrea and Robert started talking with other families and learned that Jack's story was not unique. They found family support networks that shared great information about navigating the transition process from school to adult services. However, they discovered that there were big gaps in information, available services, and access to support related to helping students plan for a successful transition from secondary school to adult services.

Andrea and Robert found that sharing Jack's story helped connect them to more resources and referred them to state agencies that could support him with employment and independent living. Colorado's state agencies and partners started talking about the gaps in information and the complexity of the transition process as they discovered more and more students were falling through the cracks without making the connection to adult services. Fortunately, partners of Colorado's state agencies had a vision to make sure Jack's story was not the standard for what happened to students with disabilities after high school. Colorado leadership set into motion a state-level effort to align and coordinate transition services and supports for students with disabilities while they were still in high school.

Sequencing of Services Initiative

In Colorado, the Department of Education and the Division of Vocational Rehabilitation have a strong partnership that focuses on bridging the gap between services from the school and the state vocational rehabilitation agency to assist students with disabilities in accessing employment supports. Hearing the voices of families such as the Mills, Colorado state leadership started to recognize that students' needs are broader than just employment supports, and the two agencies decided to bring more partners together to discuss how they could improve postsecondary outcomes for students with disabilities.

In a podcast for the Vocational Rehabilitation Technical Assistance Center for Quality Management, Katie Oliver, principal consultant and inter-agency transition liaison from the Colorado Department of Education, described the problem and the vision Colorado must address:

> We want to make sure that we're increasing outcomes for students with disabilities, ultimately getting them employed and self-sufficient and involved in their communities. Back in 2019 we said, OK, for some reason, no matter how much our best laid plans and transition planning takes place, we're still not getting the outcomes we want for our students with disabilities. We're still missing them. So how do we make these connections? We're trying to have that smooth transition process, handing the baton to the next system, whether that's other adult services, whether it's postsecondary education or employment. We're still dropping the baton somewhere. We're all speaking different languages. We're not coordinating, we're not braiding and blending funds. Let's start talking about this and let's really beef this up so that we can have more of a presence and more consistency across our systems so that our families, and ultimately the students, are knowing what's happening next.[2]

With support from the National Technical Assistance Center on Transition: The Collaborative (NTACT:C), Colorado began to engage state-level partners who supported students with disabilities during their transition years (ages 14–24). These included:

- Division of Vocational Rehabilitation
- Colorado Office of Employment First
- Career and Technical Education
- PEAK Parent Center
- Department of Labor and Employment
- Department of Healthcare Policy and Financing
- Office of Behavioral Health
- Developmental Disabilities Council
- Department of Higher Education

The exact outcome of coming together as a state team was not immediately known; however, the work quickly became unified, as a recognized gap needed to be addressed. The state team developed a vision to alleviate some of the complexities of navigating the secondary transition process, making it easier for students and families to find connections for postsecondary success. The vision was inclusive of each and every student and focused on a comprehensive transition plan for students with disabilities that included education, employment, independent living, full community participation, and the right to make decisions in and about their lives. Their vision created an interagency model for transition that extended beyond what one entity could do alone; therefore, interagency partnerships were essential.

The project was born and started to refer to itself as the Sequencing of Services (SOS) initiative, which suggested coordinating interagency partnerships; not letting students fall through the cracks; and supporting students with disabilities before, during, and after the high school years. SOS set out with its best intentions as an interagency community initiative, but it soon faced challenges that related to project implementation such as staff capacity, scope and scale of technical assistance, and overall questions about sustainability.

Andrea and Robert Mills were thrilled to see state leadership taking such an active role in addressing gaps in the system, but they questioned how this initiative would impact their community and their son Jack. The Mills family lived in rural Colorado, and the resources for supporting Jack to access transportation or be independently employed were limited. They questioned if state-level efforts encouraging the alignment of resources and the coordination of practices in Colorado communities would make an impact.

Sequencing of Services Framework

Development Phase

Initially, the state-level SOS team's goal was to align state agencies and partners' outcomes for students with disabilities by developing a new shared framework with six core student outcomes (Exhibit 1).[3]

The expectation was that not one entity or partner could support students with all six core student outcomes, but that through partner referrals and coordination, students could access more services and supports.

While the SOS framework was about partnerships, it was also unique, as it helped to map out services to support skill development along an age continuum (ages less than 14 up to ages 22–24). It recognized that services for students should change and progress as one gets older to ensure that there are high expectations of growth. To map out the SOS, a Local Workbook was developed for communities who would implement the new initiative so they could document and develop a roadmap for their partners (Exhibit 2).

In the development phase of this work, raising awareness and introducing this new framework to leadership and administration in various agencies, schools, families, workforces, and direct service providers was the main focus. Information was distributed through listservs, webinars, trainings, and communities of practice. The SOS team used this phase to gather input and feedback about the best way to implement this initiative into local communities.

Andrea and Robert Mills were key stakeholders in the initiative, representing the family voice as well as Jack, whose previous experience lacked interagency supports and partnerships. As trainings and the SOS workbook were developed, the Mills family provided valuable insight into the usability and accessibility of some of these resources. However, as they reflected on Jack's experience and the capacity of school staff to do some of this interagency work, Andrea and Robert worried that people may just not have the time to do this important work.

In meetings and presentations across the state, SOS was welcomed by stakeholders and valued as a shared vision for Colorado to achieve. During a presentation at the Transition Leadership Institute for educators in June 2021, state leadership recruited several communities interested in pursuing interagency collaboration. Four school district communities, representing urban and rural areas, enrolled in the SOS pilot: Denver, Weld, Mesa, and Pueblo.

To assist the four communities with implementing the SOS framework, the team developed guideposts for training, facilitation, and education to help establish practices around the core values of the SOS framework and the operationalization of key components (Exhibit 3). With the workbook and resources in development, the state leadership team was ready to establish a plan for moving into implementation. Specifically, they wanted to evaluate how the four pilot sites could be supported by state leadership.

Implementation Phase 1

A tiered implementation strategy was formulated starting at the state level, with a plan to move to the community level, and then eventually to a student level, thus hopefully impacting student postsecondary outcomes related to employment, education, and independent living. This tiered approach allowed for time to pilot this work in four communities and learn from local transition teams including families, educators, service providers, and state agencies.

The state-level team would need to form several management strategies to ensure progress, buy-in, and overall project management to move toward implementation at the local level. While state-level leadership was invested in the SOS initiative, they saw the project as additional work outside of their job descriptions. Fortunately, they had national support from two staff at NTACT:C as well as the Colorado Office of Employment First (COEF). In 2019, when SOS was just getting underway, COEF contracted with a transition liaison to support interagency work and, ultimately, they funded a position to act as the SOS project coordinator. As outside neutral support systems, NTACT:C and the COEF transition liaison could take on the project management of SOS and move the model into the four pilot communities. This team of three made up the SOS trio of technical assistance team, who supported the pilot sites to operationalize the key components of SOS. First, their priority was to support the communities in developing an interagency transition team. From there, the work focused on increasing the shared understanding of transition services, including the roles and responsibilities of partners.

The SOS trio of technical assistance team supported the four pilot sites through a variety of capacity building efforts. The type of technical assistance they provided was relatively time intensive, as they supported the development of meeting schedules, presentations, and trainings; facilitated interagency team conversations; promoted idea development for the team's vision and purpose; encouraged partners to embrace the values of SOS (especially to focus on younger students); hosted meetings for agencies to raise awareness and better understand their roles and responsibilities; scheduled meetings across pilot sites for shared learning; and addressed any needs that came up within the school district or with local partners that required more training or state-level engagement.

Their role was to act as an intermediary to ensure that work was completed at both the state and local levels. An important responsibility of the SOS trio of technical assistance team was to be a neutral conduit of information reporting back to state-level leadership on progress, areas of needs, and how state agency staff and partners could further support the work at the local level.

Implementation Phase 1: Lessons Learned

The four community pilot sites were each unique in their efforts to implement SOS in their districts. There were several common challenges and lessons learned in the four communities. Common challenges related to getting internal district administration and teachers to see the value of participating in the SOS initiative. Their buy-in varied, as school staff have limited capacity outside of their job descriptions to participate in additional community-based work. Another challenge was related to keeping partners invested in the work; it was critical to make sure attending monthly meetings felt like a win-win collaboration.

The four pilot sites reported some "aha" moments. Initially, they were shocked at how many partners came to the table and were invested in the work. They were also surprised to learn that most partners were having similar struggles and that, in the end, they all had the same vision for supporting students and youth in their community. They realized they needed to work smarter, not harder, and collaboratively, not in silos. Everyone also agreed about the complexities of the transition process for students with disabilities and wanted to have a better understanding of who provided which resources, thereby simplifying the system. Overall, the four pilot sites saw the value in SOS's road map of resources and services and its potential to better support students, youth, parents, teachers, and agency and service provider staff in accessing school and community resources.

While the reporting from pilot sites was positive, based on their first-year experience, they wondered, "What is next?" How would the state continue to support these first-year pilots? Could they move into Phase 2, where they would pilot this work with students? Who could support that work?

The state's vision was to have the pilot sites move forward in completing their Local Workbooks and then move into Phase 2, where they would put this work into practice with students by assessing and setting goals related to the six core student outcomes. However, Colorado faced dilemmas as to how to support the current four pilot communities as they moved into Phase 2 of the initiative and how to potentially expand the SOS initiative into more Colorado communities. The sustainability and capacity of the project were changing, and questions about how best to sustain and provide intensive technical assistance for the SOS pilots sites were at hand.

Sustainability

Regarding the sustainability of the SOS initiative in Colorado, there are a couple of different aspects to consider relating to the scale and scope of the project. One relates to funding, as the staff capacity of the state leadership team was limited, and the funding streams for the SOS trio of technical assistance team was changing as well. State leaders looked into various ideas about how to further contract with the COEF transition liaison to support the SOS project coordination, but funding streams both from agencies and grants were limited. One challenge with seeking funding for the initiative related to the infancy of the project; SOS was still in a development and piloting phase to test for feasibility, so it was not able to point to its impact for improving student outcomes.

Another consideration for sustainability related to the question of how much external state-level support from the SOS trio of technical assistance team was necessary for the local pilots. The pilots reported that a big part of their success with interagency work thus far had been because the initiative was coordinated and supported by the state and by a neutral technical assistance team. State leadership knew that, eventually, local community pilots had to take the lead in managing this initiative for the interagency work to be sustained.

The SOS initiative faced complex questions as the four local pilots were, in many ways, just getting started and about to move toward seeing student impact. The state agencies and partners had several decisions they needed to strategize around, as their capacity moving into the 2023 fiscal year was limited due to changes in the capacity and funding of the SOS trio of technical assistance team to coordinate and facilitate the pilots at the local level. Some ideas they considered for new implementation strategies to support local pilots included a train-the-trainer model, communities of practices across pilot sites for shared learning, transition champions to help spread the SOS model, and potentially bringing more state agency staff on board to be involved at the local level.

An upcoming strategic planning meeting is taking place in a couple of weeks. Before the meeting, the state leadership reconnected with Andrea and Robert Mills who had been in communication with family networks in the pilot site locations. The Mills family shared that families were enthusiastic about the efforts being made by the school districts to connect with their community agencies. They added that more professional development was being considered and that in some areas, they were targeting middle schools. Andrea and Robert encouraged state leaders to strategize and coordinate their efforts to find solutions, as the Mills family was hearing about some impact from families in the pilot site locations.

The agenda at the upcoming strategic planning meeting with key leadership members and stakeholders includes the following questions:

- How do we support the four pilot communities as they move into Phase 2, which will pilot the initiative with students accessing supports around the six core student outcomes?
- Can Colorado expand the SOS pilot into more communities and develop more interagency transition teams?
- What level of technical assistance support is necessary to facilitate, coordinate, and help local teams embrace and implement the SOS framework?
- What do we need to do to continue state leadership buy-in and propel the momentum of the initiative?
- What do we need to do to obtain future funding, whether it be through the state or external grant funding?

With enthusiasm for SOS at an all-time high, state leadership knew they needed a plan to keep the initiative going. But with less capacity, what could this new model look like?

Discussion Questions

1. What lessons from this case can help the families of students with disabilities?
2. What are the strengths and limitations of how the Sequencing of Services (SOS) initiative developed its implementation strategy?
3. What is your assessment of whether the first-year pilot sites were successful?
4. What role should the SOS trio of technical assistance team have in moving forward?
5. How do you think the SOS initiative should proceed? Should it focus on supporting the first-year pilots in Phase 2 and possibly expand to new pilot sites as well?

NOTES

1. Peter W. D. Wright and Pamela Darr Wright, "Transition, Transition Services, Transition Planning," Wrightslaw, n.d., accessed August 29, 2022, https://www.wrightslaw.com/info/trans.index.htm#:~:text=Both%20the%20IDEA%20and%20the%20Rehabilitation%20Act%20make.
2. Katie Oliver, "Leveraging Employment First Initiatives to Improve Consumer Services Across Agencies in Colorado," interview by Carol Pankow, Manager Minute, *VR Technical Assistance Center for Quality Management,* March 14, 2022, podcast, https://podtail.com/podcast/manager-minute-brought-to-you-by-the-vr-technical-/vrtac-qm-leveraging-employment-first-initiatives-t/.
3. "The 6 Core Student Outcomes," Colorado Department of Education, n.d, https://www.cde.state.co.us/sequencingofservices/coreoutcomes.

■ **EXHIBIT 1. Sequencing of Services Framework With Six Core Student Outcomes**

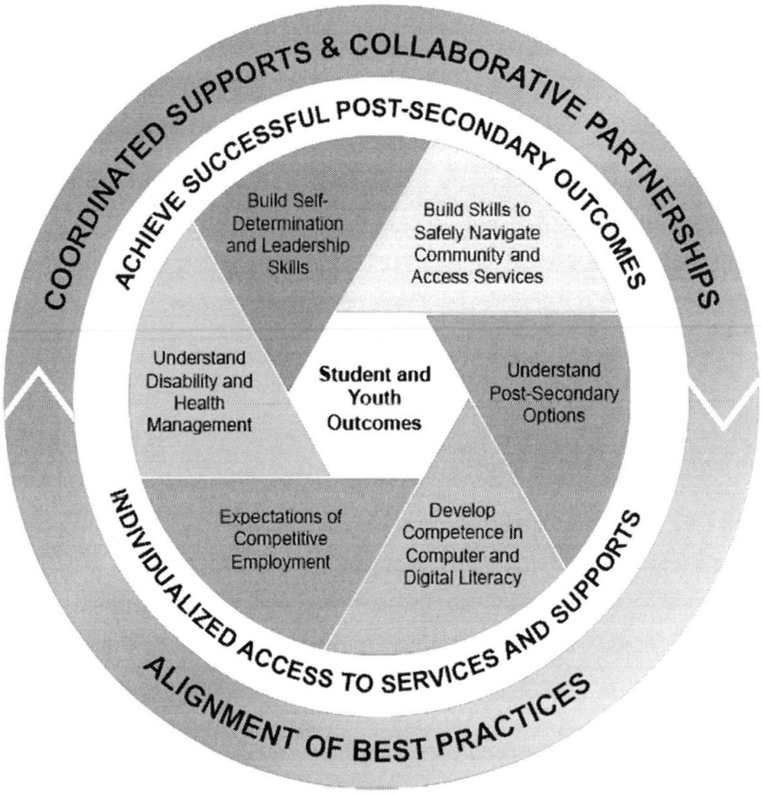

Used with permission of Colorado Sequencing of Services for Students and Youth With Disabilities.

EXHIBIT 2. Example of Local Workbook for Self-Determination and Leadership Skills Core Outcome

GOAL: To have each student develop the skills and knowledge necessary to understand their strengths and areas of need, to set and achieve goals for themselves, to work with other people, and to be a leader in their own life.

POSSIBLE SKILL DEVELOPMENT BENCHMARKS TO ACHIEVE LONG-TERM CORE OUTCOMES	
Age	**Possible skill development benchmarks**
< 14	• Develops self-reliance skills • Develops increased self-awareness and participates in making choices • Develops personal unique interests, talents, and aspirations
14	• Participates in volunteer and civic activities • Engages in person centered planning process
15–16	• Participates in student leadership activities • Identifies needs and can appropriately self-advocate
17–18	• Participates in peer mentorship • Leads personal planning sessions (IEP, ICAP, IPE, etc.) and evaluates progress toward goal
19–21	• Develops self-reliance skills • Identifies supports needed to reach personal goals and monitors progress
22–24	• Demonstrates leadership in groups and mentors others • Demonstrates self-determination and advocacy

INTERAGENCY TRANSITION TEAM PARTNERS: BUILD SELF-DETERMINATION AND LEADERSHIP SKILLS			
	Services and resources available		
Age	**Independent living center**	**Division of Vocational Rehabilitation**	**School transition teacher**
< 14	Self-advocacy training, 1:1 peer support		Self-determination instruction
14	Disability awareness, 1:1 peer support		Self-determination instruction
15–16	Advocating for accommodations, 1:1 peer support	Pre-ETS, self-advocacy training	Self-determination instruction; self-directed IEP, communication and language around physical/motor and mobility needs to self-advocate
17–18	Self-advocacy training, 1:1 peer support	Pre-ETS, Youth Leadership Forum	Self-determination instruction; self-directed IEP, communication and language around physical/motor and mobility needs to self-advocate
19–21	Community support, 1:1 peer support	Pre-ETS	Self-determination instruction; self-directed IEP, communication and language around physical/motor and mobility needs to self-advocate
22–24	Community support, 1:1 peer support	Job counseling	

Colorado Department of Education, "Sequencing of Services Framework," Colorado's Sequencing of Services for Students and Youth with Disabilities, updated August 31, 2022, https://www.cde.state.co.us/sequencingofservices. Used with permission.

EXHIBIT 3. Core Values and Key Components

Core values of SOS framework	Key components to operationalize
Partner at younger ages during high school	Building an interagency transition team
Focus on the six core student outcomes—in particular, employment	Having a shared understanding of transition services
Support self-determination and high expectations	Collaborating with families is essential
Increase agency coordination and collaboration	Making competitive integrated employment an essential goal
Create consistent language	Sharing communication practices to support the tracking of student growth Utilizing the student driven process to support the student's vision

Colorado Department of Education, "Shared Vision" and "Key Components," Colorado's Sequencing of Services for Students and Youth with Disabilities, updated August 31, 2022, https://www.cde.state.co.us/sequencingofservices. Used with permission.

CASE 4.4

The Native Plant Ordinance Meeting

ELIZABETH V. SESSIONS

General Information

You are a long-time resident of Hollybrook, a small urban city. Last year a local environmental organization, Hollybrook Green, introduced an ordinance at a city council meeting proposing that all new plantings on city property consist of 100% native species. Despite support from the newly elected mayor, the city council members unanimously rejected the ordinance based on the recommendations of the Department of Public Space and Urban Forestry (DPSUF).

A few months after the initial ordinance was proposed, DPSUF publicly published a memo to explain their opposition (Appendix A), which referenced additional sources including a letter to the editor in Akron, Ohio (Appendix B). They detailed the ecological, financial, and logistical barriers to using 100% native species in new city plantings. Proponents of the ordinance maintained that using 100% native plants was necessary to combat the environmental threats residents of Hollybrook faced. Since then, proponents have spoken at dozens of council meetings and public hearings and published op-eds (Appendix B) about the dangers of inaction, but they have failed to sway a single council member.

For months, there had been no movement on either side of the issue. But today, the mayor contacted you about arranging a meeting to discuss a possible compromise. This meeting will be attended by four individuals: the two co-founders of Hollybrook Green and sponsors of the original ordinance, the director of DPSUF, and a city council representative. The mayor is asking you to come up with an ordinance that everyone can agree on so that it can be approved by the council, incorporated into the budget, and implemented in the next fiscal year, which begins in 3 months. For this to happen, you need to meet and come to an agreement *today*. The mayor has blocked out 30 minutes for the meeting and, because of the short notice, has provided you with space to prepare yourself beforehand.

Attached is the memo from DPSUF that was prepared for the Mayor and that has been made available to all of you.

Preparation

To prepare for the meeting, you should do the following:

- Draft your opening statement (no more than one minute each)
- List what you see as your interests
- Anticipate what you think will be the interests of others
- Identify at least three options for potential agreements

APPENDIX A

Memo from the Department of Public Space and Urban Forestry

Memorandum

To: The Mayor's Office

From: Hollybrook Department of Public Space and Urban Forestry

RE: Background information for proposed Native Plant Ordinance

Introduction

In the last few decades, there has been a growing recognition that restoring and conserving natural habitats in and near urban spaces creates unique benefits to residents. Some cities, like Akron, Ohio, have updated their weed ordinances from requiring privately owned yards to be maintained at a six-inch height or less to allow for the full growth of environmentally beneficial native species like milkweed and goldenrod. Other cities, like Sanibel, Florida, have prohibited the planting of invasive species and require that all property owners remove eight different invasive species if found on their property. Many cities are incorporating native plant percentage minimums for new developments and public lands.

The Department of Public Space and Urban Forestry (DPSUF) maintains all publicly held spaces in the city, including public parks, road medians, riverbanks, floodplains, conserved forests, and multi-use forested land. Each of these categories includes lands with many different sites, all with different conditions and considerations. DPSUF recognizes the importance of native plants to the local environment, but there are financial, logistical, and environmental constraints that prevent the exclusive use of native plants. These concerns are explained in detail in the next section.

Financial Sustainability

Tree maintenance currently costs an average of $700,000 a year. This includes removing dead and diseased trees, treating viable diseased trees, pruning and training healthy trees, and planting new trees to replace the removals. Many native species are even more expensive to maintain because they are less able to thrive in city street environments and thus require more care and more frequent replacement. In addition, the city is already planning to increase the forestry budget and initiate cost saving measures in other areas of the department to deal with the anticipated early death of 20% of all trees in the city due to pests like the emerald ash borer.

We must also consider that all trees, whether native or non-native, provide ecosystem services like wildlife habitat, flood and erosion control, air and water quality improvement, noise reduction, energy savings, and carbon sinks. Norway maples, for example, while non-native, are more tolerant of harsh street conditions and grow more quickly and larger than native sugar and red maples, so they provide more of certain ecosystem services at a faster rate per planted tree.

Many native shrubs and small plants are also less viable in city environments. Planting and maintaining species that are not completely suited for the area will require more ongoing care and more frequent replacement, adding pressure to the department's budget.

Incorporating Diversity

Species diversity can provide many benefits to planted areas. This diversity protects plants from pests and provides food and habitat for more species of animals. Most importantly, it increases the ecosystem services garnered from the land by allowing for greater biomass, which provides more effective flood and erosion control, carbons sinks, and water and air filtration. At the same time, urban locations have extreme microclimates; for example, medians, also known as "hellstrips," are often exposed to full sun, with compacted soil that does not absorb water well. There may be one or two native plants that are able to tolerate such conditions, but by adding non-natives, we increase that number 10-fold. In addition, many native tree species saplings do not survive transplantation and so cannot be used as street trees. If we are able to include hardy non-native plants that are suitable for these different harsh conditions, the number of species we can install increases, allowing for diversity that can improve ecosystem benefits.

Cultural and Community Needs

Every fall, the community gathers at public sites throughout the city to plant non-native bulbs for the upcoming spring. This is a highly anticipated event that brings the community together. In the spring and through the summer, communities gather again to plant community gardens which DPSUF supports through the wholesale purchase of food crops, most of which are non-native. Any new regulations will need to provide cultural exceptions to the new native plant minimum rule.

Logistical Challenges

Currently, native plant nurseries are a new industry, and local companies have not grown large enough to supply the full needs of our department at wholesale prices. Without an affordable and dependable supply of healthy native plants, we cannot plan and install plantings in resource-efficient ways.

Conclusion

DPSUF recognizes the importance of native plants to the local environment and already acts in environmentally positive ways by removing invasives and prioritizing the use of native plants when feasible. The department welcomes the opportunity to work within practical and realistic environmentally positive regulations.

APPENDIX B

Letter to the Editor in Akron, Ohio

Organizations appreciate council support on weed ordinance

March 31, 2022

Letter to the Editor

LEAD for Pollinators and the Summit Food Coalition are appreciative of our collaboration with the City of Akron in revising Noxious Weed Ordinance 94.29 based on scientific evidence. This change allows the Akron community to legally plant native plants, goldenrod, milkweed, and daisies to support migratory Monarch butterflies and other pollinators. During the March 21 Akron City Council meeting, the revised ordinance passed unanimously. The revised ordinance aligns Akron's noxious weed criteria with the State of Ohio list of noxious and invasive plants.

This collaborative coalition led by LEAD for Pollinators and the Summit Food Coalition is to support and improve the Akron community through cleaner water, reduced storm water run-off, small business development, reduced carbon emissions, increased natural pest control, landscape beautification, and support of backyard and community gardens, urban farms, beekeeping, honey production, and a healthier ecosystem for all.

Sixty individuals, as well as local, state, and national groups, have expressed their support of changes to Akron's farming, beekeeping, and plant species ordinances.

Akron City Councilwoman Nancy Holland (D-Ward 1) has been very supportive in working with the coalition to ensure homeowners, retail nurseries, county extension, and landscape designers can support customers and landowners in creating beautiful landscapes that also support pollinators. Under the old city ordinance, it was illegal to plant and grow goldenrod, milkweed, and daisies: all vital food and habitat for honey bees and native pollinators. We are appreciative of this legislation's sponsors—Holland and Akron City Councilman Jeff Fusco (D-at large) for presenting a revised ordinance 94.29 to Akron City Council and for shepherding its progress to passage.

Michele Colopy, executive director, LEAD for Pollinators Inc.;
Beth Knorr, executive director, Summit Food Coalition

APPENDIX C

Native Plant Op-Ed

Climate change and other environmental concerns paint a dire picture. The good news is, Hollybrook residents have the power to restore the local ecology and combat these threats.

A monarch butterfly flutters aimlessly through your yard. Or, at least, to us it seems aimless. In fact, she is on a determined search for a very specific plant. Monarchs and milkweed have one of the most well-known symbiotic relationships—the monarch feeds on and pollinates the milkweed flower, lays her eggs, and a few days later the resulting caterpillars enjoy feasting on fleshy milkweed leaves. But nowadays, there is a hitch to this plan in the form of swallow-wort, a prolific vine from eastern Europe. Related to milkweed, it smells and looks similar enough to fool adult butterflies into laying eggs on the plants, but the caterpillars are not able to digest the leaves, and they quickly die.

The monarch isn't the only one in trouble—loss of habitat to development, proliferation of invasive species, and damage from modern landscaping practices have caused a precipitous decrease in insect populations around the globe. While a few less insects might not seem like a dire consequence, consider these two things. First, we are not talking about a few less insects—research suggests that insect populations all over the world have decreased by up to 80% (and if this number seems extreme, ask yourself, when was the last time you had to clean smashed bugs off your windshield? It's probably been a while.). Second, insects are integral to a well-functioning food chain and provide ecosystem services that we cannot get anywhere else. They provide food for birds, fish, amphibians, and mammals; they assist in the decomposition of all organic matter; and they pollinate plants (including our food crops).

The good news is that there are many things that Hollybrook residents can do today to help protect local insect populations and our local ecosystems.

Call your city councilor and tell them that you support the proposed Native Plant Ordinance, which would require that all new plantings on city property consist of 100% native plants. Almost all of our native insects evolved to eat specific native plants. When we use non-native plants, we are essentially creating food deserts for insects and other wildlife.

Plant native trees on your property. Everyone has heard about planting native flowers to support bees and butterflies, but did you know that it can actually be more beneficial to plant native trees? Many species of native bees nest in or near trees and rely on early flowering trees like sugar maples to provide food in spring. Native tree leaves, especially oak, native willows, black cherry, and birch, provide food for caterpillars. These protein-rich caterpillars, in turn, provide food for baby birds—it can take up to 9,000 caterpillars to raise a clutch of chickadees. That's a lot of caterpillars!

Plant other natives under those trees to create a tiered habitat and food source for even more animals. Pine and oak trees can provide a canopy over smaller tree species like black cherry and red maple and shrubs like blueberry and viburnum. Under these, native flowers like asters and violets can thrive. Packing a diverse group of plants into one area benefits animals and people: the plants can support a wider range of wildlife, strengthening the local food chain. The tiered system creates more biomass, which can act as a carbon sink and provide greater flood and erosion control than traditional landscape designs.

Leave your leaves! Did you know that many species of insects require a bed of leaf litter for food or habitat? Fireflies, for example, spend the majority of their lives in their larval form, crawling through leaf litter eating slugs and snails. When you collect and throw away your leaves, you are effectively killing these firefly larvae and the hundreds of other insects that use leaf litter as a home. Instead, try using your autumn leaves as a mulch for your garden, leave a section of your yard "unraked," or if you still want to get the leaves off your lawn, rake and leave some of them in a corner of your yard.

Even small changes can make a big difference when we all work together!

Sam Colby, Hollybrook Green

NOTE

The organization featured in this case has been disguised.

SECTION 5

Social Impact Operations Cases

CASE 5.1

Boston MedFlight

Leveraging Data to Design a New Helicopter Algorithm

MATTHEW KRIEGSMAN

Matthew Kriegsman entered Boston MedFlight's (BMF) brand new facilities and made his way to the conference room on the second level. He set up his laptop and began reviewing his notes from the previous meeting, where he and the senior leadership team had discussed a yet-to-be named concept to potentially establish a new service model for select rotor-wing scene calls. Their goals were to improve patient outcomes and increase scene call volume while also potentially reducing costs by decreasing estimated times of arrival (ETA) to first responders caring for patients in critical condition. The new service would initiate the sequence of reporting to a scene call (i.e., any transport that is not interfacility, such as a car accident on a highway) at the moment a call-source initiated contact with BMF rather than waiting for an official request for medical transport. These goals were particularly important to the senior leadership team, which noted a 10% reduction in scene calls requested for their helicopter rescues over the prior 16 months due to increasing ETA response times.

The yet-to-be named concept had not moved forward from ideation to execution. Large volumes of data needed to be synthesized and analyzed, and an actionable framework of implementation needed to be created based on those findings in collaboration with all relevant stakeholders. BMF had turned to Kriegsman to spearhead the project. He coined this new initiative "Smart Launch."

Boston MedFlight Overview

BMF is a world-renowned, nonprofit, air-ambulance and emergency transport organization that services a consortium of hospitals in the Boston area. Its mission is to "provide transport to the sickest of the sick regardless of the patient's ability to pay." Since its founding in 1985, BMF has successfully provided over 75,000 emergency medical transports to critically ill and injured patients across more than 170 cities, towns, and hospitals in the New England region. What started as a small organization became a robust operation with an annual budget exceeding $34 million. In 2018, this allowed BMF to provide free and unreimbursed care equaling $4.5 million, meaning that patients who could not afford their transport had part or most of their transport medical bill waived.

BMF's main headquarters is located at the Laurence G. Hanscom Field Airport, 15 miles northwest of Boston. It also operates three satellite locations, including Lawrence Municipal Airport, Mansfield Municipal Airport, and Plymouth Municipal Airport, which typically house at least one helicopter for quicker patient transfers from scenes in those regions. All four locations are in eastern Massachusetts.

BMF utilizes six aircraft, consisting of five rotor wings (helicopters) and one fixed wing (plane), as well as several ground transports (ambulances) that transport patients to seven main hospitals in the Boston region. The consortium includes Beth Israel Deaconess Medical Center, Boston Medical Center, Brigham and Women's Hospital, Boston Children's Hospital, Massachusetts General Hospital, Tufts Medical Center, and Lahey Hospital and Medical Center. Unlike more rural medical centers, these facilities are Level 1 trauma centers that provide more advanced and specialized care to American College of Surgeons adult and pediatric trauma centers.

Rotor-Wing Scene Call Operations

The BMF rotor-wing fleet consists of six Airbus manufactured H-145 aircraft, which were specifically designed for medical transports. Each contains most of the same equipment and medicines as a ground transport ambulance, though specific calls require retrofitting the aircraft with the appropriate patient-saving devices. The crew for each transport consists of one pilot, one critical care transport nurse, and one critical care paramedic. Clamshell doors located at the rear of the aircraft make for easy loading and unloading of the patient. In many cases, there is also room for one other person, such as a family member, to ride along. Cruising altitude is typically less than 1,500 feet above sea level at a speed of roughly 150 mph. The aircraft have a range of about 400 miles, but their capabilities depend on wind speed, wind direction, total weight of passengers, total weight of medical equipment, and total amount of fuel. Helicopter transports in 2018 accounted for roughly 1,840 of BMF's total transports, averaging about five flights per day for the system-wide operation.

Rotor-wing operations present both benefits and drawbacks. They can reach remote locations that either are too dangerous or too far for ground transport or too isolated for fixed-wing transport. For example, rotor wings can directly access select hospitals via a helipad, typically located on top of a building in a dense metropolitan area. The latter results in even faster patient transport compared with patients entering through the hospital's ground entrance. On the other hand, inclement weather such as thunderstorms, high winds, low visibility, and icing conditions prohibit safe rotor-wing operations. Additionally, BMF's helicopters typically cruise at lower than 1,500 feet above sea level, a low altitude that correlates with the highest risk of aircraft obstacle collisions approaching and departing landing zones for scene calls. Rotor-wing operating costs are also more expensive than fixed-wing operating costs by roughly 20%. These costs result in increased medical bills for patients after a rotor-wing transport compared with fixed-wing and ground transport. To stay aligned with its mission, BMF strives to ensure that rotor wings are only utilized when necessary so patients do not suffer from burdensome medical debt in addition to their physical ailments.

All rotor-wing patients are transported to the nearest Level 1 trauma center, which includes the Boston Hospital consortium, to receive more advanced and specialized care. About 15% of helicopter transports originate from a scene call rather than another hospital. A *scene call* is any rotor-wing transport where a patient is picked up from a non-hospital facility. Thus, rotor wings are an obvious choice for a scene call, such as a vehicle accident on a remote highway or a construction injury at a rural worksite, because of their ability to take off and land in hard-to-reach locations.

Whereas a physician phones from a hospital for interfacility hospital transports, scene calls are phoned to the BMF Communications Center by a first responder on the scene. For example, if there is a highway accident, first responders, who may include the local fire department, local police department, or emergency medical services crew, phone BMF for patient transport.

The Communications Center constructs and follows specific workflows known as *algorithms* to dictate their rotor-wing operations when any call from a scene is received. With an initial *inquiry*, a call source contacts Boston MedFlight only to learn if helicopter transports are operating. For example, if the weather is unsafe for flying, BMF informs the call source that no rotor-wing transports are occurring. But if helicopter operations are running and an aircraft is available for transport, BMF informs the call source of the best ETA to the scene. It is important to note that a call source will sometimes contact BMF only with this initial inquiry but never follow up to officially request transport (i.e., never call back) because either another form of transportation has been ordered for the patient or because it was decided by the call source that the patient does not need transport. Other times, the call source will re-contact BMF to change the initial inquiry into an official *request*. This means that first responders at the scene have determined a BMF rotor-wing transport for the patient is needed. At this moment, BMF will officially begin its launch process to the scene, which typically ranges between 5–12 minutes.

There are two additional facts related to scene calls that impact rotor-wing operations. First, some inquiries turn into official requests immediately. This may be because the original ETA is acceptable or because the patient requires a helicopter transport regardless of the ETA. Second, Boston MedFlight notes that the number of scene calls per location varies greatly from year to year.

The New Idea: Smart Launch

Before Kriegsman joined the team at BMF, leadership had spent the previous year brainstorming process improvements to expedite helicopter launch times and thereby increase rotor-wing utilization. Among other recommendations, they considered whether BMF should design a tiered response operation based on a scene call's inquiry location and potential urgency.

Whereas the scene call algorithm dictated that BMF wait for an inquiry to turn into an official request before launching a helicopter to the scene, this new approach would launch the rotor wing when first responders of a scene call *first contacted* BMF with an inquiry but had not yet requested an official patient transport. If an initial ETA to the scene was too long, BMF could re-contact the call source with an updated, shorter ETA midflight. Leadership believed this may persuade some call sources to request the helicopter transport when BMF followed up with a shorter ETA, resulting in increased patient care and improved utilization.

The team took note, however, that according to the Air Medical Policies and Procedures Protocols of the State of Massachusetts, medevac helicopters were not allowed to launch an air-ambulance without receiving an official call. Therefore, air-ambulances could not fly around an area actively soliciting patient transport. BMF knew that any new algorithm could not begin with a helicopter launch unless the call source had initiated contact in the form of an inquiry.

Gathering the Data

Even before beginning his analysis, Kriegsman believed it was important to put a name to the project to transition the idea from abstraction to action. He coined the term "Smart Launch" because of its emphasis on analytics to determine a launch procedure and because it was an easy name to remember. The name quickly gained acceptance across departments at BMF and motivated the team to move forward.

Having reviewed the initial notes with senior leadership, Kriegsman scheduled his first meeting with Kenneth Panciocco, EMT, CFC, and director of the Communications Center. Together, they brainstormed a draft algorithm for Smart Launch (Exhibit 1). Several key data points needed to complete the algorithm were missing. First, how long should the aircraft fly to the scene before it needed to turn back to base in the event a patient transport was not ultimately requested? Panciocco and Kriegsman uncertainly placed an "X?" in the algorithm and noted that "X?" should include the crew preparation time on the ground prior to takeoff, which could take anywhere between 5–12 minutes.

EXHIBIT 1. Smart Launch Algorithm

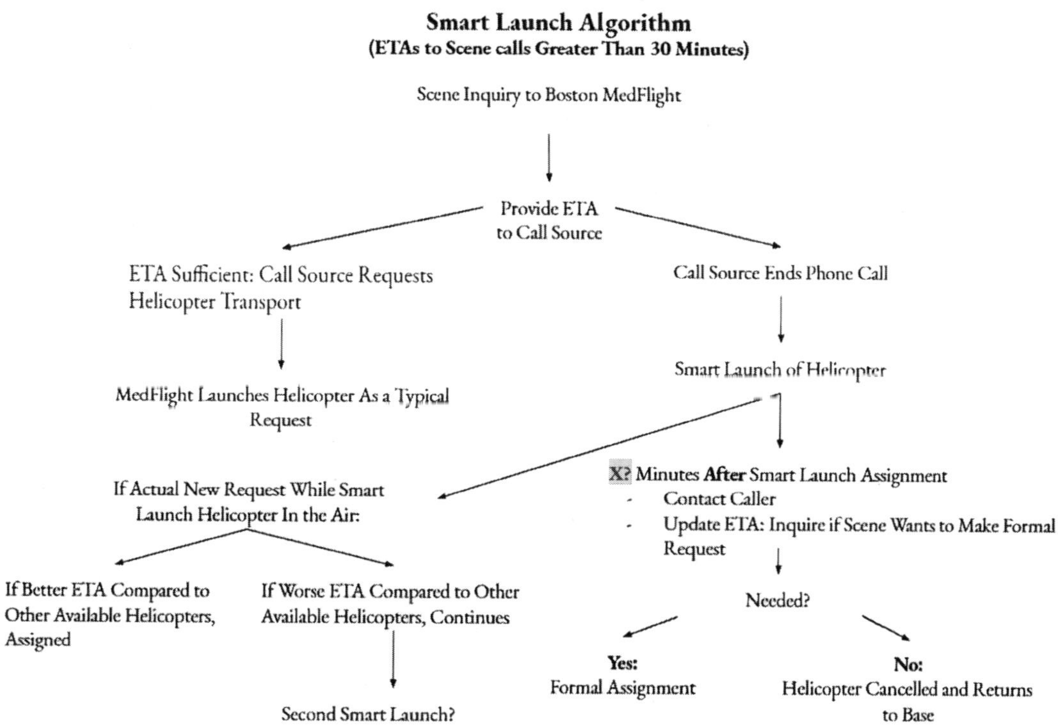

Used with permission of Matthew Kriegsman and Andrew Farkas.

Second, because Smart Launches had never actually been monitored, Panciocco and Kriegsman had no data to determine the timing of each step in the process flow. Lastly, Panciocco questioned what would happen in the event another call source requested a helicopter. He thought it was sensible to divert the Smart Launch helicopter to the new scene and see if another helicopter was available to continue the original Smart Launch, but he figured verifying an appropriate dataset might help.

Following his meeting with Panciocco and hoping to fill in these gaps with data, Kriegsman arranged a meeting with Chief Operating Officer of Clinical Care Andrew Farkas, RN, EMT-P. Farkas suggested reducing the scope of Smart Launches to only originate from their headquarters in Laurence G. Hanscom Field Airport (not from BMF's other airport locations) and to only focus on call sources in southeastern Massachusetts. Grateful that a draft algorithm had been created but acknowledging the need for data to try and answer "X?" he pulled and organized trip data collected in the ordinary course of helicopter operations in 2018 (see the corresponding case supplement, provided by the instructor). The corresponding dataset included data for the following call sources:

- Bridgewater Fire Department
- Foxborough Fire Department
- Framingham Fire Department
- Hanson Fire Department
- Middleborough Fire Department
- Norwood Fire Department
- Plymouth County Sheriff's Department
- Taunton Fire Department

Next, Kriegsman arranged a conversation with Chief Financial Officer Norma Mendilian, CPA. At the initial leadership meeting, she asked how Boston MedFlight could accurately predict the total revenue from patients who had been transferred via Smart Launches as well as the total costs to Boston MedFlight if no specific data from those operations currently existed. Supportive of innovation but cautious about significant changes that would hinder financial predictability, Mendilian put together the following information outlining the hourly cost of the H-145 helicopter:

Operating Costs of H-145 per Hour as of December 2019
Personnel Costs: $3,295
Vehicle Costs: $1,157 (not including replacement value, which should be counted into depreciation)
Depreciation: $1,008
Overhead Costs: $1,668
Total Costs: $7,128

Lastly, Kriegsman met with Rick Kenin, ATP, MPA, and chief operating officer of transport. Kenin was especially excited by the new idea but questioned how Kriegsman could design an algorithm and operation that ensured the flight crew would feel the same urgency even if no patient was guaranteed during a Smart Launch. Kenin also wondered how the crew would feel when a Smart Launch was canceled and the aircraft forced to turn back. He asked Kriegsman to come up with ideas for a later discussion.

Ready to Launch?

The individual meetings with senior leadership lasted almost 2 weeks. Glancing at all the data he had collected, Kriegsman took a moment to reflect on the bigger picture: Was Smart Launch a reasonable operation to implement in the first place? Did he have enough data, let alone the correct data, to answer fundamental operational and financial questions? How could he craft beta testing to collect missing data, and what would those test runs look like? Would the flight crew even support the idea behind Smart Launch? And how would he get so many different stakeholders on board with the final recommendations? Confident in his abilities but unsure of Smart Launch's future, Kriegsman began his analysis.

Discussion Questions

1. Looking at all the data collected, what information is missing to solve for "X?" in the newly created Smart Launch algorithm? Elaborate on how you came to your conclusion.
2. Explain why the financial data provided by the CFO either do or do not enable you to determine the costs and revenue potentials associated with the Smart Launch initiative.
3. Describe the social and organizational implications—positive or negative—that need to be seriously considered before adopting the Smart Launch approach.
4. Should Smart Launch be implemented at BMF? Whatever your conclusion, what actionable suggestions, frameworks, or beta testing methodologies would you share with the leadership team as next steps?

CASE 5.2

Ford Hall 2015

AVERY BRIEN, MÓNICA GARCÍA, SONIA KIKERI, AND MIYA WARD

Dear Reader,

The case study you are about to read contains a collection of vignettes, quotes from various panels, and primary source materials. You will come to know us as the creators of this case study; however, we are also former Brandeis students, voices speaking truth to power, and participants and supporters of the Ford Hall 2015 movement.

As you can probably already tell, the format of this case study is intentionally nontraditional. This case reflects our approach to social justice work in that we have chosen to restructure a conventional document into a format that, we believe, provides an authentic and inclusive recollection of the events of Ford Hall 2015.

Our vignettes are written in first person, as they are narratives predicated on our lived experiences. Factors such as times, dates, and locations have been fact-checked to the best of our abilities. We have also tried our best to be reliable narrators by instilling mechanisms throughout our writing process that hold us accountable for writing our stories with intentionality and accuracy. In an effort to honor our commitment to transparency, we also want to acknowledge that the perceptions of events and circumstances shared here may shift and, at times, clash based on our respective experiences. However, this does not make our accounts any less valid or true.

Finally, before you begin reading our case study, some context is necessary. This case study details the events of Ford Hall 2015 from an operational and strategic management lens. Ford Hall 2015 was the student-led occupation of the Bernstein-Marcus administrative building on Brandeis University's campus, which took place between November 20, 2015, and December 1, 2015. The occupation was given the name Ford Hall 2015 as an homage to previous student activists who executed a demonstration known as Ford Hall 1969.

On January 8, 1969, between 60–75 Black and Latinx students took control of both Ford and Sydeman Halls, presenting Brandeis's administration with 10 demands for addressing the representation and support of Black students on campus (Exhibit 1). While the founding of the African and African American Studies department was a direct result of the occupation, other demands the students put forward were not met. By naming the demonstration Ford Hall 2015, we were able to uplift an incredibly significant piece of Brandeis's history that was often overlooked or flat-out disregarded while continuing the work previous students had started.

With that said, this case study was created to capture and tell another important piece of Brandeis's history and to give current and future students the opportunity to learn from our work. We hope that while reading this case you pick up tools and learn more about processes that you can use to yield successful results in your post-graduate work. But, most importantly, we hope that this case will encourage you to think critically about your position in and contribution to society as a change agent.

In solidarity,
Ford Hall 2015 Case Study Contributors

◆ ◆ ◆

We weren't thinking about strategy on a more nuanced level but responding to the immediacy of the needs that we experienced personally and that we witnessed on campus and so it was more of a call and response.[1]

—Rima Chaudry, Ford Hall 2015 Organizer

Section 1 Community Norms

We believe that it is important to establish Community Norms before you begin reading our case study. Please take a moment to commit to the following prior to reading:

- I commit to being open to listening to the stories told in this case.
- I commit to experiencing discomfort and acknowledging the different feelings that may arise.
- I will keep the focus on this community.
- I will be mindful in thinking about the complexities of structural racism.
- I will listen to and respect the experiences of my peers as we discuss this case study.
- I will reflect on and be mindful of the experiences my perspective is rooted in as I share my thoughts

◆ ◆ ◆

The strategy very early on was: we're going to follow the leadership of Black women and Black queer people, which historically and systematically are voices that are silenced and that are not listened to or not followed across the organizational perspective. We knew that if we listened to those who are most marginalized, if we focus on lifting up and standing in solidarity with those who are the most marginalized, that we would win.

—Christian Perry, Ford Hall 2015 Organizer

Section 2 Miya's Vignette

My name is Miya Ward, and I was a first-year Master of Business Administration (MBA) student at Brandeis University's Heller School for Social Policy and Management during the demonstration referred to as Ford Hall 2015. Prior to attending Brandeis, I worked at a women's health nonprofit. Outside of my professional endeavors, I was active in racial justice movement building and organizing. Activism has always been an important part of my life, as I have been involved in intersectional environmental justice efforts since high school. I was also no stranger to organizing demonstrations in an effort to champion causes I believed in.

Raised by a registered nurse and a civil rights attorney in a small town outside of Washington, DC in southern Prince George's County, Maryland, discussions on politics, race, identity, and other topics I would later find to be taboo in most spaces were considered dinner conversation in my home. However, it wasn't until my undergraduate years that I shifted my focus from my own lived experiences to thinking more critically about race, racism, and identity on a macro level.

Then, shortly after I graduated, an unarmed, 17-year-old Black boy named Trayvon Martin was killed. His murderer, George Zimmerman, was tried and acquitted of the crime. The verdict of the trial that became national news launched me deeper into racial justice work, as I used my organizing background to help dismantle systematic racism. I decided to apply to and, ultimately, attend Brandeis because I was interested in one day starting my own nonprofit centered on racial justice initiatives. I was attracted to the school's legacy of social justice work and the Heller School's MBA curriculum, which promised a healthy mix of courses focused on social justice, nonprofit management, and traditional business school topics.

With that said, my involvement in helping to further diversity, equity, and inclusion efforts at Brandeis prior to Ford Hall 2015 was limited. This was mainly due to the fact that I had not attended Brandeis for very long. The occupation took place in late November, and I had just matriculated in August of that same year. However, even in my limited experience, I quickly became aware of the various hardships people of marginalized identities on campus had experienced before I began my graduate program and were, in many ways, still experiencing. I learned about these negative experiences from my peers, friends, acquaintances, and strangers and through my personal encounters as a Black woman navigating the terrain of a predominantly white institution. It wasn't long before I felt myself wanting to act, wanting to see some change occur on campus so that all students, staff, and faculty felt safe, valued, and supported by the larger Brandeis community.

An Education

Although I found myself wanting to pursue some course of action to incite positive change at Brandeis, I also knew it was important to educate myself on similar efforts that had been made, or at least attempted, already by others at the school. My organizing background had taught me the usefulness of building upon an already stable foundation if one was present. Therefore, I spent my first 2–3 months at Brandeis attending working group meetings pertaining to diversity work; talking to other graduate students involved in diversity, equity, and inclusion (DEI) initiatives; and gaining further insight into how the system of higher education functioned.

By educating myself, I was able to better understand where the institution stood in regard to social justice, activism, and the furthering of DEI initiatives. I also knew more about what work had already been done and what changes had yet to be made. Finally, I had a firmer grasp on the protests that had been led in the past in attempts to achieve the outcomes that many students, myself included, still wanted to see.

Call to Action

The catalyst for Ford Hall 2015 was a call to action put forth by a group of students at the University of Missouri (informally known as "Mizzou"), who collectively referred to themselves as "Concerned Students 1950." This group issued a list of demands to the university's executive leadership, which required the administration to address the racism Black students experienced on campus at the hands of other members of the Mizzou community. It is also important to note that episodes of anti-Blackness, racism, and exacerbated racial tensions occurring at the time were arguably the driving forces behind the demonstrations led by Mizzou students and prompted the call to action.

The call asked other campuses to stand in solidarity with the Concerned Students of Mizzou. Graduate students from the Heller School who had been active in organizing work on campus responded by quickly organizing a rally and march to be held the next day. The rally was held on the steps of Rabb Graduate Center. Dozens of students participated in the rally, and a group photo was taken and posted on social media.

The rally then turned into a march to the Shapiro Campus Center, where an impromptu "Speak Out" session occurred over the next 2.5 hours. During this time, several undergraduate and graduate students of marginalized identities held the floor, speaking about some of the negative experiences they'd had on campus. These stories ranged from microaggressions experienced in the classroom at the hands of faculty members to harmful situations involving other students.

For many, this was the first time both undergraduate and graduate students had interacted within the same space, let alone shared deeply personal information with one another. It became clear to me in that moment that what my peers and I had been experiencing at Heller extended beyond the walls of our building.

The BBSO Meeting

During the Speak Out session, it also became clear to me that if any change was going to be made, it needed to be a campus-wide rather than Heller-specific. Therefore, the first step was to break down the wall that seemed to exist between undergraduate and graduate studies, as many programs operated in silos. Fortunately, the Heller students I had befriended who were actively pushing forward DEI efforts long before my arrival at Brandeis had also come to this conclusion. They had even formed relationships with undergraduate organizers and were, therefore, clued into the meetings and gatherings occurring on campus about other demonstrations that would be held in response to Mizzou's call to action.

Students first discussed the idea of presenting a list of demands to Brandeis's senior leadership at a meeting of the Brandeis Black Student Organization (BBSO) on Tuesday, November 17, 2015, in the Intercultural Center, which I attended with my friends. It was my understanding that members of BBSO met weekly and that because the rally, march, and subsequent Speak Out session had recently occurred, the group had decided to hold space for members of the community to reflect and discuss next steps. For that reason, of the two dozen or so students present, there were several who did not normally attend these meetings, myself included.

The discussion at the meeting quickly transitioned from reflection to response. It became clear that many students were looking to demand more from their school administrators with regard to addressing inequality and inequity on campus. Someone proposed issuing a list of our own demands to the administration; most of the students present agreed that this was the best option. We then quickly shifted to talk about what demands should be included on the list.

Next Steps

The BBSO meeting, which was only scheduled to last for an hour ended up lasting roughly two, with me along with a few other students staying an additional half hour to debrief. During this initial meeting, where roughly two dozen people crowded into a small classroom with a table and chalkboard to shout out demand ideas to a volunteer notetaker, it became clear that if we were going to go through with this action, we needed to develop a strong strategy.

In the last half hour, after many attendees had left, we discussed relegating revising the demands into clearer, more precise language to a group of undergraduates. They would work with me and two other Heller students who had attended the BBSO meeting to flesh out the finer points with any accompanying actions. We would then have another meeting with the larger group to review the drafted list of demands and discuss action ideas.

However, about a day after making that decision, I was included on an email chain with three other organizers—one undergraduate representative and two Heller students—where it was made clear that our initial plan still had us operating in silos. There was a general uneasiness regarding the planned actions due to a lack of clarity about roles and next steps.

Also, sensitive information about the list of demands and other aspects of our organizing process had been shared on social media and circulated in other ways, threatening the overall success of what was, so far, only a half-baked action. A Heller student proposed meeting again, but as a smaller group, as doing so would allow us to more easily discuss the demands and any accompanying actions. The student noted that we would remain transparent with the larger group about what was happening. Those included on the email chain agreed that this was the best course of action. We informed the larger group that we would cancel the meeting, explaining why and what the planning process would look like for the demonstration later.

We also discussed who should take part in revising the demands and planning for the demonstration. Because we had been operating in silos, another organizing group on campus had begun crafting their own demands. We reached out to them and requested that they attend the small group meeting as a way to join forces so that the administration didn't receive multiple lists of demands. From there, recipients of the email chain listed the names of other students they believed should be in the room due to their organizing work on campus, attendance at the BBSO meeting, skill sets, and/or previous leadership experiences that would make them assets to the Planning Team. All the people suggested were agreed upon by those included on the email.

The Planning Meetings

In the next meeting, 10 of us, including the leader of the organizing group in the process of constructing their own demands, met on campus to discuss a draft of the demands and the overall action. We opened the meeting by establishing ground rules for how the meeting would proceed. We then reviewed the agenda I had proposed so that others in the room could add to it as needed. The first two items on the agenda called for a discussion about what brought us to this meeting and a conversation about any confusing moments or concerns that had arisen in the past 2 days with regard to planning. We also had a discussion about our individual organizing efforts on Brandeis's campus. Doing so gave me greater insight into each person's values, interactions with civil disobedience (or lack thereof), and organizing skills and weaknesses.

As the conversation moved onto the list of demands, several questions arose about the action we were planning. These questions dealt with a variety of issues, such as who should be sent the list, who we should center through our actions (e.g., Black students, students of color, etc.), and what the escalation tactics for the action should look like. After working through these strategic elements, we made a series of important decisions by discussing and voting until we reached consensus.

We ultimately decided that we would present a list of demands to the interim president and would, subsequently, occupy the campus administration building until the demands were met. After the meeting concluded, we worked in our assigned roles to pull off an effective demonstration. I, along with another Heller student, was tasked with making final revisions to the list of demands. During this time, we mainly communicated via our Brandeis email accounts, a method of communication we would decide not to use once the occupation began.

We met again the following day, Thursday, November 19, 2015. Twelve students, including myself, were present at the meeting, but one of the students involved the day before was unable to attend, making the true number of our makeshift planning committee 13. Earlier that day, our committee had delivered the list of demands (Appendix C) along with an accompanying letter to the interim president (Appendix B) via email. We also blind copied other members of the administration who we believed should be made aware of its existence. Therefore, we primarily spent this meeting discussing the campus's current climate and the communications aspects of the impending demonstration, including messaging and media outreach. We also solidified our action plans.

Part of the process for detailing our action plans involved assigning roles that we believed were integral to executing an effective action. I believe this is why a member of the group suggested that if we were to demonstrate via occupation, it would be prudent to have a small collective serve as a direct point of contact with whom the administration could discuss meeting the demands. This collective would serve as both representatives of those demonstrating and a liaison between the administration and the demonstrators. With this structure, the students participating in the occupation could focus on other important aspects of the demonstration. The meeting group agreed to this proposal. However, it then became a question of who would serve as a member of this small collective.

The Negotiations Team

The process of choosing who would serve as a member of this small collective was a relatively quick process. It was verbally agreed upon by all at the start that we would apply the same principles that guided the formation of our list of demands to all aspects of our planning processes and strategizing. Since the action we organized was predicated on the need to shift equity and the principle that uplifting the most marginalized uplifts us all, we thought it imperative to center Black women in the work we were doing. Therefore, we suggested that Black women who operated at various intersections of identity should represent the group of demonstrators, who would be referred to as "Concerned Students 2015," thereby forcing the administration representing a traditional system to interact with the reality we wanted them to see. Furthermore, other factors, such as organizing experience and experience serving as a negotiator during previous demonstrations, contributed to the nominations for this collective.

After we settled on the factors that would inform our choices through verbal consensus, we began the selection process. The process was fairly informal and proceeded on a nomination basis. Each member of the meeting group stated the name of another person in the room who they believed should act as a negotiator on behalf of the Concerned Students. From there, we went around the room and each of us offered another name and/or "seconded" or "thirded" another nomination. While this round robin was occurring, the people whose names were put forth more than once either accepted or declined to take on the role.

My name was one that came up more than once. I was hesitant to accept the role because I knew from past experience in other demonstrations how difficult a position it actually was. However, I was also eager to affect change and represent the amazing students I shared space with during that moment and the previous night. I also felt that I was up to the challenge, even though I was nervous about whether my presence would benefit the group.

I accepted the role along with four other women of color, and from that point on, we were collectively referred to as the Negotiations Team.

The Occupation

In the emailed letter we sent to the interim president, we stated that she had exactly 24 hours to devise and publicly share a plan to meet our demands. When Interim President Lisa Lynch did not respond to our demands within that 24-hour period, we escalated our tactics and executed the plan we had devised during our meetings. We held another rally and Speak Out session on the Rabb steps at noon on Friday, November 20, 2015. Once our action started, I found myself primarily interacting with the rest of the organizing group in a private mobile chatroom, which a member of our freshly formed Communications Team (another byproduct of the second planning meeting) created on the day the demands were sent. The chat allowed us to communicate with each other quickly and efficiently in real-time.

After the rally at Rabb, instead of marching to the Shapiro Campus Center, as we had done the week prior, roughly 100 students marched to the Bernstein-Marcus administration building, chanting for the duration of the march. Once inside the building, we instructed students to sit down and to continue the chants until the interim president appeared. After the interim president said a few words to the students indicating that our demands would not be met at that time, myself along with a few of the 13 demonstration organizers said that the action had officially become a sit-in. The Negotiations Team then stepped forward, identifying ourselves to the interim president, so that negotiations regarding the list of demands could begin.

The Evolution of the Occupation

For me, the first 24 hours of the occupation felt like a blur. I remember being pulled into a meeting in the president's office along with the rest of the Negotiations Team and senior leadership. I remember the meeting lasting a long time and leaving it feeling as though nothing productive had been accomplished. I remember sending the list of demands to personal acquaintances and family members in the area to try to help spread the news about what was happening. I remember not getting enough sleep. I also remember leading a centering exercise with some of the demonstrators the following morning. I remember my fellow protestors rejecting the food the interim president sent over to us in Bernstein-Marcus, and placing the donuts and coffee delivered to us in common areas around campus for other students to enjoy. I also remember accepting the food and materials sympathetic faculty and staff sent over.

The significance of our acceptance and rejection of these items was tied to whether or not the donations came from contributors who were actively leveraging their power and privilege to make a difference. I saw our rejection of the food from senior leadership as a way of saying that the only "contribution" we would accept would be that of them meeting our demands. Whereas, we accepted contributions from faculty and staff who risked their own social standing by providing us with items that would help us continue the demonstration and, ultimately, achieve our goal.

After the first day, it became apparent that we would be occupying the space for longer than even I had initially anticipated. It also became clear to me and the other organizers that we would have to begin creating infrastructure that would allow us to sustain a demonstration that was quickly developing into a movement. In order to do this, we honored the values and principles we had asked the administration to consider in our deliverance of the list of demands. This included upholding transparency, rooting oneself in community, and centering Blackness.

Using the aforementioned guiding principles, we begin building the community we wanted to be a part of. This included having daily town halls, during which updates, concerns, and proposals were shared with the group. It was at these town halls that the Negotiations Team described how the negotiations process with senior leadership was going, where necessary groups like the food and resources committee were voted into existence, and where proposals on who we should and should not allow into the space were also debated and voted on. We also laid ground rules as a community by employing rules, such as step-up/step-back, which allowed us to elevate the voices of the most marginalized who are not as frequently heard.

This methodology allowed us to remain flexible in the ever-changing landscape of the demonstration, which was heavily influenced by what occurred in the communications room. Developing committees as needed also allowed for better exchange of information and subsequent planning to occur within the group. No one committee's or individual's opinion or direction superseded another's, as all of the actions that took place were done via group consensus.

These processes allowed for the movement to be "leader-full" in that every participant in the demonstration had the ability to step up and into roles they were enthusiastic about and/or believed were necessary. Being a "leader-full" movement was a principle that the "Original 13," the initial organizers of the demonstration, had committed to before executing the action. It meant that no single person or group of people were the leaders of what had become a movement. Rather, we were a collective, working together toward one shared goal, and everyone's role was an important one.

Reflections

One of my biggest takeaways from my experience with Ford Hall 2015 is the power and importance of community. I truly believe that if we hadn't worked to build a community founded on a shared goal and guiding principles inherent in our list of demands, the occupation would not have been a success. I also believe that we developed a community that empowered participants in the demonstration in ways I had never really seen before. For example, I saw students who had little to no experience in the field of communications working alongside those who did to ensure we had consistent messaging and a strong media presence throughout the duration of the occupation.

With that said, I think the biggest challenge was maintaining the movement after the demonstration. The demonstration took a toll on me mentally and physically in ways for which I was not fully prepared. It also challenged my relationships with staff and faculty in ways I did not see coming. Therefore, directly after the occupation, it became extremely difficult to figure out a way to continue the work of Ford Hall 2015.

◆ ◆ ◆

[The demonstration] was not glamorous, it's not something that I would want to experience again or want others to have to experience . . . It was hard, as much as we tried to create this community, there was still a lot of learning, a lot of tensions we had to solve together. There was a point at which being on the Negotiations Team I really didn't have any real, substantive daily relationship with the sit-in because on a daily basis we were in these, at times, extremely hostile negotiations with senior leadership. So, we would go from that 10–12 hours on any given day and come back from that and a whole day's worth of building, working group creation, op-ed writing, problem-solving, all of these things would have taken place. So, there were these two different tracks operating parallel to each other that were informing each other.

—Rima Chaudry, Ford Hall 2015 Organizer

Section 3 Avery's Vignette

My name is Avery Brien. I was a first-year, first semester Master of Public Policy (MPP) student at the Heller School at the time of the occupation of the Bernstein-Marcus Administration Center, known as Ford Hall 2015. Prior to attending the Heller School, I worked at a local youth development nonprofit, where I focused on volunteer recruitment and community partnership development. I decided to pursue an MPP to address the broader systems that create barriers to health and well-being across our society.

My connection to activism and organizing started while I was an undergraduate student at the University of New Hampshire, somewhere between 2006–2010. I grew up in a working-class family in a predominantly white, middle-income, heteronormative community. To name some of my own identities, I am white, able-bodied, trans-masculine, and queer. Although I witnessed injustice throughout my childhood, my family was mostly apathetic, and it took me a long time to question the world around me. It wasn't until undergrad that I realized that injustice can be addressed, that systems are constructed, and that people have the power to shape them.

When I started at Heller, I was in the midst of deepening my understanding of identity, specifically the histories through which our identities have been constructed and the ways in which they are politicized today to meet the demands of mostly profit-driven systems (i.e., capitalism and white supremacy). I was excited to be accepted into a program with a focus on social policy and the slogan "knowledge advancing social justice." In that first semester, it became clear that the institution had yet to figure out how to practice these values. The MPP curriculum centered the voices of prominent white, cisgender, heterosexual men and often lacked perspectives from women of color, queer and trans people, folks living in poverty, and other historically marginalized communities. Because of this, much of what we learned aligned with a status quo that reinforces colonial systems and structural inequity. The solutions and policy approaches promoted by professors in the classroom were developed without the influence and voices of those most adversely affected by them. To me, this seemed more like "paternalism maintaining the status quo" than "knowledge advancing social justice."

During this time, state-sponsored violence was pervasive in the media, and the Black Lives Matter movement was gaining momentum as protesters organized to address the murder of unarmed Black people, mass incarceration, and systemic racism. As a white person, I asked myself the following questions: What is this violence rooted in? What is my role in this violence? How is this violence tied to challenges I face? And, what can I do to address it? I was paying close attention to myself and my immediate community and thinking critically about what we could all do to challenge ideologies and systems that create and justify such violence and tragedy.

In early November, I was informed by Black students in my cohort who had been organizing with other students of color that there would be a rally and Speak Out in solidarity with students at the University of Missouri. I was not planning to be on campus that day, but I knew that being present was necessary. I wasn't sure what would happen at the rally or if it would make a difference, but community, to me, means showing up for people when they need you, when things aren't okay.

During the Speak Out, I heard my Black peers and other students of color express their frustrations with Brandeis and the Heller School, as well as the pain and hurt they faced on a daily basis. Student after student shared stories of interpersonal and structural racism on campus and how their physical health, mental health, safety, and general humanity was jeopardized. I left with heartache, sadness, anger, frustration, and a commitment to the work, to continue to show up.

A week later, another rally was planned. Again, I was not part of the organizing; this was activism led by students of color on campus. I was unsure what to expect or what would come of it, but when I got word that folks needed people to show up, that's what I did. We rallied again on the steps of the Rabb Graduate Center, where students of color read a list of demands that were shared with university administration earlier that week. We marched to the Bernstein-Marcus building to address the concerns and the inaction of the administration. Four students went into a closed room with the interim president while the rest of us waited. Hours went by, and we continued to sit. The hallways were packed with students sitting on the floor, waiting for an update. As someone who had very little information going into the event, I wondered: What is taking so long? Would the administration see that work needed to be done to achieve racial justice in academia, in the institution in which they worked? Would they commit needed resources to advance this work? What is my role in this? What am I bringing to this action, to this space? How long would we be here?

I'm not sure how long the conversation between the students and administration lasted, but at one point the door opened, the students negotiating with the dean came out, and one of them announced, "This is a sit-in." So, we kept sitting.

The Challenge: Safety and Planning in the Midst of Uncertainty

As the night evolved, I took cues from the people around me. Those who appeared to have a leadership role in the organizing efforts made occasional announcements. It became clear pretty quickly that the group of concerned students was not leaving until their demands were taken seriously. I, and many of those around me, had no idea how long it would take. It was a Friday night. I didn't initially imagine that we would have to stay through the weekend to continue negotiations with the administration.

The next day, after spending our first night in the building, we were visited by a prominent Brandeis professor who encouraged us to stay strong in our efforts. The interim president also sent us breakfast. While we needed food, we did not want to accept breakfast from someone we felt should be with us trying to work things out. So, we returned the food.

When the administration did not show up to continue the conversation, it became clear that we might be in the building for a while. We also ran into a security issue that morning, as a group of white students came into the space to laugh, stare, and invalidate those participating in the sit-in. Immediately, questions and conversations centered around maintaining safety and organizing to meet our needs started: What can we put in place to ensure people have what they need to last however long this takes? How will we feed each other? How will we sleep? Do people have access to medication? How do we keep people safe?

Co-Creating Solutions: Police and Campus Liaisons

At this point, I still didn't fully understand what my role should be. As a white person, I wanted to put my body on the line alongside my peers of color. I wanted to contribute in the ways that people needed me to while being mindful of how my contributions shaped the work around me. It was established very early on that this was an action that aimed to center the most marginalized on campus—those living at the intersections of oppressive systems and ideologies, those experiencing the brunt of injustice on campus. Counter to the approach of the MPP pedagogy, centering the most marginalized meant that the most marginalized were leading the action, shaping the demands, and using their voices at the negotiating table. This meant that I was doing a lot of listening. I listened to learn, and I listened to identify opportunities to support the work in ways that didn't center my ideas or experiences.

During that initial weekend, committees were created to organize the work that needed to be done. The Negotiations Team would be present at the table with administration and function as liaisons between the university and the students, moving forward the work we were all there to accomplish. There was a committee for organizing food and donations of blankets and other materials for sleeping. There was a committee strategizing about direct action and escalation tactics as the week proceeded. There was a Communications Team shaping the movement's messaging and doing PR. And there was a group of liaisons establishing relationships with the police and functioning as their point of contact for updates or messages they needed to get to the larger group.

These committees were formed and shared with the larger group. I assessed both my skills and the group's needs. I have a background in writing and communications, but the communications group had a number of people involved, and I didn't necessarily want to be the one shaping the narrative. I decided to join the police liaison group for a couple reasons. First, as a white, able-bodied, middle-class United States citizen, my interactions with the police would be less risky than other people's. I didn't have reason to fear them, and I knew that stepping into this role as someone with less anxiety around anticipating that interaction made sense. I also had some prior de-escalation training.

Before stepping into this role, it was clearly communicated to us what the expectations of police liaisons were. Those in the group with experience in direct actions knew exactly what police liaisons would need to do. The situations we would find ourselves in were described, as well as our objectives and how our role fit into the bigger picture. Those who had experience with de-escalation organized a quick training, and the people who chose to serve in this role held a meeting. We thought through what we were tasked to do and how to best organize ourselves to accomplish the work. We set up a schedule where each liaison signed up for shifts. We got to know each other, sharing our experiences, what we were worried about, and how we could support each other. Communication and trust allowed us to figure out next steps with flexibility and confidence.

Over the course of the week, there were some interactions that caught us off guard. As time went on, the space evolved, as well as the climate on campus. Students were back from the weekend; word had spread about the actions, and hundreds of students and faculty showed up to voice their support as well as their opposition. We made a decision collectively that in order to maintain comfort and a sense of safety in the space, we had to limit the number of people present. Those there from the beginning would remain inside, and those willing to support but who weren't there from the beginning were given opportunities to do so from outside the space. This helped people maintain their mental health and feel less overwhelmed as days turned into weeks. To assist with the communication with the larger campus community, the police liaison role evolved from communicating exclusively with cops to communicating with anyone who approached the building. We communicated on behalf of those inside and shared the messages of those approaching the building.

The evolution of this role is just one example of how the work and space developed over the course of 12 days to meet the emerging needs of those in our community. We committed ourselves to living the values we wished to see on the broader campus. We changed bathroom signs to ensure trans-inclusivity. We shared pronouns during introductions for the same reason. At one point, a survivor of sexual assault informed the group that their perpetrator was present in the space. The group identified people with Title IX training to handle the issue according to their training and best practices. That issue was resolved through a survivor-led process.

Conclusion

While there was a core group of organizers that had a plan going into Ford Hall 2015, none of us knew exactly what to expect, how long we would be there, or how the situation would evolve over time. As I reflect back, I see clearly the characteristics of our work together that allowed us to be successful: flexibility, adaptability, transparent communication, and a focus on mission and values, including accountability, love, patience, and support for each other. The space we created was well-organized and a reflection of what we wanted to see in our broader society. This allowed those involved to feel seen and affirmed and to stay motivated. Our shared vision and values functioned as the glue that held us together. Everyone in that space had a commitment to each other and to the work. This allowed us to show up day after day, to listen, to be present for town hall meetings, to challenge ourselves, to step into different roles, and to be flexible with the evolution of events. We believed in the work, in the vision. The competitive culture that dominates many professional and academic spaces didn't exist. Organizers within the space shared the idea that our movement was leader-full rather than hierarchically structured. This was an approach to community organizing and collectivism that came from Black civil rights activist Ella Baker. We embodied this and functioned as a collective working toward a shared goal, honoring each other along the way. We all brought different skills and experiences that allowed us to fill specific roles and functions. All contributions mattered. When there was conflict, we worked through it without disposing of each other. When things were hard, we uplifted each other, reminded each other why we were there. No one was more important, and nothing we did would have been successful if people didn't feel valued for their contributions or connected to the reasons we were there.

◆ ◆ ◆

I felt the exhaustion because in addition to being students and paying this institution lots of money to educate us, we were also expected to be on any given day an educator, an advocate, an ally, an accomplice, and that's very taxing.

—Rima Chaudry, Ford Hall 2015 Organizer

Section 4 Sonia's Vignette

My name is Sonia Kikeri, and I was a first year Conflict Resolution and Coexistence (COEX) and Master of Business Administration (MBA) student at Brandeis University's Heller School for Social Policy and Management during the Ford Hall 2015 demonstration. Prior to attending Brandeis, I worked as a project director and research assistant at Georgia State University. My background at the time was in global conflict analysis, and my intention in going to Heller was to grow an intersectional skillset to actively work toward dismantling neocolonial structures and achieving higher standards of individual and collective human rights.

Prior to Heller, I had minimal experience in the world of activism and organizing in the United States, having lived abroad so frequently. I participated in the Occupy Movement in Melbourne during a semester abroad, and I supported Black student movements on my undergraduate campus virtually while I lived in France the year after graduating. I had shown up to a few rallies and marches in my hometown of Atlanta and in Washington, DC, during undergrad, but those were large and, what I would consider, safe and low-risk for participation, meaning there was no fear for my body nor my liberties. It was when I moved back to Atlanta in 2014 that I slowly began unpacking my identity as a non-Black woman of color in America. The journey I took that year was rooted in anti-Islamophobia work and being in community with people of color in a way I had never experienced before.

My first semester at Heller was turbulent. I was starting off my coursework in both the MBA and COEX programs, and in the former I was elected to serve as a student representative to the Program Committee. I was also hired as the Diversity and Inclusion Admissions graduate research assistant and joined the Teaching Excellence Committee as a student representative. I was active in the Students of Color Working Group and also attended meetings of the Anti-Oppression and LGBTQ+ Working Groups. During the first half of the semester, I witnessed and lived through violent classrooms, derogatory workplace behaviors, and the silencing of people of color's truths through institutional suppression and erasure.

Call to Action: Solidarity with Concerned Students 1950 of Mizzou

During my first semester, I also began forming friendships and building community with my amazing peers, including first and second-year graduate students who had a strong background in advocacy and organizing as well as those of us who were still learning about white supremacy and systemic oppression and how to dismantle it. By being a part of a community who shared their lived experiences and institutional knowledge, I was allowed insight into the decades of abuse students of color and people of other marginalized identities faced while attending Heller. Therefore, when the call to action came from the Concerned Students 1950 of Mizzou, a few of the second-year students of color at Heller, who had previously organized die-ins and other protests, included me in a Facebook message group and started to organize an action in solidarity with Mizzou's Concerned Students. The night before that initial demonstration, I was involved in the planning and logistics, helping to gather materials and spread information to students about the walk out.

On Thursday, November 12, we did a school-wide call to action, where students walked out of their classes and gathered at the steps of the Rabb Graduate Center for a rally. This gathering evolved into a march to the Shapiro Student Center, the ground where the Ford Hall Communications building once stood: the same building students of color occupied in 1969 to protest the oppression they were experiencing on Brandeis's campus. In this space, students spoke out about their lived experiences on campus, which further illustrated how marginalized populations were facing violence and oppression throughout campus. It was now clear to both undergraduate and graduate students on Brandeis's campus that students of color, particularly Black students, still faced high barriers of racism and systemic oppression.

Call to Action: Ford Hall 2015

On the night of Thursday, November 19, I received an email from one of the Black women in my cohort informing me that 13 demands, which were also attached in the email, were sent to the interim president of Brandeis, Lisa Lynch. The email stated that Interim President Lynch had "24 hours to devise and publicly issue a plan that will address the demands." If that did not happen, there was a call to action for students to walk out and gather at Rabb steps, this time to fight for our rights at Brandeis.

As noon approached on Friday, November 20, it was clear that the demands were not going to be recognized and that the action would occur. At 11:45 a.m., myself and others walked out of Heller classrooms, marching to the chants "no justice, no peace" and Assata Shakur's words: "It is our duty to fight for freedom. It is our duty to win. We must love and support each other. We have nothing to lose but our chains."

It was evident that the undergraduate and graduate students had planned the action together because those graduate students with whom I had worked before acted in accordance with undergraduates. Three students were in charge of speaking truth to power on Rabb steps, a couple were documenting the moment via photos and videos, there were pre-made banners, and over all, there seemed to be a plan of action that moved the crowd forward.

After getting the consent of the students who had gathered at Rabb, we marched through campus chanting again. Some students walking through campus during this time joined as we passed the dining hall, the library, dormitories, and classroom buildings. We made our way to the center of campus and, instead of going back to the Shapiro Student Center, we veered left to the administration building, Bernstein-Marcus. We did not lower the volume of our chants as we went inside and reached the doors of the interim president's office until the interim president herself emerged. We then followed cues from the organizers to let one of the graduate students and women of color speak; she asked Interim President Lisa Lynch if the demands were to be met. When she did not give us an answer, the student told us to sit down, and we sat.

While the sit-in lasted 12 days, I was only there for the first one. The next morning, I flew home a bit early for fall break, with the expectation that by the following Tuesday, the administration would have come to an agreement that met the demands put forth by Ford Hall 2015. As I virtually joined the secondary tiers of the research and communications groups, I quickly learned that my assumption was grossly incorrect. In the comfort of my home, I worked to get statements from my program directors and deans at Heller, and I researched things like hiring practices and other institutional policies. This was a huge privilege compared to those students who gave up the comfort of their beds; their Thanksgiving breaks; spending time with their families; and, ultimately, their daily lives to put their bodies on the line for the rights of Black and other marginalized students on Brandeis's campus.

Coming back to Brandeis on the last day of the sit-in—what I think is now known by the misnomer "Unity Day"—I realized I faced a huge division from my comrades who had lived through this trauma. I needed to learn quickly how to subvert my power and privilege to empower their efforts moving forward.

Now What?

Now that the official demonstration was over, the community who had been physically present at the event, in my perspective, faced the difficult challenge of maintaining the same level of organization, communication, and action they had built an entire culture around during the sit-in. This stood in stark contrast to the brutal bureaucracy of the administration, who had institutionalized structures and power working in their favor. Having tangentially participated in and virtually supported the movement, how could I rejoin this community who had just lived through a traumatic experience that I had not? How could I authentically participate and contribute my truth and lived experiences in a meaningful and impactful way that alleviated some of the burden? How could I contribute efforts to make sure this movement did not burn out and become erased by the institution as so many others had?

My fear was that Ford Hall 2015 would be like Ford Hall 1969, the sociology sit-in of the 1980s, the Heller PhD demands of 2001, and so many other student movements that had been largely erased from the campus memory and history. I learned of these movements not through institutional resources but from current students or student-made structures that archived previous students' stories. I was afraid Ford Hall 2015 would burn out. The student labor in this movement was free and largely unsupported. Students' mental and physical health were deeply affected. We did not have the same resources as the institutions did to move forward; the only resource we had readily available was each other. We also faced high turnover rates with students graduating every 2 or 4 years. How would this movement and its legacy be passed on? How would we make sure our story and knowledge were accessible and available to future generations?

While I did not physically participate in the sit-in, I still had strong connections to and support for the movement, and I came back to a tense campus in a unique position. Because I had close friendships with a few of the participants who had sat in for the 12 days, I began learning of the oppression and backlash they had experienced and would come to face in the days, months, and semesters following the demonstration. Because I was not facing the same burnout and backlash, I could step in and contribute my energy and access to the work we still faced at Heller.

Community Day Spring 2016

While the campus-wide Ford Hall 2015 community continued holding town halls and monitoring the implementation plan that would meet their demands, a group of about 10 students at Heller designed what would be the first Community Day for the graduate school. These 10 students were a mixed group of second-year students who had organized prior events at Heller, as well as first-year students who would go on to be key figures in Ford Hall 2015 and related movements. This event had been scheduled before any of our demonstrations took place, and we had been meeting since early November to plan it. The initial meetings prior to Ford Hall 2015 continued the work of student organizers who had planned an orientation workshop and led die-ins the previous year.

After Ford Hall 2015, we formalized this group of unpaid student organizers into what was initially named "The Diversity Committee," as our group represented a myriad of diverse identities, including students of color, LGBTQ+ students, domestic and international students, and differently abled and disabled students. As we worked together, we recognized our individual strengths as facilitators, negotiators, and organizers and used this knowledge to create subgroups. One group was in charge of formal communication, both through email and in-person, with administration to negotiate space and acknowledgement of our work. Another group organized the logistics: room reservations, lunch provisions, gathering supplies, etc. A group of expert facilitators lead the morning general sessions, and each of us stepped up to create content-specific breakout workshops for the afternoon sessions. At each preparation meeting, we had a group facilitator, a note taker, someone who kept track of the speaking order ("stack"), and at times a "knowledge harvester" to make sure we stayed on task and summarized the big takeaways as the conversation progressed. These roles rotated as to give those without much practice facilitating an opportunity to develop this skill.

As Community Day approached, I, along with other organizers, felt the need to cement this organization's identity with a better name. The word "diversity" had been tokenized by the institution and, therefore, felt inauthentic to who we were as a group. During one of our last group meetings, we came up with the name "Heller Forward," and one of our members even came up with a logo. This was a really important tool, as it was how we identified ourselves to the administration: as a collective rather than a group of individual students. We even printed our name and logo on all the materials and handouts.

On Community Day, Heller Forward executed the day-long agenda we created, established operations for the welcome and check-in, facilitated morning and afternoon workshops, organized lunch, and distributed entry and exit surveys that we wrote and would later publish in our first official report. This work, alongside all of our preparation, was unpaid labor. Two-thirds of the group had been involved in the sit-in and were, therefore, burnt out. Also, spring semester started the next day.

Heller Forward

After Community Day, one of the Heller Forwarders hosted a potluck to celebrate our labor and provide an informal gathering space where we could debrief outside the structure of one of our meetings. By the end of the evening, it was clear that there was still a lot of work to be done and that the institution needed to be held accountable to its supposed commitment to social justice. In the basement over a cup of tea, a group of five of us who stayed after dinner audio recorded a brainstorm session on my phone that outlined potential language for Heller Forward's goals, vision, and function. After transcribing the main takeaways, we brought that information back to the group at our next meeting.

Our next two to three meetings were essential to our development as a group. We had strong and difficult discussions about what the group would center on and what our purpose would be. We had live editing sessions where we went through the language drafted that night word by word, ending up with a mission, vision, and goals that spoke to an organization both continuing the work of Ford Hall 2015 within Heller and to the work of previous Heller generations who had faced similar oppression. This process was essential to our group because those of us who continued with Heller Forward after the Community Day held in Spring 2016 now had a fundamental level of trust and a structure we had co-created.

Heller Forward became a solution to continuing the work of Ford Hall 2015 and previous student demonstrations on campus. We led two community days; wrote multiple open letters to Heller and the larger Brandeis communities that included data gathered from surveys we developed; created student-centered institutional knowledge regarding acts of oppression and erasure; and led solidarity actions with campus, local, national, and international movements and communities such as #noDAPL, Standing in Solidarity with Standing Rock, union movements with Harvard cafeteria staff, and Black Lives Matter Cambridge. Heller Forward also applied pressure to both Heller and the larger Brandeis administration to stand up against oppression and to honor their commitment to adopt the 13 demands of Ford Hall 2015, as well as to act as a sanctuary campus during the Trump administration's Islamophobic immigration initiatives. We were able to accomplish all of this and more because of the community we had intentionally built.

Moving Forward

I strongly believe that the successes of Ford Hall 2015 and Heller Forward are grounded in community. These student-led movements and organizations were able to accomplish complex and high-level functions because of the core values that centered, guided, and aligned us as a group, the foremost being "uplifting the most marginalized uplifts us all."

Ultimately, this work was liberation work, which is hard work that isn't done alone. Our efforts were sustainable because our levels of trust allowed members to be honest about how much they could step up and when they needed to step back. Organizing in an institution that has turnover rates of 2–4 years makes continuity a challenge. The biggest obstacle we faced and continue to face is how to make sure that our work continues to empower future generations and make their experience better than ours. This case study is a tool that can educate and empower those looking to learn from our lived experiences.

◆ ◆ ◆

The strategy of a system is to make it seem like you're alone and that you're the only one experiencing [oppression] and that you're the first one to experience it.

—Christian Perry, Ford Hall 2015 Organizer

Section 5 Mónica's Vignette

My name is Mónica García. I am originally from El Paso, Texas, a border city of Ciudad Juárez, Chihuahua, México. I initially came to Brandeis University's Heller School for Social Policy and Management to pursue a dual master's degree in Conflict Resolution and Coexistence (COEX) and International Law and Human Rights (UPEACE). I ended up dropping the dual degree once I arrived on campus because I was not provided critical information from the department about the logistics and details of the program despite numerous inquiry attempts. Conversations with a head administrator confirmed that no previous student had successfully completed the COEX/UPEACE program, despite this dual degree being marketed as a successful program for several years at the university.

I chose to attend the Heller School because of its focus and self-reported dedication to "knowledge advancing social justice" in its marketing brochures and website. Additionally, I read Mitch Albom's book *Tuesdays with Morrie* in my undergraduate philosophy class, which helped to paint Brandeis as a school dedicated to rich academic experiences, student diversity, and growth and as an institution with professors who were both experts in their respective fields and dedicated mentors. For this reason, I selected Brandeis over other programs—a decision I have thought about many times since I graduated.

In the first few weeks of arriving at Heller, it became immediately clear to me that "knowledge advancing social justice" was a slogan and not a practiced value. My chosen program's curriculum lacked discussions on race, culture, and equity and avoided discussions about racial justice entirely. As I combed through the syllabi professors distributed during the first week of classes, I immediately noticed that the curriculum in almost every class largely centered the perspectives of white, cisgender, male scholars. In the moments when I brought my perspective as a woman of color and a daughter of immigrant parents living at the border with a working-class background into the classroom through my comments on the assigned readings, I felt isolated by my professors, who poorly facilitated our classroom discussions on race and social justice.

I was in my first semester at Heller during the student-led occupation referred to as Ford Hall 2015. I had taken several years off after completing my bachelor's degree at Gonzaga University in Washington State before pursuing my master's degree. In between my degree programs, I worked in a variety of sectors: education, health and human rights, and public service, both domestically and internationally. Right before attending Heller, I worked as a case manager at an international children's shelter in San Antonio, Texas, serving unaccompanied children who were seeking asylum in the United States. In my role as a case manager, I translated communications and formal documentation, interviewed children to document their journeys to the United States, and liaised with various stakeholders, which included families, communities, and governmental agencies. This specific work experience inspired me to professionalize my knowledge of conflict resolution and human rights by enrolling at the Heller School. I thought Heller would give me the opportunity to learn about the ways in which I could contribute to social justice movements at the Mexico-United States border in aims of advocating for equity and justice in a more global context.

Growing up in a border city, surrounded by native and Latinx people, cultivated my deep understanding of and respect for all living things and for those in which we are in relation, including plants, insects, animals, earth, and people. Growing up in El Paso, I watched the progressive militarization of my community as it was used as a pawn for political advancement. Experiencing these conditions time after time almost forces you into activism because you are fighting to have basic human rights on a land you grew up on and want to protect. I fought for equity in resources and services in my communities. In these places, being forced into activism means that you are fighting daily against injustices at different scales, both large and small. I continued my community organizing from high school through college and participated in racial justice movements, immigration protests, and environmental justice efforts. My politics are very much rooted in my community because they are my lifeblood, so the vantage point of this story is reflective of my positionality in that.

I bring my own personal narrative into this vignette so that I can share my experience of Ford Hall 2015, the occupation *and* movement. I write about Ford Hall 2015 because, as people who are constantly marginalized due to our identities, it is important for us to write our own narratives so that others do not inaccurately portray our struggles and co-opt our work. Writing and preserving our perspectives and our experiences is the true work of advancing social justice, and it is one way that I/we reclaim our time.

Why Ford Hall 2015?

Inequitable Education: An Example

I specifically remember being targeted and alienated at Heller for ideas I expressed in response to one of my professor's comments about the *Black Lives Matter* movement. The unwanted dispute with the professor started when he said the following in one of our first classes of the semester:

> If we want to talk about stupid movements, we should think of the Black Lives Matter movement. Black Lives Matter is a stupid movement . . . ALL LIVES MATTER! [emphasized by writing "ALL" on the whiteboard at the front of the room]

I sat frozen for a second as he continued:

> There is no reason to be divisive. This is why we need to have empathy for people like Donald Trump. White people are seeing their country being taken over [. . .] White people have lost so much in this country, and they have been the biggest contributors to creating such a great country.

After his comments, I snapped out of my trance and raised my hand to share my disagreement with the statement and offered my reasoning, which included a combination of historical knowledge and my lived experience. I was thoughtful and calculated in my response. One of my earliest lessons, inculcated from childhood as a person of color in a working-class family, was: speak clearly, organize your thoughts in a coherent message *prior* to speaking, and express yourself in a way that is non-threatening.

I challenged this comment while exercising restraint since he was my professor. I felt compelled to speak up at the time because my peers remained silent. I felt compelled to speak up because my humanity and the humanity of other disenfranchised folks is non-negotiable. Furthermore, his comment was not made to further discussion in the classroom and discuss social justice, but to intimidate, silence, and fuel white supremacy.

My professor exhibited this kind of behavior on several occasions, causing me to withdraw from fully participating in classroom discussions and affecting my sense of self and belonging at Brandeis. Throughout my education at Heller, I never saw myself in the scholarship and programming promoted in my degree program.

Immediately after this first encounter, I began to experience retaliation from the professor. I received different grades from my groupmates—the lowest—despite our nearly indistinguishable work. When I asked for details or clarification regarding my grade, I was told that "life wasn't fair." I initially attempted to work within the university structures by reporting this behavior to deans, program administrators, the campus Ombudsman Representative, Human Resources, and the diversity chair at Heller; everyone was aware of the problem, and everyone performatively empathized, but *no one took action*. I sat in countless meetings with each of the listed individuals, but the result remained the same: no one was willing to help me. I eventually also reported my professor's behavior externally to the Office of Civil Rights, Department of Education, which I was initially discouraged from doing by a dean. I believe this is just one example of the motivations behind Ford Hall 2015.

My experiences in the classroom with faculty, in combination with the difficulties I had with administration, left me in a mode of panic. Disappointed and hopeless, I sought out working groups and other activities on campus to supplement my master's education. It is from this point of disarray that I found community in the Students of Color Working Group and became involved more with students of color in my cohort.

Call to Action: Solidarity with Mizzou

On November 11, 2015, I was cooking dinner when I received a text from a friend that I had met in my program saying that she was (1) coming over for dinner and (2) wanted me to accompany her to the store to buy duct tape for a planned demonstration standing in solidarity with students at Mizzou. I immediately agreed to both, as I was trying to become more active in forging relationships with new peers since I had intentionally distanced myself from my own cohort due to their silence and inability to disrupt oppressive rhetoric in the classroom.

We initially stopped at CVS, but the selection was limited. We sat in the aisle for a few minutes contemplating our next move: Should we go to another store? Were the five rolls of silver duct tape sufficient? How many people would be participating in the demonstration? We decided to purchase the five available rolls and then try the Walgreens a few minutes away. There were seven more rolls available there, so we bought them quickly and left.

The next day, November 12, 2015, students, faculty, and staff gathered on the steps of Rabb Graduate Center, using the duct tape as messaging on their clothing, signs, and bodies. Students were creative and had fashioned multiple uses for the duct tape; some used it to create an "X" on their shirts, some wrote the word "silenced" on the tape and placed it over their mouths, and others wrote intricate messages on the tape and attached it to their bodies. A few students spoke to the purpose of the demonstration: to stand in solidarity with Mizzou as they fought back against racial hostility and violence against students of color on their campus. For over 30 minutes we collectively chanted messages of solidarity and resistance. Students shared poetry and other writings from Black revolutionaries such as Assata Shakur. As students continued to fill the space of the steps with their voices, the energy grew, and we marched.

I marched alongside over 150 students from the Rabb steps to the Shapiro Student Center. I believe the Shapiro Student Center was intentionally chosen as our gathering site because it was the original ground of the Ford Hall Communications building where, in 1969, roughly 70 students of color occupied the building to protest the racism and educational inequality that they were experiencing during their studies at Brandeis. I was not taught the significance of this location during orientation or in any classes or student workshops. Rather, students of color provided me, and our peers, with this institutional knowledge and history as it had been preserved in writing by alumni of color.

As we entered the Shapiro Student Center, our chants filled the entirety of the building as we continued to pour in, occupying the entire first floor. Once everyone participating in the demonstration was inside, a more seasoned graduate student calmed the chants and invited us to sit as she re-grounded the demonstration by providing context to folks who had just joined. The importance of sharing contextual and historical information appeared to be central to the organizers. They made sure it was clear that we were gathering in solidarity with students at Mizzou who were applying pressure to their university and its administration, which had been unresponsive to racial incidents and discriminatory practices.

They then opened up the floor for students, faculty, and staff to share their stories. However, they asked to center the voices of students of color. In this space, students (and, that I can recall, one staff member) spoke powerfully on their experiences at Brandeis and detailed the ways in which the institution had sat idly by without utilizing the *knowledge* of racial incidents on campus as opportunities to *advance social justice*.

As demonstrators continued to share about their experiences on Brandeis's campus, I felt their pain. After about 2 hours, I left the demonstration to go to class. Despite wanting to stay and participate, the professor whose class I left to attend was the same professor I had the dispute with and, therefore, I did not want to jeopardize my academic career by missing class. This professor's attendance policy was already strict, and he made an announcement during a previous class stating that if we were caught participating in any demonstrations, we would receive an automatic letter grade deduction. The inner discord and anxiety I felt caused by being unable to participate in this liberation demonstration and live my truth were overwhelming.

Perceptions of Ford Hall 2015

During the early morning of November 20, 2015, the same friend who I went to the store with for the call to action for Mizzou texted me about another possible action. I was quickly updated via text and email about the list of demands that were sent to Interim President Lisa Lynch. The email included reasoning for the demands, the 13 actionable demands, and a request to have the demands met by Fall 2016, the start of the next academic year.

Had my friend not texted me the details of students organizing this movement, I would not have been aware of the communications and actions happening. As I mentioned earlier, I was new to Brandeis and did not know the students who were organizing, as we did not have any classes together. In addition, I did not have a Facebook account, which was, from my understanding, one of the main platforms on which they shared information.

As noon approached on November 20, 2015, it was clear that the interim president and the university were not going to respond to the demands in any foreseeable or meaningful way; there was complete silence from the administration. Within a few minutes, I received a text from the same friend who informed me of the Mizzou solidarity demonstration; she said we were gathering on the Rabb steps to fight for our right to learn, study, and exist at Brandeis.

This demonstration was slightly different than the last, as multiple groups of graduate and undergraduate students had joined. Once again, we chanted, listened, and took a moment of silence for the Black men and women who were victims of state violence and police brutality. After collectively agreeing that we were ready to move, we marched through campus, chanting the entire way. However, instead of marching toward the Shapiro Student Center again, we marched to the operational hub of Brandeis: the Bernstein-Marcus administration building. This demonstration would come to be known as Ford Hall 2015.

The chants were intentional, powerful, and so beautifully loud that administrators working in the building couldn't ignore our presence or ignore the fact that we were looking for a response. We entered into Bernstein-Marcus maintaining the same volume and combination of passion and collective pain. The chants continued until the front of the group reached the doors of the interim president's office and she emerged from it. In these moments, I remember feeling trapped; trapped between wanting to stay to speak my truth and support my peers or attending a mandatory class where I was in the midst of my own personal battle. Ultimately, I left. I went to class, then home, completely unaware that the action had turned into an occupation. My involvement in the marches was the extent of my involvement in the occupation of Ford Hall 2015.

Synergy: Ford Hall the Movement

Ford Hall 2015 generated many beautiful and essential learnings—most notably, the collective power of the masses. To keep the momentum after the occupation, students who participated in the demonstration continued the conversation. My friend who included me in the marches once again connected me to the ongoing efforts; she looped me into the inner workings of the group that had led the occupation by providing my contact information to their listserv, through which they sent communications. From these conversations, students created innovative spaces and opportunities for student-led programming. From these correspondences, Heller Forward emerged.

Heller Forward was a manifestation of the Ford Hall 2015 movement. We met for months in both university spaces and our own homes to develop a vision, mission, and organizational design for transforming Heller both institutionally and culturally. During our meetings, we strategized both short-term and long-term goals essential for our learning and existence on campus. We thought about how our work would continue beyond the current group. We employed innovative ways of working and thinking by allowing for flexibility and encouraging one another to self-identify skills, talents, and passions that could contribute to Heller Forward in organic and meaningful ways. In this way, we forged an uplifting community that utilized our own funds of knowledge.[2]

We created "living documents" that were, first and foremost, rooted in radical community and in service of anti-racism, decolonizing academia, and dismantling systems of oppression. As a collective, we led two Community Days at Heller, created systems to preserve institutional memory, and led actions alongside larger movements that unfolded both domestically and internationally. Heller Forward *was* community.

Reflection

For me, inequitable education and campus culture largely sparked my involvement in the Ford Hall 2015 movement. I became increasingly frustrated with how my degree program reinforced a narrow colonial history and narratives that did not develop my conflict resolution skills or intellectual scholarship in any meaningful ways. Reflecting back throughout graduate school, I was overwhelmed for reasons not associated with the rigor of my courses, but with the culture and environment of the space.

For me, participating in Heller Forward was a way to speak truth to power and stand in solidarity with my peers. I did not get to participate in the occupation beyond the marches. From my own attempts at trying to resolve racial incidents on campus by working within the university structures, I knew firsthand that it didn't work if you yourself did not hold a certain amount of social and white cultural capital. I learned quickly through my previous experiences on campus that working *within the system* was not the best way to undo the university's cyclic patterns of racism and discriminatory practices. Compared to the collective efforts I participated in with my peers, trying to make amends and find collaborative solutions solely by working within the university system wasted my time, energy, and efforts. Ford Hall 2015 was a *necessary response for us* to collectively address racial disparities on campus.

The efforts of Ford Hall 2015 transformed my experience and my education at Brandeis. As a result of watching students fiercely and strategically advocate for themselves and one another, I also began to learn and internalize the tactics. I learned about negotiations, mediation, organizing, and the importance of uplifting community, not in the classroom but from my peers; they taught and guided me. To this day, these friends make up an important network that enables me to search for my best self.

I believe Ford Hall 2015 forced Brandeis's administration to enter conversations about structural racism at large and within the university's institutionally racist practices. Avoiding conversations to better understand and address the root causes of racist practices prevented Heller from truly providing an equitable and inclusive education for its students. Although I did not receive the global and equitable education promised by the Heller School at Brandeis, Ford Hall 2015 provided me with a relevant education by organizing, strategizing, and furthering a movement.

Concluding Thoughts

The process of unlearning oppressive behavior is hard work, but *vale la pena*. With that said, I believe it is critical to hold each other and others participating in this hard work accountable for their actions and contributions to furthering efforts related to diversity, equity, and inclusion.

To be honest, I am not sure how much I believe that universities in their current state *can* be inclusive or equitable. Universities' disavowal of racist practices, denial of responsibility for continuing the production of state violence, and willingness to retreat to liberal positions that promise to improve are evidence of the university's *insistence* that institutional and structural oppression continues. More specifically, I believe that the Heller School operates from a deficit model, where they believe that they can continue to "time students out"—waiting until the activist students cycle out, and the next cohort comes in with little institutional knowledge. It takes time to understand what is happening, and the university knows this. Brandeis should focus on shifting the school's culture to support an identity-safe campus and intellectual capacity building by examining social inequalities, inequitable policies, and preferential treatment throughout the university. Additionally, Brandeis needs to accept its responsibility to students of color and other marginalized identities on campus beyond saying "thank you" and "celebrating us" through veneers of multiculturalism. This means fighting with and for us against the valences of violence that structure racism and heteropatriarchy in our everyday lives.

Thank you for reading my story. I hope that this small piece of history provides insight into and reflection on the movement that was Ford Hall 2015. I hope that you all leave your respective universities with a better space than when you arrived. Alumni did this for us, and this case is testament to how we continued the efforts for future scholars at Brandeis and beyond. Consider this as a call to action to pay it forward.

◆ ◆ ◆

We focused a lot of the narrative on diversity and inclusion and, seeing how this has panned out, not just at Brandeis but across the country—and not just on college campuses. But how we see systems of oppression operate, we know that the words "diversity and inclusion" have a very different meaning for different people; they can be very corporate and conservative terms depending on who's viewing them and who's wielding them. I think that what we really wanted to get ourselves toward, and what I would have wanted to center, is liberation. What does liberation look like on a campus? What does liberation look like in an institution that was never built for us to exist within and has never really adapted now that students of color, and Black students in particular, exist in these spaces, and Black faculty and staff across the board. We are expected to conform to a white supremacist model as opposed to breaking that model and re-envisioning what this should look like and not having whiteness so centered.

We assumed that "diversity and inclusion" meant the same thing to everybody. Reflecting now—especially graduating having had decades of professional experience prior to going to school—going back into the workforce, diversity and inclusion are boxes people check off of employment applications or fundraising applications, and we didn't want to reach a quota with the work we did. We wanted to re-envision what academic spaces would look like; we wanted to re-envision what the world would look like in abolishing these systems of oppression that continue to marginalize our people.

I don't think that the implementation plan fully holds that vision, and my hope is that as the implementation plan continues to (1) get implemented and (2) evolve, that new students . . . pick up that charge and continue to move the institution into a radical revisioning. So, we did what we could, we learned our lessons, and I'm always happy to share those with the next generation of folks who are willing to continue the work as well.

—Rima Chaudry, Ford Hall 2015 Organizer

Discussion Questions

1. How would you define a social justice movement? What are the components?
2. This isn't a "traditional MBA case study." What were your expectations going into this case study? How did they shift or change as you were reading it?
3. What did you see as the catalyst for Ford Hall 2015?
4. Do you think the Ford Hall 2015 demonstrators were successful in their mission? Why or why not?
5. What did you see as the main challenges for the Ford Hall 2015 demonstrators? How would you address them?
6. Did you identify any gaps in the retelling of the Ford Hall 2015 story? What other perspectives would you have liked to have read?
7. What operational decisions had to be made?
8. What were some strategic choices made?
9. What was the role of strategy in an evolving and organic movement?
10. What were the guiding principles and values of the movement?

APPENDIX A

Ford Hall 1969 Demands

"In 1969, the occupying students of Ford Hall made a list of 10 demands that they wanted the University to agree to before they ended their occupation. The students first announced their demands at a news conference in the Ford Hall office of Lathan Johnson, black student advisor, shortly after the students had taken control of the building. At the news conference, spokesmen Ricardo Millet '68, GRAD, Ridgewood Residence Counselor; and Roy DeBerry '70, Brandeis Afro-American Society President, read a prepared statement along with the 10 demands, which they said were non-negotiable. The spokesmen also called for the university to guarantee complete amnesty for all those involved in the protest. At 5:00 p.m. that same evening, some of the occupying students held a meeting in Mailman Hall to announce the reasons for the takeover. Phyllis Raynor '69, a representative of the Afro-American Society, again presented the group's demands to let the white students on campus decide among themselves what kind of support they wished to offer. Following are the 10 demands as they appeared in the January 14, 1969 issue of *The Justice* (vol. 21, no. 14, page 9)."[3]

The 10 Demands

My name is Roy DeBerry from the Brandeis Afro-American Organization, and first of all I want to say that the black students and also the group here is in sympathy with the striking students at San Francisco State and also we support the Timilty coalition in Boston. Let me add that all students, faculty, and staff and administrators involved in the action that we have taken should get complete amnesty. The essentials of all the demands is that they must be controlled by black people and in the interests of the black community at Brandeis. Demands are non-negotiable and must be answered in black and white and with the appropriate signatories.

The demands are as follows:

1. An African Studies Department with the power to hire and fire. This means that the committee must have an independent budget of its own.
2. Year-round recruitment of black students by black students and headed by a black director. The number of students in the TYP Program should be doubled next year and the administration should support and actively campaign for the necessary funds.
3. There must be black directors for the Upward Bound and TYP Program.
4. Immediate action on the part of the administration to have black professors added to the various departments.
5. The establishment of an Afro-American center designed by black students.
6. Written clarification of the position of TYP students within the University structure encompassing the areas of financial aid, admission to Brandeis, [and] criteria for satisfactory work.
7. Expulsion of a white student who shot a black student before the Christmas holiday.

8. The brochure (for black student recruitment) must be accepted in its present form or only with changes accepted by black students. The brochure must be published immediately.
9. Intensify the recruitment of African students in the Wien program.
10. Ten Martin Luther King automatic full scholarships for on and off campus black students. This should include transportation from the TYP Program on up to graduation from the University.

APPENDIX B

Concerned Students 2015 Email

Date: Thu, Nov 19, 2015 at 1:33 p.m.

Subject: URGENT: Demands from Concerned Students 2015

Dear President Lynch,

> "The university that carries the name of the justice who stood for the rights of individuals must be distinguished by academic excellence, by truth pursued wherever it may lead and by awareness of the power and responsibilities that come with knowledge."
>
> —Last paragraph of Brandeis University's Mission

We, the concerned students of Brandeis University, take pride in being Brandeis students. We care deeply about the future and progress of this university and want this university to continue to attract and produce the world's greatest and most critical minds. This is why we are dedicated to the needs of our fellow students and believe we must hold this beloved university to its mission.

As a University we have failed. We have failed our Black students. We have failed our Black professors. We have failed our Black staff members. We have failed our Black community. We, as a university, must not continue to claim ignorance of said failures. Black students across the nation are standing up against racial injustice on their campuses. We, as concerned students, need our university to stand with us and to work with us on addressing issues of injustice, as they unfold on our own campus. The only way for this institution to move forward is to address these failures directly. This is what we, as concerned student leaders of Brandeis University, have done.

Attached to this letter you will find a list of demands, which we feel will resolve a few of the most pressing issues Brandeis students, faculty, and administration face today. We write these demands as we reflect on the social justice values upon which Brandeis University was founded upon in 1948. This list is a call for action This is a call for Brandeis to acknowledge its failures and to correct them as soon as possible. You have 24 hours to devise and publicly issue a plan that will address the demands we have presented to you.

We are moving our people toward a liberation that has long been denied. This is a liberation that those of all races can understand. By uplifting one facet of our community that has been kept down or simply ignored, we uplift us all. Therefore, we ask that our brothers and sisters from all backgrounds stand with us, as Black students are granted the rights they have been denied for far too long at this institution.

"The proof that one truly believes is in action."—Bayard Rustin

#ConcernedStudents2015

APPENDIX C

Ford Hall 2015 Demands

Ford Hall 2015 demands presented to Brandeis University by Concerned Students 2015:

1. Increase the percentage of full-time Black faculty and staff to 10% across ALL departments and schools, while prioritizing the following: Anthropology, Heller, History, HSSP, Fine Arts, IBS, NEJS, Sciences, Sociology, and Theatre.
2. Increase the number of tenure tracks for Black faculty across ALL departments and schools.
3. Implement educational pedagogies and curriculums that increase racial awareness and inclusion within ALL departments and schools.
4. Mandate yearly diversity and inclusion workshops for all faculty and staff with optional workshops being offered consistently throughout the academic year.
5. Employ additional clinical staff of color within the Psychological Counseling Center in order to provide culturally relevant support to students of all backgrounds.
6. Increase funding of Black student organizations and programs.
7. Appoint a Vice President of Diversity and Inclusion.
8. Increase the admittance of Black students via the general admission process to 15% within both undergraduate and graduate schools.
9. Establish an Office of Ombuds within Academic Services.
    a. Ombuds is an intermediary administrative body appointed to receive and investigate complaints made by students against abuses or capricious acts of university officials, faculty, and staff.
10. Increase minimum wage for all hourly paid university employees by 15%.
11. Increase the number of professional development workshops specifically tailored for Black students.
12. Issue a public apology to Khadijah Lynch from Senior Vice President Andrew Flagel.
13. Brandeis's current Interim President and the Brandeis Board of Trustees will fulfill these demands:
    a. Interim President Lisa Lynch will call an emergency meeting with the Brandeis Board of Trustees and will hold this meeting in the next 24 hours.
    b. The Board of Trustees will meet all of these demands and write these demands into the contract of the new Brandeis president-elect for the president-elect to sign.

All demands are to be met by the start of the Fall 2016 academic semester.

EXHIBIT 1. Ford Hall 2015 Timeline

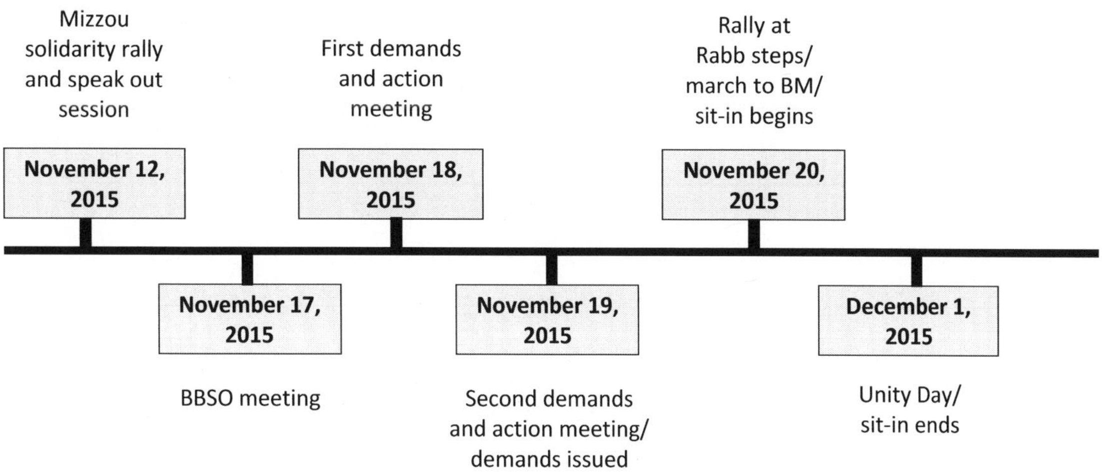

Created by case authors.

NOTES

1. Quotes throughout from session notes captured live and visible to the participants, Heller School Operations Management Class, April 20, 2018. Used with permission.
2. Funds of knowledge are essential cultural practices and bodies of knowledge used to survive, get ahead, and thrive. Norma González, Luis C. Moll, and Cathy Amanti, eds., *Funds of Knowledge: Theorizing Practices in Households, Communities, and Classrooms* (New York: Routledge, 2005).
3. Demands and introduction quoted from Brandeis University, "Remembering Ford and Sydeman Hall," Robert D. Farber University Archives and Special Collections, accessed August 29, 2022, https://lts.brandeis.edu/research/archives-speccoll/exhibits/ford/occupation/tendemands.html.

CASE 5.3

The Interfaith Worker Rights Council Call Center

JOEL CUTCHER-GERSHENFELD

> ***I don't know where to go or what to do. I have not been paid overtime, but the boss insists that I work the extra hours. I was promised health benefits and there are none. I have a good chance of getting citizenship, I am told, but right now I am undocumented. What can I do?***
>
> **—Caller to the IWRC Call Center**

The question hung in the air while the call center representative (CCR) reflected on whether this was a labor rights call or an immigrant rights call. There were two types of calls that came into the Interfaith Worker Rights Council (IWRC), from workers and from immigrants, and this could go either way—one person could fit into both categories. Of course, the call was also heartbreaking, one of 10 that had already come in this afternoon. The work was stressful not just because of the volume of calls, but also because of what was happening in these people's lives. In this case, this person needed help and, if it was an immigrant rights call, it needed to be documented by one of the case managers (CM) as required under the grant that was funding the immigrant rights work. There were nine CCRs, all volunteers, in the organization (with four and a supervisor on duty at any one time); three CMS, who were paid; and two executive leaders (the founding CEO and long-time CFO).

To make matters more complicated, calls also came into the call center from lawyers representing workers as well as from state and local legislators involved in worker and immigrant rights issues. The call center also received calls from partners at sister organizations. The CCRs fielded all incoming calls. The calls from workers might come in English, Spanish, Hmong, or other languages. Some of the CCRs and all of the CMs were multilingual. In addition, translators for languages staff didn't speak could be invited to come on the line. The CMs not only had to record the immigrant rights calls but also had to track calls involving lawyers and state and local legislators. The last two categories of calls needed to be promptly followed up by the appropriate CCR or executive leader. Follow up didn't always happen. There were many complaints similar to this lawyer's:

> I had a client facing harassment on the job. She was not the only one, I was sure. There was the potential for a class action response, but I needed to know if you had records of others who might be in the same class. First, I was kept on hold for 7 minutes—time that I didn't have. Then the person answering my call asked me a series of questions. That was fine. But I was transferred to another person who asked many of the same questions. A week went by before I heard back from

> someone who, of course, asked the same questions again before we could even begin to explore if there was an opportunity here. I just can't work with you if you continue to operate this way.

A state representative had this complaint, which was not unusual:

> We had a chance to organize a coalition regarding a legislative amendment on immigrant youth health care. It was a time-sensitive situation. I needed to talk with the IWRC executive director right away. Not only did I have to explain the urgency to two different people, with long hold times in each case, but in the end I wasn't put through to the executive director. I had to wait for a call back, at which time the window of opportunity had passed. How can we make any progress on the very issues you were set up to advance?

Worst of all, the governor's chief of staff had this complaint:

> Instead of having my admin do it, I called IWRC directly and was on hold for 5 minutes with the loud music blaring. I had another pressing issue so I hung up and had my admin set up the needed call for later in the week. If this is how you treat your callers, something needs to change.

It was not all bad, however; there were also dozens of individuals every month who were able to get accurate information and specific assistance on immigration and employment matters. Every individual helped was a considerable accomplishment.

IWRC Background

The IWRC had been set up 3 years prior by a coalition of religious leaders concerned about some of the most vulnerable people in the community. The mission centered on providing direct service to people who were experiencing mistreatment or who needed information with respect to employment rights and immigrant rights. There were two tracks for service delivery. On weekdays, IWRC had a walk-in clinic with three paid CMs. Beginning on Friday evenings and extending through Saturday and Sunday, it also operated a call center operation with CCRs and with the CMs also present. There was a supervisor who oversaw the CCRs on weekends and, as a lawyer, they were able to handle legal issues that arose during the week for the CMs.

The call center's weekend hours had been carefully crafted to be appropriate for a volunteer organization made up of people who still had day jobs or school commitments. These hours also matched when the target clients were most likely to call. It was decided early on that IWRC would only be sustainable if it did not need a great deal of office space. As a result, there was a physical call center, which also included a meeting room where the CCRs and CMs all worked (Exhibit 1). The executive leadership staff (two people) operated from their homes, coming into the office for meetings and other essential activities. During operations, there were four CCRs taking calls, with the supervisor overseeing the work and providing orientation and training to new volunteers. In a separate room, there were three CMs, who operated as a self-managing team with no direct supervision for their work (except when they needed legal guidance from the supervisor).

EXHIBIT 1. IWRC Call Center Layout

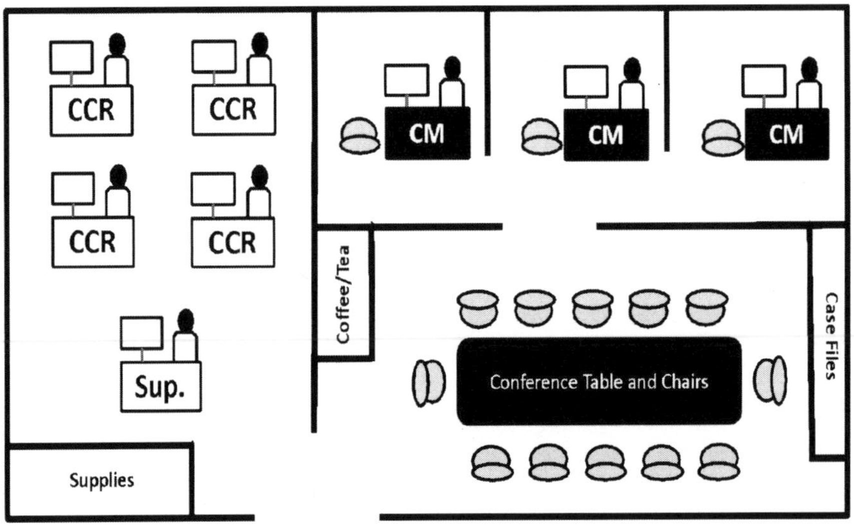

Created by case author.

CCR Responsibilities

There were six types of calls that came into the call center:

- Employment Calls: Workers with fair labor standards, discrimination, and other workplace issues (average length of time was 8 minutes, with a range of 6–15 minutes), accounting for 30% of incoming calls. Associated recordkeeping took an additional 5 minutes.
- Immigration Calls: Immigrant workers with immigrant rights and related issues (average length of time was 10 minutes, with a range of 7–16 minutes), accounting for 25% of incoming calls. Associated recordkeeping took an additional 4 minutes.
- Combined Employment and Immigration Calls: Immigrant workers with a combination of employment and immigration issues (average length of time was 12 minutes, with a range of 10–18 minutes), accounting for 15% of incoming calls. Associated recordkeeping took an additional 10 minutes.
- Legal Calls: Lawyers calling in to coordinate the handling of cases (average length of time was 3 minutes with the CCR, with a range of 1–5 minutes to connect them to the appropriate CM, who was sometimes unavailable), accounting for 10% of incoming calls. Associated recordkeeping took an additional 2 minutes for the CCR. Correspondence with the CM or any other professional handling the call (such as the supervisor, who was a lawyer) lasted an additional average of 30 minutes per call, plus 10 minutes of recordkeeping.
- Legislative Calls: Legislators and legislative staff calling in to coordinate policy initiatives (average length of time was 5 minutes with the CCR, with a range of 2–7 minutes to connect them to the appropriate member of the executive leadership

staff, who was sometimes unavailable), accounting for 10% of incoming calls. Associated recordkeeping took an additional 5 minutes.

- Other Calls: These could be calls from concerned citizens, religious leaders, employers, sister organizations, and others (average length of time was 6 minutes with the CCR, with a range of 5–15 minutes to connect them to the appropriate CM or member of the executive leadership, who was sometimes unavailable), accounting for 10% of incoming calls. Associated recordkeeping took an additional 4 minutes.

The nine CCRs worked on Friday evenings (3 hours), Saturdays (6 hours), and Sundays (6 hours). All came in with good knowledge of employment and immigrant rights issues. Some were AmeriCorps members and graduate interns between the ages of 23–29. Others were retirees in their late 60s and 70s. The nine individuals were all deeply committed to the values of the organization and put in their own personal time to make a difference on these issues. Still, every 2 hours each CCR needed a 15-minute break.

All calls came first to the CCRs. When they were on a call with a worker or immigrant, CCRs were trained to give that person their undivided attention. Everyone calling in had a story to tell, and it was important to hear that story. If all four of the on-duty CCRs were handling calls, the next caller had to wait on hold. The younger CCRs picked the music that played while someone was on hold—always some of the best music from the local arts scene. On the call, a CCR had to get the person's first name (last name was optional to protect privacy), a call-back number, their story, and a statement of the problem(s) (which was paraphrased back to the caller to ensure it had been heard correctly). CCRs would then provide information on a variety of online resources to answer relatively common questions. Following the call, the CCR had to enter the case information into both the online system and physical files. When calls backed up, recordkeeping suffered. For more complex immigration and employment issues, calls would be handed-off to one of the CMs; this happened about half of the time. The CMs could also serve as translators if they spoke a language that was not spoken by the CCR.

This was an interfaith operation, and religious observances meant that the CCRs were not available at all times. Four CCRs were Christian (CCRs F, G, H, I), three were Jewish (CCRs B, C, E), and two were Muslim (CCRs A, D). All were observant in their respective religions. Among the nine CCRs, four were AmeriCorps members (CCRs D, E, G, H), two were graduate interns (CCRs B, C), and three were retirees (CCRs A, F, I). The following table shows call averages per CCR from one month's operations (not including the recordkeeping times):

Table 1 shows that on Friday evenings, on average, there were two abandoned calls per hour. On Saturdays and Sundays, the abandonment rate increased to three calls per hour. Other than the average number of calls handled and the average number of abandoned calls, no other metrics were tracked.

The CCR position was stressful, with high turnover, particularly among the student volunteers. The typical tenure for a volunteer was 3 months, with departures based on burnout half of the time and other life changes (including graduate students completing their internships, AmeriCorps members moving on, and retirees focusing more on family or other matters) for the other half. Orientation and training for a new volunteer took one month. Training and orientation were provided side-by-side with the lead supervisor, who did not handle any calls directly.

TABLE 1. CCR PERFORMANCE

CCR	Months volunteering	Friday (3 hr) average calls handled/night	Saturday (6 hr) average calls handled/night	Sunday (6 hr) average calls handled/night	Average calls per hour
A	9	16	28	–	5.0
B	5	–	–	23	3.8
C	3	–	–	27	4.5
D	2	10	17	–	3.1
E	1	–	–	12	2.0
F	10	–	27	33	4.8
G	1	9	14	–	2.7
H	2	–	15	18	2.8
I	12	18	–	–	6.0
Average per person		13.3	20.2	22.6	
Total abandoned calls		6	18	18	
Total calls per shift		59	119	131	

Note. Averages are shown for five CCRs on Saturdays and Sundays because these were monthly averages, and in any given month, five individuals would have volunteered but only four would have been working at a time.

As a lawyer, one issue of great concern to the supervisor was the lack of proper security for digital and physical files. The digital files were not on a secure server with encryption. The physical files were in open filing cabinets in the conference room, which was used by many people, including clients waiting to see a CM during the week.

Some of the younger CCRs wanted to be in a regular paid position, doing the work of the CMs. The CCRs were swamped with emotionally demanding calls. The CCRs also worked in an open space, while all the CMs had their own separate office spaces. The meeting room was also a shared space located outside the CM offices. The CCRs looked on the other side of the wall and saw people who were not nearly as stressed. The wall was more than a physical barrier—for the younger CCRs, all of whom had strong political views, it was a symbol of a two-class system.

CM Responsibilities

The three CMs all worked the same Friday, Saturday, and Sunday hours as the CCRs and then split coverage of the other weekday hours, ensuring two were present at all times. The work schedule was as follows:

- Monday 9–5: CM A, CM B (8 hours)
- Tuesday 9–5: CM A, CM B (8 hours)
- Wednesday 9–5: CM A, CM C (8 hours)
- Thursday 9–5: CM B, CM C (8 hours)
- Friday 9–5: CM B, CM C (8 hours) and Friday 6–9: CM B, CM A (3 hours)
- Saturday 10–4: CM A, CM C (6 hours)
- Sunday 10–4: CM B, CM C (6 hours)

There were six relevant CM tasks:

- Walk-In Support: Providing walk-in support on all relevant employment and immigration issues during regular business hours.
- Immigration Case Tracking: Ensuring appropriate tracking of all immigration cases, including completing reports for funders.
- Legal Case Coordination: Coordinating with lawyers as appropriate for legal issues involving immigrant workers.
- Translation/Interpretation: Serving as a translator/interpreter when needed by a CCR who did not speak the language of the caller.
- Employment Case Review: Overseeing trends and emergent issues in the employment rights cases handled by the CCRs.
- Updating/Correcting Case Files: Finding information for case files, which were essential for legal reasons and created out of respect for the clients, yet were frequently incomplete.

There was no record for how long it took to complete these tasks, but the CMs were aware that there was a wide variance for each. This reflected their commitment to dealing with each case with complete focus. In addition, there were both digital and physical files that needed to be accurate and current. The foundation funding the immigration work had threatened to pull the grant if the files were not maintained properly.

During the week, the CMs did the very demanding work of handling walk-in cases. This involved not just talking on the phone (as happened on the weekends) but being physically "present" for people face-to-face. It could be highly emotionally demanding. The office walls were essential for privacy during these conversations. Often there would be a line of people waiting for a turn to see one of the CMs. They were supposed to finish work at 5 p.m., but when there were people waiting, the CMs would often stay over since they knew how hard it was for people to come in. They also knew that this work did not count for overtime until it was more than 40 hours in a week, but it should be paid time. Given the tight budget at IWRC, however, they rarely reported this on their time cards.

Weekends were used to catch up on the files and other aspects of case management as well as to field calls forwarded from the CCRs. There was also the occasional need to help out with translation/interpretation. Moreover, it was not just necessary to catch up on the files; there was also the frustration of trying to figure out how to complete electronic and physical files that had been left incomplete by the CCRs.

The CMs were all paid on an hourly basis. All wanted to be full-time, and there was some resentment around differences between the hours each worked. All were in their late 30s and 40s, each with young families, making work-life balance a priority. Unfortunately, there was no budgetary room to increase the number of paid hours for the CMs.

Discussion Questions

Assume you are a graduate student intern CCR who has collected all of the above information. You were asked the following:

1. How can we ensure that key stakeholders are not frustrated by the way our call center operates—so that their interests are clearly advanced in the way that the call center operates? While many problems could be addressed, focus your analysis on a few key issues.

2. Are the CCRs working at full capacity? If so, what would you recommend (noting that there is a cost to recruit and train additional volunteers)?
3. What can be done to optimize and coordinate the work of the CCRs and the CMs so that both can best advance the mission of the IWRC and ensure compliance with protocols and procedures? Include a process flow map in your analysis.
4. Can anything be learned from the way that commercial call centers operate (see Appendix A)—such as applying relevant metrics, staffing standards, and other lessons learned—or is this situation fundamentally different?
5. What will it take to implement your recommendations in terms of cost, timing, and other considerations? In other words, how do you recommend that the IWRC manage change?

You may not be able to address all of these issues given the available time, so choose what to prioritize for a deep dive and what to address in less detail. Your choices should be based on what you believe is best for the organization, not just on what may be easiest to do.

APPENDIX A

Comparative Data on Commercial Call Centers

Commercial Call Center Metrics (average per person per shift):

- Average speed for handling call
- Average after-call work time
- Average delay in queue
- Longest delay in queue
- First call resolution
- Error/rework rate
- Customer complaints and compliments
- Percentage of calls monitored by supervisor
- Number of call abandons
- Hours of operation
- Number of supervisors and representatives working

Individual Employee Metrics in a Commercial Call Center (per person per shift)

- Average speed for handling call
- Average after-call work time
- Average delay in queue
- Longest delay in queue
- First call resolution
- Error/rework rate
- Customer complaints and compliments
- Random call monitoring by supervisor

Benchmarking Standards for Commercial Call Centers
Industry benchmarks for staffing are well established. Here is a standard table that you can use:

TABLE 2. BENCHMARKING STANDARDS FOR COMMERCIAL CALL CENTERS

Calls per hour	Workload hours	Staff required	Staff occupancy (workload/staff)
100	8.33	12	.69
200	16.67	21	.79
400	33.33	39	.85
800	66.67	74	.90
1600	133.33	142	.94

North American Quitline Consortium, "Call Center Metrics: Best Practices in Performance Measurement and Management to Maximize Quitline Efficiency and Quality," North American Quitline Consortium, 2010, issue paper, 16, https://www.naquitline.org/resource/resmgr/issue_papers/callcentermetricspaperbestpr.pdf.

Benchmarking Workflow for Commercial Call Centers

There are also industry benchmark standards for the workflow of handling commercial calls, which are as follows:

TABLE 3. BENCHMARKING WORKFLOW FOR COMMERCIAL CALL CENTERS

1. Opening	2. Discovery
• Uses standard greeting • Verifies customer account • Updates customer information • Offers assistance	• Clarifies purpose of call • Asks fact-finding questions • Identifies correct nature of call
3. Resolution	**4. Closing**
• Matches best option to need • Explains delivery schedule • Follows resolution procedure • Promotes additional services	• Summarizes actions taken • Offers additional assistance • Thanks customer for business

North American Quitline Consortium, "Call Center Metrics: Best Practices in Performance Measurement and Management to Maximize Quitline Efficiency and Quality," North American Quitline Consortium, 2010, issue paper, 22, https://www.naquitline.org/resource/resmgr/issue_papers/callcentermetricspaperbestpr.pdf.

NOTES

This is a hypothetical case developed for teaching purposes.

SECTION 6

Social Impact Marketing Case

CASE 6.1

JA Worldwide

Creating a Global Brand

KESHIA ENGWENYI, JULIA ROBINSON-ROSENDORFF,
AND SEAN C. RUSH

We're one of the world's best-kept secrets.

—Members of the JA Worldwide Board of Governors in 2008

This comment was made to Sean Rush during his first few days as president and CEO of JA Worldwide (JAW) in January 2008. By this time, JAW had become a sizable organization compared to most social service nonprofits; its annual worldwide operating budget was close to $300 million, it served almost 8 million young people around the world, it employed nearly 3,000 people and 270,000 volunteers, and it provided services in 127 countries. In terms of sheer statistics, it was one of the largest and oldest NGOs in the world. Yet, even as JAW was approaching its 100th anniversary, Rush often received a quizzical response when he told people he worked for the organization.

History and Evolution of JA Worldwide

The Early Years

JA Worldwide was founded as the Boys' and Girls' Bureau Committee in 1919 in Springfield, Massachusetts. The goal of the new organization was to provide students with experiential education in financial literacy, workforce readiness, and entrepreneurship. During its second year of operation, it changed its name to the Junior Achievement (JA) Bureau to better reflect the organization's purpose. JA's first program, the Company Program, was established by Theodore Vail, president of American Telephone and Telegraph; Horace Moses, president of Strathmore Paper Co.; and United States Senator Murray Crane of Massachusetts. This program became the foundational building block of JA's work and was offered to high school students on an after-school basis.

As JA's informational literature states:

> The JA Company Program empowers high school students to fill a need or solve a problem in their community and teaches them practical skills required to conceptualize, capitalize, and manage their own business venture. Throughout the process of building their own company, students collaborate, make crucial business decisions, communicate with multiple stakeholders, and develop entrepreneurial knowledge and skills.[1] Community volunteers and mentors provide real-world guidance and experience to the student-led startup.

The Company Program targeted high school students with an after-school course focused on developing business skills. As part of the program, participants elected company officers; raised capital through the sale of shares of stock; developed a business plan; purchased materials; and produced, promoted, and sold a product. Upon dissolution of a company at the end of the school year, students would pay back capital and dividends to their shareholders before pocketing, spending, or donating any remaining profit.

JA relied on volunteers from the general business community to serve as advisors to the clubs. The adult leaders were expected to help the students learn basic principles of finance, production, marketing, and sales but were not to intrude directly in the operations of the company. The success or failure of the company was considered to be part of the JA learning experience.

The Company Program became the bedrock of JA's work. Early on, JA was recognized by United States President Calvin Coolidge for its efforts to help young people who relocated from farms to the city adapt to the booming industrial economy. Over time, JA began to slowly expand in the Northeastern United States.

The geographic expansion of JA occurred in a highly decentralized manner. New chapter expansion was primarily attributed to word-of-mouth growth, as businesspeople described the Company Program to peers and colleagues in neighboring communities. There was no central JA organization to coordinate growth, maintain quality control over programs, create operating standards, or raise money to support JA activities. Each JA chapter raised all of its funding from local businesses and sourced all of its volunteers from those same companies. The chapters were completely private in operations and funding. Additionally, each chapter was established as its own nonprofit organization.

Post-World War II: HQ Creation and Accelerated Growth

Shortly after World War II, JA decided to expand more aggressively. A "National Headquarters" was established to catalyze this increased growth and to better coordinate JA activities. However, despite the name "Headquarters," JA was decidedly decentralized, with the real organizational power resting within each local chapter. During this period of growth, JA's branding evolved as well. Its logo, for example, assumed different forms over time (Exhibit 1).

Furthermore, as American corporate executives were increasingly transferred to postings around the world, they wanted to see JA in the countries where they lived and worked. This international interest began to gain traction in the 1950s, when local chapters in Canada and the United Kingdom were founded through the initiatives of local businesspeople. However, this decentralized method of growth, compounded by cultural differences, resulted in very little consistency among global chapters. In the United Kingdom, for example, the term "junior" was problematic. There, as well as in other countries, the word junior could connote someone of low rank or status as well as reference a small child. For this reason, a chapter in the United Kingdom was founded under the name Young Enterprise (YE).

Over time, YE spread to Norway, Sweden, Belgium, and eventually most countries in Western Europe. However, at the center of all YE activities was JA's Company Program, or a slight variation thereof (Exhibit 2).

The 1990s: The JA USA Growth Initiative and the Creation of JA International (JAI)

In order to tackle their continued growth, JA leadership decided to create two distinct entities: JA USA, to oversee operations in the United States, and JA International (JAI) to oversee international expansion in all other participating countries or Member Nations. JAI pursued its mission by zealously creating JA chapters in many additional countries throughout the world. By the early 2000s, JAI had a presence in 97 countries. Many countries did business under the banner of Junior Achievement or JA. However, even when the name was used, it was translated to the local language and combined with a variety of unrelated colors and graphics. Not included in the total number of JAI countries were the 19 YE operations in Western Europe.

Another factor contributing to JAI's growth was the fall of the Iron Curtain. The collapse of the Soviet Union in 1989 led to the "creation" of many new countries that had previously been part of the USSR. JAI quickly exploited these opportunities, establishing a formidable presence in Eastern Europe. All of these Eastern European countries did business as JA or Junior Achievement upon their creation, but again, their titles were often translated and contextualized for the local communities (Exhibit 3).

The Creation of JA Worldwide

As the organization grew, challenges arose with respect to JA's many corporate funders. The overwhelming bulk of donations to JA was from American domestic companies as well as United States–based global companies. Given JA's high degree of decentralization, many companies were solicited multiple times by various JA USA chapters and Member Nations. Many of JA's funders had offices throughout the United States and the world. Each local JA chapter or Member Nation would approach the company's local office seeking support. Within a short period of time, the companies began to push back: "Aren't you one organization? Why don't you approach us once on behalf of all of your various chapters and Member Nations?"

This and other issues came to a head in 2001. Concerned about not just the fracturing of the organization but also its possible collapse, the JA USA Board proposed a merger with JAI to create one coalesced global entity: JA Worldwide. After over 2 years of complex negotiations, the merger was finally consummated in 2004.

However, even after the merger dust had settled, JAW still was not a coherent whole. In addition to JAW itself, there were now six Regional Operating Centers (ROCs) around the world (Exhibit 4):

1. JA/YE Europe
2. JA Asia-Pacific
3. JA Africa
4. Junior Achievement USA
5. JA Americas (Central and South America)
6. INJAZ al-Arab

A New JA Worldwide CEO

In early 2007, the CEO who had guided the organization through its merger and the attendant politics, David Chernow, resigned after 6 years on the job. After many months, the JAW Board of Governors selected Sean Rush to become the new CEO of JAW in 2008. Rush had taken early retirement from IBM the year before and had embarked on a one-year master's degree program at the Harvard Kennedy School in 2006 at the age of 55.

Rush had spent the first part of his career at PricewaterhouseCoopers (PWC)—an international, "big four" accounting firm, where he had been a partner and chairman of the education and nonprofit practice in the United States. At IBM, he had been general manager of the Global Education Industry Group, a $2.4 billion business within the company. However, despite these decidedly "corporate" roles, Rush had a deep passion for nonprofit organizations and their management. All of his work at PWC had been focused on the nonprofit sector, and his recruitment to IBM was based on that nonprofit market experience. When asked about his interest in pivoting to the role of CEO at JA, Rush stated:

> I've been fascinated by nonprofit organizations since business school. They play such an important role in our world through the delivery of education, health care, art, culture, and social services. Yet, they are often neglected managerially. Mission often overrides the need for solid strategic thinking, financial management, technology, and human resource development. My year at the Kennedy School was intended to be a career inflection point. Up to that point, I had consulted with many of these organizations. Now, I want to work in a nonprofit and apply my experiences in a single organization.

The Challenge

Five months into Rush's tenure at JAW, an article came out ranking the 100 most impactful NGOs of 2008 (Exhibit 4). While JA Worldwide was nowhere to be found on the list, INJAZ al-Arab, one of JAW's Regional Operating Centers, was ranked number 92. Additionally, during a speech to the JAW leadership team, a prominent journalist from *The New York Times* suggested that JAW try to emulate INJAZ al-Arab in its work. Clearly, the organizational structure of JAW was completely unknown to the speaker. Though INJAZ al-Arab was doing the same work as the rest of the organization, in this moment, a small piece of JAW was more widely renowned than JAW as a whole. Because of this disconnect in public perception, Rush concluded that addressing the fractured JAW brand was of extraordinary importance. He thought:

> When I put all of the various logos from around the world on a single page [Exhibit 5], it looked like a kaleidoscope. In essence, it showed over 50 years of decentralized uncoordinated growth. No standards had been established. And where standards were in place, nobody paid attention to them, nor were they enforced. Each piece of JAW could do what it wanted. We had no coherent brand.

His experience at IBM told him that brand was a promise to an organization's customers. Rush continued to reflect:

> It's much more than a logo. Brand encompasses your mission, values, customer perceptions, personality, voice, and positioning. The logo is the visual symbol of a host of organizational attributes that you want your customers to perceive . . . At IBM, the logo was sacrosanct. You never tinkered with it. Yes, that logo changed over time as the company evolved. But while that logo was in place, it was untouchable. It was deployed consistently and meant the same thing to customers anywhere in the world.

Compounding these challenges, a crushing reality emerged—JAW was in deep financial trouble. The suddenness of JAW's financial crisis was brought about by the global financial meltdown of 2008, which was considered the worst financial crisis since the Great Depression of 1929. JAW's corporate funding began to shrink rapidly relative to its budget plans, the ramifications of which were huge and potentially devastating.

As Rush considered these challenges and addressed the many options that would enable JA to meet its full potential and overcome its problems, he kept returning to branding as a way to unify the organization. Although he was not a brand expert, he knew that solving this problem would be a critically important step in unifying JAW. After consulting with his team, he took out a piece of paper and started to sketch out options for the short, medium, and long terms.

Discussion Questions

1. What is the JAW brand? Is there a brand at all? What does it mean to be a global brand?
2. How do you address cultural differences in global branding? Should Rush stick with the word "Junior?"
3. How do the financial challenges facing JAW affect its brand and vice versa?
4. If you were in Rush's shoes, how would you address these challenges?

EXHIBIT 1. PRESENT DAY JA LOGO

Used with permission of Junior Achievement Worldwide.

EXHIBIT 2. JA History Fact Sheet

Beginnings

- Junior Achievement, originally called the Boys' and Girls' Bureau of the Eastern States League, was started in 1919 in Springfield, Massachusetts by AT&T Chairman Theodore Vail, Strathmore Paper Company Founder Horace Moses and Massachusetts Senator Murray Crane.
- The official start date for Junior Achievement is considered to be December 1, 1919. That's when the first director of Junior Achievement, O. H. Benson, began working for Junior Achievement after his previous career at the U.S. Department of Agriculture and at another youth-serving organization, 4-H.
- Even though Junior Achievement started out focusing on younger participants, it soon shifted its programs to serve high school-aged kids who started student-run businesses with the guidance of Advisors from the business community.
- Early on, Junior Achievement was recognized by U.S. President Calvin Coolidge for its efforts to help young people who relocated from farms to the city adapt to the booming industrial economy.

Growth

- Junior Achievement was not immune to the Great Depression. The organization remained concentrated primarily in the Northeastern United States during the 1930s with the support of businesses.
- Junior Achievement began to expand in the Midwest just before World War II.
- Prior to the War, Junior Achievement's leadership made the decision to become a national organization. Those plans were put on hold with the start of World War II.
- During the War, JA student companies supported the war effort through recycling drives and by supplying the armed forces with items such as clothes hangers.
- Following World War II, Junior Achievement began to expand nationally in earnest.
- In 1944, the first National Junior Achievers Conference (NAJAC) was held. NAJAC would eventually find an ongoing home at Indiana University (IU) and grew to hosting more than 2,000 JA Company students each year. NAJAC continued in various forms until the mid-1990s.
- The first international JA office opened in Canada in the 1950s.
- In the 1960s, the first overseas Junior Achievement-affiliated organization, Young Enterprise (YE), started in the United Kingdom.
- In the 1969, Junior Achievement marked its 50th Anniversary by delivering programs in all 50 U.S. states.
- By the mid-1970s, it became apparent that Junior Achievement needed to expand from being strictly an after-school program for high schoolers into offering in-school programs in other grades. JA launched Project Business, designed to teach middle school students business concepts during in-classroom sessions.
- In the late 1970s, Junior Achievement launched Business Basics, a program for elementary school students that utilized JA Company Program students as volunteers. Later, JA began to engage business professionals as volunteers for Business Basics.
- In the early 1980s, Junior Achievement began to offer Applied Economics, an in-depth economics program for high school students. Applied Economics was one of the first programs to use Personal Computers (PCs) in the classrooms setting.

- During its peak in the early 1970s, the JA Company Program reached nearly 300,000 teens in a year. By 1987 Junior Achievement, combining both after-school and in-school programs, was reaching 1 million students a year.
- With the fall of the Berlin Wall in 1989, there was increased global interest in Junior Achievement programs.
- In 1992, Junior Achievement was offering programs in the former Soviet Union. The 1990s saw a spike in the offerings of JA programs around the world, with JA expanding in Europe, Latin America, Asia, Africa and the Middle East. During this time, Junior Achievement International, which would eventually become JA Worldwide, was established.
- In the 1990s, Junior Achievement in the U.S. developed a complete suite of in-school programs for all grades K-12.
- By 2000, Junior Achievement was implementing JA Finance Park, an experiential program that lets middle school students make adult financial decisions in life-like simulations. This was soon followed by the launch of JA BizTown, designed for elementary school-aged children to run a simulated town for a day. Around this time, Junior Achievement also became involved with JJA Job Shadow, a program that allow high school students to "shadow" working professionals in their places of work.

Today and Beyond

- Today, Junior Achievement reaches nearly 5 million students a year in the United States with the support of nearly a quarter-million volunteers in over 100 communities. Globally, JA reaches 10 million students in more than 100 countries.
- JA is pushing the education envelope with the implementation of blended-learning, augmented reality and project-based programs.

Used with permission of Junior Achievement.

■ EXHIBIT 3. JAW Regional Operating Structure

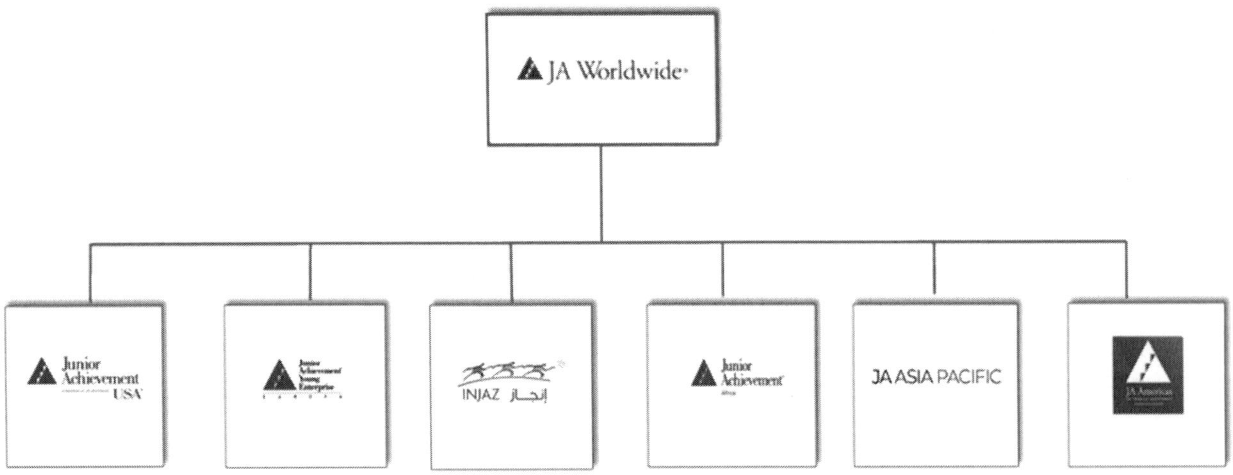

Used with permission of Junior Achievement Worldwide.

EXHIBIT 4. 2013 Top 100 Global NGO Rankings

1. BRAC
2. Wikimedia Foundation
3. Acumen Fund
4. Danish Refugee Council
5. Partners in Health
6. Ceres
7. CARE International
8. Médecins Sans Frontières
9. Cure Violence
10. Mercy Corps
11. APOPO
12. Root Capital
13. Handicap International
14. International Rescue Committee
15. Barefoot College
16. Landesa
17. Ashoka
18. One Acre Fund
19. Clinton Health Access Initiative
20. Heifer International
21. Human Rights Watch
22. Rare
23. Digital Divide Data
24. Akshaya Patra Foundation
25. Gram Vikas
26. Room to Read
27. Amnesty International
28. AMREF
29. Pratham
30. iDE
31. Riders for Health
32. MERLIN
33. Fonkoze
34. Helen Keller International
35. Water for People
36. Aflatoun
37. FrontlineSMA
38. Marie Stopes International
39. International Planned Parenthood
40. Search for Common Ground
41. PLAN International
42. Tostan
43. Fred Hollows Foundation
44. Transparency International
45. Saude Crianca
46. Escuela Nueva
47. Open Society Foundations
48. Operation ASHA
49. International Medical Corps
50. GAIN
51. Save the Children International
52. WITNESS
53. Friends of the Earth Middle East
54. CAMBIA
55. Common Ground
56. Viva Rio
57. International Crisis Group
58. Habitat for Humanity
59. Kickstart International
60. ZOA
61. Friends-International
62. Architecture for Humanity
63. Concern
64. Center for Digital Inclusion
65. American Refugee Committee
66. International Center for Transitional Justice
67. Interpeace
68. Geneva Call
69. Rainforest Alliance
70. FAWE
71. Code for America
72. Child & Youth Finance International
73. Asylum Access
74. Ycab Foundation
75. PlanetRead
76. Dhaka Ahsania Mission
77. International Commission of Jurists
78. World Vision
79. Movember Foundation
80. PlaNet Finance
81. Free the Children
82. Terre des Hommes International Federation
83. TRIAL
84. International Bridges to Justice
85. Skateistan
86. International Alert
87. Libera
88. Krousar Thmey Cambodia
89. Greenpeace
90. Global Footprint Network
91. Luz Portatil Brasil
92. **INJAZ al-Arab (Note: This is a JA Affiliate)**
93. CIVICUS
94. Generations for Peace
95. Send a Cow Uganda
96. Project WET Foundation
97. Instituto da Crianca
98. Diplo Foundation
99. Born Free Foundation
100. Akilah Institute for Women

"The Global Journal (January 2013) Special Edition: The Global Top 100 NGOs," The Global Journal, 2013.

EXHIBIT 5. JA Logos Around the World

Used with permission of Junior Achievement Worldwide.

NOTE

1. Junior Achievement USA, "JA Company Program," n.d., https://jausa.ja.org/programs/ja-company-program.

SECTION 7

Social Impact Human Resources Cases

CASE 7.1

Breaking Down Silos to Build Collaborative Systems

LAUREN HAJJAR, JODY HOFFER GITTELL, NINNA MEIER, AND BILL GUNN

As the new director of the Integrated Delivery Network in one New Hampshire region in 2016, Nora Evans had her work cut out for her. Under a federal program that had recently been implemented in New Hampshire, Evans was responsible for delivering needed services in a more impactful way. Her target population included 25,440 people who were eligible for services under the federal Medicaid health insurance program due to having income near or below the poverty line.[1] Until now, service providers—municipal agencies, social service agencies, behavioral health providers, community health centers, local hospitals, etc.—had carried out their work in silos separated by disparate information systems, payment structures, and accountabilities. The new federal program, called the Delivery System Reform Incentive Payment Program, was designed to overcome these silos through payments that would reimburse health, mental health, and social support services for work they carried out together.

Though Evans had played leadership roles in multiple sectors over the past 2 decades and understood the need for integrated models of service delivery, her current role came with a new set of challenges. In her new role, she was often disconnected from the front-line work due to the nature of her responsibilities, so she was dependent upon her management team and community partners to understand the evolving needs of the target population. Due to time and resource constraints, she was unable to meet with everyone who was engaged in providing services to clients, and yet, she was responsible for making sure the right stakeholders were around the table to represent and address client needs.

Early on in her role, Evans began meeting with service providers to better understand their experiences with delivering services to low-income residents of the region. During a conversation with a care coordinator at the local hospital, Evans was informed:

> When patients come into the hospital, we often don't know enough about the other providers they have seen or whose care they are under regularly. Sometimes they have a community support person or advocate with them, sometimes they don't. We don't get the full health history. We also have to make sure that we are reimbursed by Medicaid for the care that is provided, and we get a lot of pressure from our leadership team to minimize costs related to unreimbursed care, especially acute care.

Based on what she learned, Evans was curious how the challenge of service integration might be experienced by others in the network. In her next meeting with a behavioral health provider, Evans heard skepticism about the feasibility of service integration:

> It will never work. Health care providers don't have the same goals for the clients as behavioral health providers. They also don't understand what we do and the importance of behavioral health treatment compliance and engagement. We approach and measure care provision differently because we need to focus on the role of trust in our relationships with our clients and on understanding the constraints and barriers that they experience on a day-to-day basis.

Evans left that meeting wondering how integration could ever be achieved. She wondered whether differences she was hearing in language—with health care providers referring to the target population as patients, and behavioral health providers referring to them as clients—might signal deeper differences that would be challenging to overcome.

Following these conversations, Evans knew she had to meet with more stakeholder groups, then bring them together to better understand how to meet the needs of clients. The stakes were high for Evans: she would have to report outcomes to the state next year in order to sustain funding. She also knew that addressing the fragmented relationships among service providers would take time. She needed an effective way to help them work better together to provide improved, integrated care to clients.

Background

There is a movement around the world to integrate health and social care in order to better address the *social determinants (or drivers) of health*. These social determinants include homelessness, joblessness, racial discrimination, childhood trauma, addiction, hopelessness, and lack of access to care. Together, they are root causes of negative health outcomes. But even health systems that are accountable for the cost and quality of population health outcomes are not able to address these social determinants on their own. They need partners. According to a survey by the Physicians Foundation, most physicians are falling short in meeting the social determinants of health, citing inadequate time and restricted ability due to lack of resources as their major challenges.[2]

New Hampshire Integrated Delivery Networks

This case is situated in the New Hampshire Integrated Delivery Network (IDN), seven of which were formed in 2016 in response to a United States federal program called the Delivery System Reform Incentive Payment (DSRIP) Program (Exhibit 1). DSRIP funded states to bring local service providers together to develop demonstration projects that coordinated services for Medicaid recipients. As of 2016, a total of 12 states had signed up for five-year DSRIP contracts, including New Hampshire.

The goal of the New Hampshire DSRIP Program was to support the development and implementation of regional Integrated Delivery Networks to improve the physical and behavioral health of low-income residents and ultimately to reduce health care costs by addressing the social factors that created poor health outcomes. Each Integrated Delivery Network was required to include the following roles: administrative lead office, physical health providers, mental health/substance use disorder providers, and community supports (Exhibit 2).

In Evans' region, several experienced individuals came together to form the administrative lead office, including the former New Hampshire State Secretary of Health and

EXHIBIT 1. New Hampshire Integrated Delivery Networks

IDNs Will be Organized into 7 Regions

Illustrative IDN	Regional Public Health Networks (RPHN) Included	# of Medicaid members
1. Monadnock, Sullivan, Upper Valley	Greater Monadnock, Greater Sullivan County, Upper Valley	21,550
2. Capital	Capital Area	15,520
3. Nashua	Greater Nashua	19,110
4. Derry & Manchester	Greater Derry, Greater Manchester	34,900
5. Central, Winnipesaukee	Central NH, Winnipesaukee	15,230
6. Seacoast & Strafford	Strafford County, Seacoast	25,440
7. North Country & Carroll	North Country RHPN, Carroll County RHPN	15,300

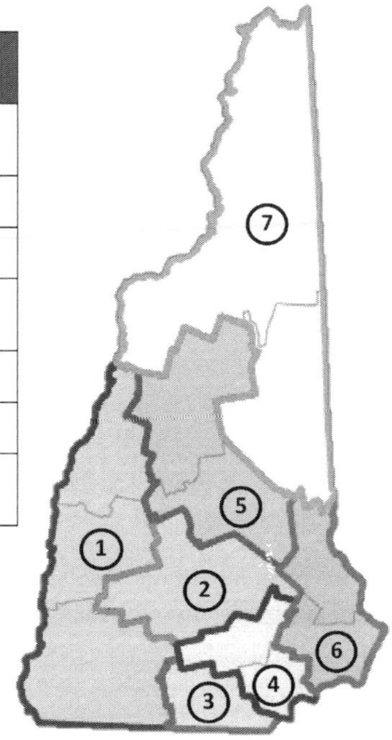

Providers in each IDN region are encouraged to work together to form one IDN, particularly in less populated parts of the State.

From the presentation, "Building Capacity for Transformation: New Hampshire's DSRIP Waiver Program," National Organization of State Health Offices of Rural Health, May 2016.

EXHIBIT 2. Roles in Each Integrated Delivery Network

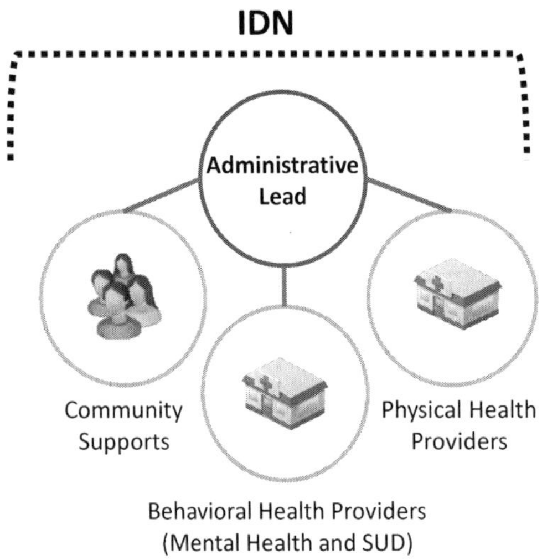

From the presentation, "Building Capacity for Transformation: New Hampshire's DSRIP Waiver Program," National Organization of State Health Offices of Rural Health, May 2016.

Human Services, a primary care behavioral health provider, a community engagement expert, and a social service operations expert. They invited all three regional hospitals, both community health centers, and multiple social service agencies to participate in the Integrated Delivery Network. All invited organizations agreed to participate, and the IDN was established. Once the IDN was formed, the organizations participated to varying degrees based on their own internal capacities and strategic priorities. Even though the IDN invested funds in integration, the incentives for organizations to act independently were still quite strong.

Evans was proud of the early innovations that had emerged in her region, which included:

1. Forming a team of community-facing care coordinators,
2. Developing a network of primary care behavioral health providers,
3. Bringing organizations together each month at Community Care Team meetings to discuss some of the most complex client cases, and
4. Creating a release form that allowed the Community Care Team to talk about particular client cases.

Although the release form seemed like a minor thing, it was essential for addressing privacy concerns. According to the former State Secretary of Health and Human Services:

> Depending on the state you are working in, privacy could be a big issue or not. For New Hampshire, it is a big deal, and for the federal government it is a big deal, especially with substance use and behavioral health issues. My employer could use that information against me. There are tremendous efforts to maintain that confidentiality. The federal government on one hand wants you to work together, but their rules put a number of different barriers in the way. For the Community Care Team to work, these privacy issues had to be addressed. The client had to give a group of service providers, some of whom are not working directly with the client, the ability to talk about them. Based on what one of us had used in Connecticut, we created a release form that allowed the Community Care Team to talk about a particular case.

In November 2016, Evans and several direct service providers in the region were particularly concerned about an individual named Justin Collins and decided, with his permission, to bring his case to the November Community Care Team meeting.

Justin Collins

Justin Collins was a 38-year-old man, who camped in the woods during much of the year and slept in various homeless shelters during the coldest parts of winter. He struggled with anxiety related to childhood trauma and substance use, had not completed high school, and had been unemployed for more than a decade. He had met on occasion with substance use and mental health counselors and visited the health care van when it parked near his campsite in the woods. His willingness to seek help had built slowly, based on personal trust with individual staff, but it was easily disrupted by the turnover of key staff. Collins had been diagnosed with hypertension and borderline Type 2 diabetes, and both conditions were being poorly managed at the time his case was discussed by the Community Care Team.

Collins had a primary care provider who worked with a behavioral health provider. His peer recovery support person had allowed him to use their address, which had enabled him to apply for Medicaid health insurance, unemployment, and housing. He was therefore covered by Medicaid health insurance, so he had access to care. But he had some issues with transportation, remembering appointments, and staying in touch with his providers. He had inconsistent cell phone and email access. At the time the Community Care Teams met, Collins was at risk of being discharged from the community mental health center due to not following through with his treatment plan, including his prescribed medication. His community-facing care coordinator brought his case to the Community Care Team after Collins had signed the release form allowing them to discuss his care.

Evans proposed to discuss Collins at the next Community Care Team meeting. Evans knew that the upcoming meeting would be critical for assisting Justin Collins and for setting the standard for future collaboration.

Community Care Team Meeting: Role-Play Simulation

You are a participant in the monthly Community Care Team meeting. The purpose of the meeting is to discuss how to provide integrated health and social care for low-income residents in the region. Each month the team focuses on some of the most complex cases that service providers are facing. Community Care Team meetings are important because existing information systems and payment and accountability structures tend to create silos that break down service delivery. In this November meeting, you will discuss the case of Justin Collins and develop a plan of action for him going forward.

How do you propose the group move forward with Justin's care? Which long-term changes should Evans and the NH IDN leaders consider making?

APPENDIX A

Role Cards

TABLE 1. STAKEHOLDERS IN THE INTEGRATED DELIVERY NETWORK (IDN)

Stakeholder group	Administrative leads for organizing IDN	Physical health providers	Mental health providers/substance use counselors	Community supports	Patient/client
Roles represented in today's meeting	Director of care coordination	Care coordinator in hospital emergency room	Mental health/ substance abuse (MH/SA) treatment provider	Community-facing care coordinator	Patient/client advocacy group leader

Role Card 1: IDN Director of Care Coordination

Tasks: Your tasks as the IDN director of care coordination are to convene partners from around the region to serve the needs of people living near or below the poverty line and to facilitate the integration of their services in innovative ways. This includes *facilitating the Community Care Team meetings* by creating shared knowledge between the stakeholders at the table, developing shared goals, and moving from blaming or blame avoidance to problem-solving. Part of this facilitator role is to ensure that everyone participates and that every voice is heard.

Main Concerns: You are most concerned with providing high-quality care to people living near or below the poverty line in your affluent region. Funders are keeping tabs on how funds are spent and what outcomes are achieved for the target population. The time spent in these meetings is precious because everyone has other commitments in addition to coordinating care. You often say things like, "We've got four people to talk about today and only one hour: Let's go!" Also, you often ask, "Who do we need who's not at this table?"

Challenges: As a director of care coordination, you must get diverse stakeholders with different incentives, perspectives, knowledge, and expertise to come together to integrate care. You have been in leadership roles for the past 2 decades and sometimes feel disconnected from the frontline work. There is not enough time to meet with everyone providing services to any one patient, so you have to make sure the right people are representing patients' needs.

Role Card 2: Care Coordinator in Hospital Emergency Room

Tasks: As the care coordinator in the hospital emergency room, you work directly with the hospital clinical staff and with patients that have arrived at the ER in need of urgent treatment and care. You also work with staff in other units, e.g., the community health center and people providing community support. Some of your primary tasks include:

- Sharing knowledge with clinicians who assess patients' clinical needs
- Coordinating activities that are found in the patients' individualized treatment plans
- Maintaining an updated overview of available services within the network

Main Concerns: You are most concerned with coordinating care for patients' physical health, particularly between those providing urgent acute care services and long-term social and mental health services in the community. You believe deeply that everyone needs to see doctors and other health care professionals regularly to catch issues early, before they become costly and life-threatening.

Challenges: As a care coordinator for the hospital ER, you often lack information/knowledge that is shared with other providers, and you have only a partial perspective of patients' histories and needs. You must also ensure that the issues of insurance and Medicaid coverage are addressed. The hospital leadership appreciates your coordination role, but they are just as concerned with minimizing the costs of unreimbursed care. You also know that hypertension and Type 2 diabetes together dramatically increase the risk of a heart attack or stroke, both of which would require acute care treatment.

Role Card 3: Mental Health and Substance Use Treatment Provider

Tasks: You work directly with clients in addiction treatment and recovery. You may also work with families and friends of the client. Some of your primary tasks are:

- Assessing clients for clinical needs
- Creating individualized treatment plans
- Providing service coordination and case management services
- Making appropriate referrals to other community supports and providers
- Managing medication
- Documenting client interactions and activities

Main Concerns: You are most concerned with engaging clients in mental health or substance abuse treatment, e.g., engaging them to attend appointments and follow-up visits and to manage their medications. While maintaining a client-centered approach is important to you, you are not confident that this goal is shared by others.

Challenges: As a mental health and substance use treatment provider, you often lack information and knowledge from the client's physical health providers, and you do not always have the same goals. You also often see funding and resources going toward hospital care rather than prevention. You see these Community Care Team meetings as one way to shift the balance toward prevention.

Role Card 4: Community-Facing Care Coordinator

Tasks: You work in the community, neighborhoods, and/or client homes and serve as a liaison between clinical and community settings. An important part of your work is translating across linguistic and cultural boundaries. Your main tasks include:

- Navigating resources, enabling client access to available community supports, and providing warm handoffs to the appropriate health and social service providers
- Supporting health literacy by providing clients with information about health, the health system, and their eligibility for benefits
- Engaging clients by building their readiness for change through motivational interviewing; supporting goal setting, prioritization, and attainment; and facilitating the implementation of their care plans
- Providing clients with logistical support, including appointment management, transportation assistance, translation resources, medication supply/refills, and/or access to food/meals

Main Concerns: You are most concerned about your clients' well-being and making sure they are engaged in their care plan. It's a lot to manage. Clients have many needs across the system (mental health, physical health, transportation, housing, etc.), but these parts of the system do not coordinate well with one another.

Challenges: As a frontline provider, you often experience a disconnect between the organizational and community leaders who are making decisions and the needs of the clients you are serving. You see opportunities for positive change, but you do not always feel that your voice is valued. You are less confident to speak up in meetings because there are lots of people there with higher degrees than you. You feel strongly that devoting community resources to housing, food, transportation, employment, and other essential needs gets at the root causes of health disparities and needs to be the top priority.

Role Card 5: Client Advocacy Group Leader

Tasks: You work in the community in a local not-for-profit organization. Your task as client advocacy group leader is to represent the concerns and challenges of the target population. This entails acting as a bridge between client perspectives and the IDN's activities. You are also responsible for sharing knowledge about activities and initiatives that are relevant to clients with the community.

Main Concerns: You are dedicated to making sure that the experiences and perspectives of clients are included in conversations and decisions about them. You believe deeply in the saying: "Nothing about us without us."

Challenges: As an advocacy group leader, you often experience a disconnect between clients' needs and the system's resources. You also have the challenge of representing a heterogenous group of people with diverse needs and preferences, given that not all people who are homeless, for example, have the same needs and concerns.

NOTES

This case is intended for teaching purposes and is based on fictional characters in a real-life policy context.

1. Created in 1965, Medicaid is a public insurance program that provides health coverage to families and individuals living near or below the poverty line, as well as those with disabilities. It is jointly funded by the federal government and the states.
2. Sari Rodriguez, "Most Physicians Lack Ability, Time, to Address Patient SDOH," *Patient Care Access News*, March 25, 2022.

CASE 7.2

The Unit-Based Team Meeting

JOEL CUTCHER-GERSHENFELD

General Simulation Information

You are a staff member serving on a newly created Unit-Based Team (UBT) in the imaging area of your hospital. Each team includes representatives from the work area who have volunteered to meet on a weekly basis in order to identify and support process improvement initiatives in your workplace. There are 20 people who work in your unit, five of whom are elected members. They are joined by the union representative responsible for this area and the area supervisor. You are all charged with taking everyone's interests into account. The radiologists in the unit asked not to be included in the election as they did not have time for a 1-hour meeting each week.

The United States health care system is facing deeply challenging times. Labor costs are high; hospitals are experiencing financial pressures, extensive regulatory oversight, and increased consolidation; new technologies are emerging; and practitioners are pushing for more patient-centric care—all during a global pandemic. In this context, many health care systems see UBTs as key drivers for needed improvements in front-line operations. This is true both in settings where unions represent the workforce and in non-union settings. In both cases, UBTs represent a culture change. Supervisors (often re-designated as "advisors") have to be inclusive and participatory in decision-making; unions have to be collaborative and take responsibility for workplace operations; and workers need to be open to suggestions for better ways of getting work done. When everyone comes together, the effects can be transformative. As one leading union-management partnership put it: "We need to be the best place to give care so we can be the best place to get care."

Of the five staff on the UBT, one is absent today and one is attending a 2-day electronic medical records training session. As a result, there are three team members at today's meeting: the newly elected UBT coordinator (also the area receptionist), a high-seniority imaging technician, and a newly hired, certified radiology nurse. In addition to the UBT members, this meeting includes the unit supervisor, who is now referred to as the unit advisor, as well as the union representative.

Recently, many workers in your unit have taken on more responsibility for daily decisions such as job assignments, overtime balancing, and supply orders. There has been more teamwork lately, but there has also been more conflict as UBT members have been more honest about what is bothering them.

Your weekly team meetings are 1 hour long, and you are halfway into this meeting. The team coordinator opened the meeting with a review of the agenda, followed by reports on safety, patient satisfaction, and efficiency utilization of the imaging equipment. The team learned that safety performance has been good, but there have been some problems with efficiency utilization. Apparently, your work area has been identified as a "bottleneck" in the overall patient flow—things get backed up at some of the imaging equipment, which then creates problems in other units.

There are just 25 minutes left in the meeting. For each of the remaining agenda items, the time you have for discussion is listed along with the name of the person who put the item on the agenda:

1. Skills progression/job rotation (6 minutes—newly hired certified radiology nurse)
2. Preventative maintenance (6 minutes—high-seniority imaging technician)
3. Absenteeism issues (5 minutes—unit advisor)
4. Respect and cultural sensitivity (5 minutes—union representative)
5. Summary of decisions and assignments and next meeting agenda (3 minutes—UBT coordinator)

Each person will take the lead in presenting the item that they put on the agenda. The newly hired certified radiology nurse has agreed to be the team's recorder. You have a few moments now to reflect on each of the agenda items using the information provided regarding your specific role. To prepare for the meeting, everyone needs to consider the following questions:

1. When the team gets to your agenda item, how will you present it?
2. What do you need to do to be ready to address the other agenda items?
3. What would be acceptable or desirable outcomes for each of the agenda items? Consider each item from your perspective, from the perspectives of the other team members, and from the perspectives of the hospital and the union.

Please see the teaching manual for roles and guidance on teaching this simulation. Role cards are included in the teaching notes.

NOTE

This case has been adapted from experiences in multiple organizations.